PASCON AGAN AR
PASSHYON AGAN AR

(KAN AN PASSHYON)
(THE PASSION POEM)
(MOUNT CALVARY)

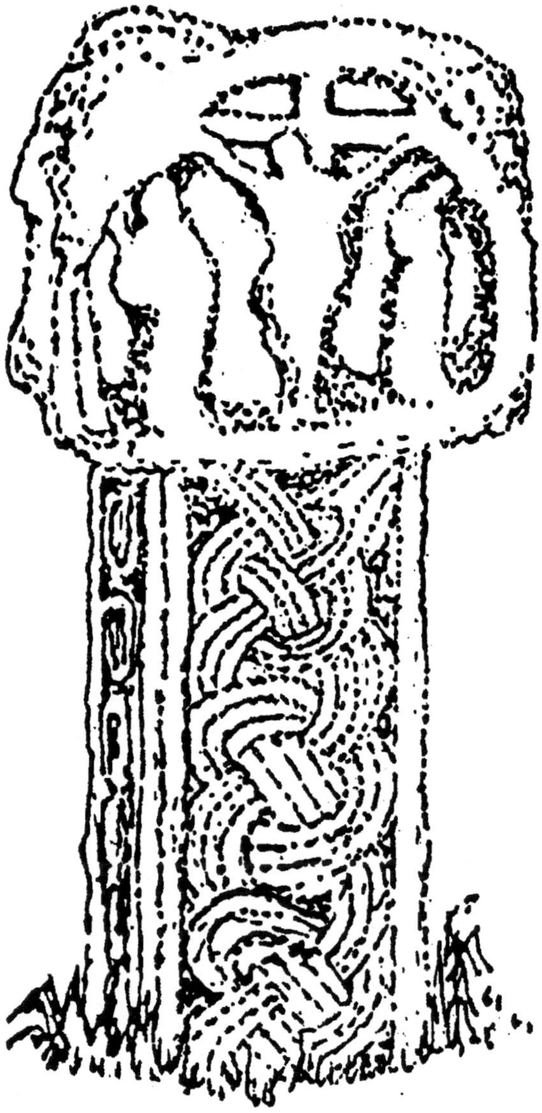

Edited by Ray Edwards

First Edition, 1993

First Reprint, May 1993. Errors detailed in an eleven page list received from Dr David Balhatchet within days of his receiving the first print have been corrected. Just as the first print was made ready, the second edition of Wella Brown's *A Grammar of Modern Cornish* was published. There has not yet been time to update all the references made to the first edition in the notes but two references have been made to the second edition where this is particularly relevant.

Second Reprint, October 1993. The second Edition of *A Grammar of Modern Cornish* and the *Gerlyver Kernewek Kemmyn; an Gerlyver Meur* by Dr Ken George have now both been taken fully into account. A number of errors which survived the second print have been corrected but there are probably still some left and it would be appreciated if readers would indicate them.

Third Reprint, October 1995. This takes into account the recently published book, *Cornish Today,* by Dr Nicholas Williams of University College, Dublin.

Fourth Reprint, May 1996. The MS text has now been checked against the 1860-61 edition of Whitley Stokes and a number of corrections made. Further amendments have also been made with help from Nicholas Williams and Keith Syed.

Second Edition, September 2008. The Board has taken the opportunity to enhance the appearance of the cover and binding and to update a small number of spellings in KK. This edition includes a dedication to Ray Edwards who died during its preparation.

First Reprint, August 2017

Kesva an Taves Kernewek
(Cornish Language Board)

ISBN 978-1-902917-72-6

CONTENTS

Profyans

Y ferwis pennskrifer a'n obereth ma, Map Mercya, prys mayth esa an dyllans ma yn darbar. Kesva an Taves Kernewek a vynn y sakra dhe gov Map Mercya owth aswonn y skolheygieth ha'y dhiwysogneth heb par hag ev owth oberi a-barth Kernewek dres 30 blydhen.

Dedication

The editor of this work, Ray Edwards, died while this edition was in preparation. The Cornish Language Board wishes to dedicate it to the memory of Ray Edwards in appreciation of his peerless scholarship and diligence in working for Cornish over 30 years.

Preface

In 1985 I went to the Scrif-Celt Exhibition in London and when I tried to brush up my French at the stall of a Breton bookseller I had a little brown book thrust into my hand. This turned out to be an edition of the famous Cornish Passion Poem, not only in Unified Cornish but also in the original spelling of the Manuscript, with a Breton translation. It was the first time I had seen a piece of Cornish of any length in the MS spelling so I bought it. When I got it home I turned over the pages rather than read it, and put it on the bookshelf...

Two years later Kernewek Kemmyn was accepted by the Cornish Language Board and I realised that sooner or later the Board would need versions of the Cornish Texts in K.K. for their examinations as well as for general interest. From that time the idea formed in my mind to convert the Poem to K.K. One thing I did not have was an English translation, and the Breton one was of very limited use. I wrote to the Board to order their edition by Talek (E. G. R. Hooper) but was told it was out of print. Dr Ken George very kindly lent me his own copy which I photocopied. When I told Talek of my plan he sent me a correction list to his edition and a copy of the Manuscript made by Robert Morton Nance and published in instalments in the Cornish magazine *Kernow*. This was of great value as I was able to compare the two readings of the MS. There is more about this in the Notes on the Manuscript on page 7.

I cannot do better than quote verbatim, and with permission, the greater part of Talek's introduction to his edition of 1972.

The "Passion Poem" is a Cornish treasure and equivalent to good poetry in any language; every Cornish student ought to know it and it is with this aim that it is presented in "unified" or "modern standard" spelling. There are five manuscript copies. One, in the British Museum, Harl. N.1782 is a small quarto on rough vellum said to have been found in the church of Sancreed, was used by Whitley Stokes for his edition and English translation, published by the Philological Society of London in their transactions 1860-61.

There are two copies in the Bodleian Library, Oxford, and one in the Archbishop's Library, Lambeth. This is the one used by John Keigwin for translation and published by Davies Gilbert in 1826 under the title "Mount Calvary" - printed for the first time. But Keigwin was badly treated by his publisher: after giving thanks that Cornish was no longer heard, Gilbert "proceeds to butcher its remains," to quote R. Morton Nance, so that this edition is worthless.

There is an incomplete copy in the Gwavas collection, and a fragment of one with a Welsh and English translation (Add. MS 14,934) which perhaps was used by Hals (1665-1737) for he miscopies and attempts to translate verses in his "History of Cornwall" as under the parish of Boyton.

The Rev. Robert Williams adopted the title "Mount Calvary" in his Lexicon Cornu-britannicum, 1865, giving references under "M.C." The scholarly edition of R. Morton Nance (Mordon) was printed by A. S. D. Smith (Caradar) in his all Cornish magazine "KERNOW," serially in 14 parts, 1934-36 with the original text and a greatly improved English translation. Later the two collaborated in a close study of the text with the aid of photostats, constantly consulting similar forms of expression in the Ordinalia and other texts. After this work they sometimes made notes independently or in letters, all of which I have studied, using them in printing a plain text without translation in the successor to Kernow, An Lef Kernewek. Nos. 81 to 103 (1968).

The B.M. text is not easily read but Nance excelled in the reading, and writing of medieval script, and in so far as concerns the mutation of initial consonants, this text is easily the most accurate as was found by Caradar in his study of mutation (lenition) that one mutation was missed in 74 lines whereas in Bewnans Meryasek it is one in 9²/₃rds.

Nance wrote "Such a poem, intended for popular devotional use, must have been copied over and over again, and this copy has some obvious blunders of which the author would have been incapable. It is unlike other Passion Poems, English, French, or Breton in having no final verse to promise 100 to 500 days of pardon to those who learn or listen to it. Here and there a later pen has inked over words that have grown faint, not always correctly. This is the only Cornish MS that has the added interest of illuminations...they are rather more in the mood of modernist art than typical of the fifteenth century."

I am very grateful to Talek for the help he has given and also to Wella Brown and Dr Ken George who have read and annotated my rough draft. Many of their comments are incorporated in the notes. I am most grateful to Dr David Balhatchet who has done a lot of research in Sussex University Library. Much of the information on the sources of the Poem (page 24) is the result of this. He has also been through the whole book with his ruthless tooth comb and made many valuable suggestions. I am fully responsible for any errors that remain. And not least, I am grateful to Les Pierce who has provided the cover illustration, based on Celtic crosses at Bodmin and Sancreed. Thus there is a link with the Manuscript which is "said to have been found in the church of Sancreed". Maybe the writer actually saw this cross!

If any reader disagrees with any comments made or can add to the information given, I shall be very glad to hear.

Ray Edwards

Mis Ebryl, 1993

The Manuscript

I have worked from two copies of the British Museum MS Harleian N. 1782. I started with the copy printed in *Passyon agan Arluth* edited by Goulven Pennaod and published by Preder in Brittany in 1980. In his preface, which Dr Ken George has kindly translated for me from the Breton, Pennaod tells us that he copied the Whitley Stokes edition in the *Bibliothèque Nationale* in Paris and had it corrected by Talek. After I had begun work, Talek very kindly sent me the version that was printed in *Kernow* in 1934-36 from Nance's reading of the MS Although both readings are from the same MS there is a large number of small discrepancies between the two. These are listed on pages 9-13, with the version which I have used in the text shown in bold type. I have chosen whichever seemed the more appropriate.

When reading the MS the following points have to borne in mind:

1) **v** and **u** are interchangeable; e.g. in 1/2, **levn** = **leun** and in 1/6, **lauarow** = **lavarow.**

2) **z** usually represents **dh**; e.g. 1/3, **zeugh** = **dhywgh**.

3) **th** may represent **dh:** e.g. in 1/7, **worthyans** = **wordhyans,**
or **th**: e.g. in 11/8, **worthebys** = **worthybis.**

4) **sc** represents **sh** or **sshy**; e.g. in 1/4, **basconn** = **basshyon.**

5) **j** was really an alternative form of **i** and was used both for the vowel **i** and for the consonant **j** that was coming into use. It seems likely that the initial sound of names like *Yesu* and *Yowann* was beginning to move from *Y* to *J* about the time of the MS. **j** was not used exclusively for the modern **j** sound until the 17th century (*Chambers*).

6) The guttural sound spelled **gh** in K.K. and K.U. may appear as **h**; e.g. in 3/4, **werhas** = **wyrghes**, or as **gh**; e.g. in 7/1, **begha**.

7) **Yesu(s)** is almost always written **ihesu(s).** The *h* crept into the name because very few scribes knew Greek. The *h* actually represents the Greek letter □ (eta, the long *e*) which is exactly the same as *H* in the capital form and which was written as well as the normal letter *e.* It is still met in modern editions of the Cornish texts published in Unified Cornish.

Up to the nineteenth century **s** often looked like **f** which explains the occasional confused readings. Mostly, editors have printed **s.**

The mutation of the initial letters of proper names, in particular *Crist/Cryst* and *Pylat/Pelat* is inconsistent in the MS. Following *G.M.C.* §19(8); *G.M.C.(2)* §23(3h) I have not mutated them in the Kernewek Kemmyn version as they are not Celtic names.

The rather haphazard rhyming scheme of unstressed final syllables suggests that there were often, if not always, pronounced as neutral vowels. It is unfortunate that Kernewek Kemmyn does not have a symbol for these, but neither does English. The MS seems to use *e* most frequently to show a neutral vowel, though any vowel letter seems possible. Nicholas Williams is of the opinion that in general unstressed syllables contain neutral vowels (§13.33) and he tells me he does not feel a special symbol for schwa is necessary if they are treated as such.

Letters shown in brackets are ones which are illegible in the Manuscript and have been supplied by conjecture, presumably by Stokes or Nance or both.

There is a facsimile of the first page of the MS in *The Cornish Language and its Literature* by Peter Berresford Ellis. It is set out in lines of fourteen syllables. The first page of the MS contains the first four and a half verses as currently edited, but the page does not show these verses clearly and although there are some Arabic numbers to the right of the lettering they do not seem to refer to lines or verses. At the foot of the page is one of the illustrations mentioned by Talek in his Introduction.

The present edition has followed Hooper and Pennaod in dividing these lines into two lines each of seven syllables. The tradition of doing so goes back to Edward Lhuyd who printed the first four lines of seven syllables in his “Catalogue of unprinted writings in the Ancient Language of Britain” (*Antiqua Britanniæ Lingua scriptorum quæ non impressa sunt Catalogus*) which he included in his *Archæologia Britannica*. They are reproduced below. Lhuyd explains (in Latin) that the MS was given him by Mr John Anstey whom he praises highly. It is on parchment but without any title, indication of the author or when it was written though the handwriting indicates the fifteenth century.

Tays ha mâb ha ſperis ſans
Wy a bŷs a leun golon;
Re wronte dheugh gras ha whans
Dhe wolſowas y baſſyon.

However, the *Kernow* edition of the MS preserves the long-line format.

Since writing the above and publishing the Fourth Print I have had the opportunity of comparing the MS readings I had with those of Stokes. At the 1995 Gorsedd Keith Syed kindly gave me a photocopy of these and Harry Woodhouse checked them through for me and gave me a list of discrepancies. I am most grateful to both for their valuable help.The list showed that in general Nance was in agreement with Stokes with very few differences but Pennaod had made a large number of errors in copying from Stokes and I had made even more in copying from Pennaod and Nance! I have therefore now corrected the present MS version to agree with Stokes/Nance and have preferred Nance to Stokes in the very few cases of difference unless there were special reasons for not doing so. These have usually given rise to a note to the text but having Stokes to support Nance has made unnecessary the list of discrepancies between Nance and Pennaod which was included in previous prints and is mentioned at the top of page 7. It is therefore now omitted. Most of the changes are minor and of little consequence and only rarely have they occasioned an alteration to the Kernewek Kemmyn text. In a few cases there is a slight change of meaning and therefore to the translation.

The Stokes edition has copious and very interesting notes though no doubt many of these are out of date now. Due to the need to prepare this fifth print quickly I have not worked through them as yet.

Language

Confusion of Present and Imperfect Subjunctive. As is to be expected in a narrative poem, most of the verbs are in the past tense, exceptions being where conversation occurs. In the narrative passages, I have counted fifteen cases where the MS appears to have a present tense verb, usually a third person singular ending in *-o*, while the grammar calls for an imperfect. Conversely in conversations there are six cases of an imperfect subjunctive where the grammar requires a present. The verbs involved are *bos*, *mos*, *klywes*, *galloes*, *gul*, *y'm beus* and *kavoes*. Each case is indicated in the notes on the text. In the Unified versions Hooper "corrected" thirteen cases and left eight as in the MS, whilst Pennaod "corrected" seven and left fourteen. I have "corrected" all twenty-one as an aid to comprehension though such a degree of confusion leaves open the question as to which form actually is "correct."

Nicholas Williams (§12.4) maintains that this confusion is due to the vowel ending in each case becoming neutral and so always sounding the same though the confusion is not limited to the third person singular as he suggests.

***Unn* used as an Indefinite Article.** Current grammars of Cornish state that the Indefinite Article ('a, an') is not usually expressed. See *Cornish Simplified*, §1, and *Cornish for Beginners*, lesson 1. *Grammar of Modern Cornish* §92(3) [Second Edition, §95(3)] gives *unn* as meaning 'one', or 'a certain'. Similar definitions are found in the Nance *Dictionary* and the *Gerlyver Meur*.

I have counted *unn* used eight times in our Poem where the only sense compatible with the context is that of the indefinite article, and four times which would admit this, or 'a certain.' All these cases are indicated in the notes on the text. Edward Lhuyd recognises this usage on page 240 of the *Archaeologia Britannica*, as does J.C. Zeuss on page 239 of *Grammatica Celtica* where he quotes 16/2, *war ben un meneth*; 84/1, *un venyn*; 214/1, *on burges*; and 217/2, *on mareg* (his spelling) as examples.

Insertion of particle *a* between a part of *bos* and a preceding complement. This occurs in 29/8 and 44/6, and is unusual. See notes on text. According to *Cornish Simplified* §100 and *G.M.C.* §317(4a); *G.M.C.(2)* §333(4a) a complement preceding *bos* is usually followed by the particle *y* or the part of *bos* with soft mutation but without a particle, e.g. *marow y fydhons* or *marow vydhons*. The latter is more usual in current use.

Use of *gweles*. Although few modern Cornish writers realise this, the tendency seems to be to omit any auxiliary verb before *gweles*, similar to the French idiom, although 'can' is commonly used in English. In other words:-

My a wel. = *Je vois.* = 'I **can** see.'

I have noticed two examples in our Poem, in 64/6 and 220/5. They are similar to each other, the first being *Ny welens yn fas* and the second, *Ny welen yn fas*. They both refer to seeing in the literal physical sense, and the obvious translation into normal, idiomatic English is: 'They/We **could** not see very well.'

On the other hand, there is an example in 60/1, *Ni a **yll** gweles,* which implies an ability to follow an argument as to how Christ died for mankind. Similarly in 12/6, *Ni a **yll** gweles.* = 'We **can** see', understanding, not physical seeing is meant. 96/1-2, *Gans kweth y benn y kwethens; Gweles banna na ylli* clearly uses *ylli* with *gweles* because Jesus literally <u>could</u> not see as he was blindfolded.

Yn krows. When one is familiar with the English expression 'On *the* Cross', it is a little disconcerting to find *yn krows* on no less than eight occasions and one instinctively suspects a missed mutation and an omitted apostrophe. However, it becomes apparent that following verbs like *ladha, gorra,* and *synsi*, it is the equivalent of 'crucify'. The examples are indicated in the text notes.

Adjective plus *rag/dhe* plus verb noun = '....enough to'. There are four examples of this interesting and useful construction which could drive *lowr* out of business. They are as follows:-

105/8	....*krev rag y synsi*	= 'strong enough to hold him'
214/8	....*hardh dh'y notya*	= 'bold enough to make it known'
234/3	....*hardh dh'y notya*	= 'bold enough to make it known'
250/7	....*hardh dhe wortos*	= 'bold enough to stay'

The construction is mentioned in *G.M.C.* §141(17); *G.M.C.(2)* §141(18) and the examples are indicated in the notes on the text.

***Dell* with Indirect Question/Statement**. In his book, *Notes on Spoken Cornish*, Rod Lyon gives some examples from Wella Rowe and Nicholas Boson of what he describes as indirect statements introduced by *dell.* The *Gerlyver Meur* suggests that *dell* and *fatell* are of the same origin and in fact that *fa-* is an interrogative prefix. From this it seems that both words can mean 'how', with *fatell* being the more directly interrogative. In most of Rod Lyon's examples the *dell* would translate as 'how' or as 'that', suggesting that the following clauses could be regarded as indirect questions rather than statements.

I have found six similar examples in our Poem and in all cases the *dell* would translate as either 'how' or 'that'. They are as follows:-

8/2-4 *Lavarav.....akord dell veu kemmerys.*
= 'I will tell how/that an accord was made.'

12/6-7 ...*ni a yll gweles lavar Duw maga dell wra....*
= 'We can see how/that the Word of God nourishes....'

61/6-8 ...*dyskys fatell dhons dh'ow hemmeres ha dell vydhav hembrynkys.*
= '...learned how/that they will come to take me and how/that I shall be led away.'

123/1-2 *Dh'y gour hi a dhannvonas a Krist kepar dell welsa,*
= To her husband she sent how/that she had seen of Christ,

177/1-2 *Unn venyn dha a welas dell o Yesus destryppys.*
= 'A good woman saw how/that Jesus was stripped.'

221/2-6 ...*welas ... an goes ha'n lin anodho dell dheveras.*
= 'saw ... how/that the blood and water ran from him.'

It is a matter of opinion whether 'how' or 'that' is better in each of the above cases; and whether the clauses are statements or questions becomes rather academic. I have used 'how' in the text translation but it does suggest that the tendency was for *dell* in such cases to mean 'that' rather than 'how' as time went on. It will be noticed in 61/7 above that *fatell* is used in the same way as *dell* to introduce the indirect question/statement.

Nicholas Williams (§21.17) regards this as a legitimate usage in Revived Cornish.

***O* plus past participle.**

"With the Imperfect tense (of *bos*), the Past Participle denotes a continuous state and is descriptive: e.g. *shyndys en* 'I was hurt.'"

[*G.M.C.* §229(3); *G.M.C.(2)* §245(3a)].

One cannot disagree with this as a general principle but I have noticed four cases where the 'continuous state' was the result of an action which had immediately preceded the time of the narration and as far as modern English is concerned 'had been' seems a more appropriate translation than 'was'. I have used 'had been' in some cases in the translation and Hooper has done so in one case (233/4). The examples are as follows:-

177/1-2 *Unn venyn dha a welas dell o Yesus destryppys.*
= 'A good woman saw how Jesus had been/was stripped.'

219/5-6 *Y hwolghas y dhewlagas gans y eyl leuv o goesys.*
= 'He washed his eyes with his one hand which had been/was covered in blood.'

219/7-8 *Dre ras an goes y hwelas Yesus Krist dell o dyghtys.*
= 'By virtue of the blood he saw how Jesus Christ had been/was treated.'

233/4 *Nowydh parys, nyns o usys.*
= "Newly prepared, it had not been/was not used."

Maybe 'was' is better in 219/6 but I certainly prefer 'had been' in the other cases. They are all indicated in the text.

***Mynnes* without verb-noun.** *Mynnes* is normally used as an auxiliary verb followed by a verb-noun. However the poem has the following examples of *mynnes* governing a noun or pronoun object:

54/4 *an kig ny vynna henna* = "the flesh did not want that."
67/4 *Pandra yw a vynnowgh hwi?* = "What do you want?"

Use of the Present Participle. The present participle formed with *ow* and the verb-noun is normally a verbal adjective, or is used with the long forms of *bos* to form continuous tenses. However, the Poem also contains the following examples of the present participle used as an oblique gerund meaning "*by/in/through* doing", similar to the ablative of the gerund in Latin or the present participle in Spanish:

86/7 *Ow nagha Duw* = "by denying God."
104/4 *ow kwertha* = "by/in selling."

Long forms of *bos* in nominal sentences. *G.M.C.* §315(4); *G.M.C.(2)* §332(4) states that the long forms of *bos* are used only in verbal sentences and the verb is therefore always preceded by the particle *yth*. However, I have found the following examples of *bos* used in nominal sentences without *yth*:

124/1 *Onan esa y'n pryson.* = "There was one in the prison."
131/1-2 ...*prennyer esa yn diwla an dhew Edhow.* = "there were sticks in the hands of the two Jews."

140/6 Kweth esa a-dro dhodho.

140/7-8 *Prest an Edhewon debel dhe Yesus esens a-dro.* = "The wicked Jews were always around Jesus."

I do not see any reason why the verb is plural in the fourth example but not in the second.

3rd singular imperative. *G.M.C.(2)* §183/3 states "The 3rd sing (imperative) in Modern Cornish has restored the use of the forms in *-es*. The 3rd sing. in *-ens* had taken its place in many instances." However there are fourteen examples in the MS of the poem of the form in *-ens* being used with a singular subject and only one of *-es*. They are indicated in the notes on the text.

Double consonants in subjunctive stems. In *G.M.C. §185 and G.M.C. (2) §182* Wella Brown introduces the principle of doubling and hardening the stem vowel in the present and imperfect subjunctive. As far as I know this had not been given in earlier grammars but it is confirmed by the following examples in our Poem:

teffa, 27/7, 162/7, 249/7; *caffans*, 67/6; *caffons*, 114/7, 154/4; *caffan*, 240/6; *wozaffo*, 14/5; *geffo*, 51/3; *deppro*, 44/7.

Spelling

The main purpose of this book is to make available a version of the Poem in Kernewek Kemmyn, and I have adhered wherever possible to the spellings given in the *Gerlyver Meur*, published in 1993 and have used conjectural spelling only where *G.M.* spellings are not available. However there are some words, the spelling of which calls for comment, as follows:

The diphthong *ay*. There are a number of words of French origin containing this diphthong which rhymes with 'tie' in English. Most of them are spelled with *ey* in the MS, and their original forms in Old French and Middle English would have had roughly the same sound as the vowel in 'say,' sometimes shortened to 'said.' This is still the sound in the Modern English and French forms of these words, so it is difficult to see how they could have reverted to the sound indicated by *ay* which was an older form going back to very old French as it developed from Latin and Gallo-Roman.

However both Ken George and Nicholas Williams seem to agree that this is the case. Nicholas Williams (§6.8) asserts that words with the *ey* diphthong borrowed from English as well as native Cornish words did change the diphthong to *ay* but then points out that both spellings are found in this poem for *paynys* and *traytor* and quotes other cases where the same word is found with both spellings. This, he says is evidence that the two diphthongs were not distinct and it is unlikely that Lhuyd considered them as separate, which to me suggests a rather colourless sound, varying between the two. The only definite support he offers for his *ey* becoming *ay* thesis is a number of place names where the word *dreyn* meaning "thorns" is spelt "-drine". These are Trendrine, Landrine and Halldrine. But his conclusion is that *ey* did become *ay* which supports the KK spelling.

Nyns and **Nans.** *nyns* occurs twenty-one times in our Poem and in every case the MS spelling is *nyn. Nyns* is the form used in K.U. and K.K. when followed by a part of *mos* or *bos* beginning with a vowel. In the MS this verb is always prefixed with *g* or *i* (=*j*) suggesting a *j* rather than an *s* sound, e.g. 6/8, *nyn io man.* On this basis it seems better to spell *nyns* as *nynj.* Similarly we have *nango* twice for *nans o* suggesting that *nans* would be better spelt *nanj.*

Marghek. I have counted this word fourteen times in either the singular or the plural and in no case does the MS show a *g* or an *h* or anything to indicate a guttural consonant between the two syllables. Ken George informs me that this is also the case in all the other texts. Etymologically it should be there, he says, and he has followed Nance in keeping the *-gh-* in K.K. spelling. This is contrary to the principle stated in *P.S.R.C.* of basing Kernewek Kemmyn on Cornish as it was *spoken* around 1500. If all the evidence suggests that there was no *-gh-* sound in *marghek*, why put one there?

Tochya/toch. These words occur in 14/6 and 158/4. It is strange to find *o* instead of *ou* as is normally the case with words derived from Old French with the *ou* spelling. However *o,* not *ou* is in the MS in both cases and there is an alternative Old French spelling *tochier* in *Larousse* which may justify it.

Lagha. Nance offers two words as meaning 'law'; *lagha* and *lay,* corresponding to the English words 'law' and 'lay' which seem to be of Norse and French origin respectively. The meaning of *lay* in both Cornish and English is 'religious law or faith.' *G.M.* gives only *lagha. Lagha* or *lay* in singular or plural occur eight times in the Poem and show a certain disagreement between the two readings of the MS. Pennaod has it spelled five times without any *h* to suggest a guttural, and so indicating *lay* and only three times with the *h* which would suggest *lagha.* However the Nance version has *h* shown in brackets in every case where Pennaod omits it. As *G.M.* and Nance agree together I have used the *lagha* form in the K.K. text.

O'ta (sy). Although the form *osta* ('you are' or 'are you') is in common use in both Unified Cornish and *Kernewek Kemmyn*, Ken George pointed out several years ago that it is not found in the texts (though it is in *C.W.*) It is always *ota* or *osa*. This is confirmed by the seven examples I have found in our Poem. The MS spelling is *ota* in three cases, *ote* in two cases, *ose* in one case and *oge* in one case. Both Pennaod and Hooper Unified versions have *ota* wherever there is a *t,* and *osa* where there is *s* or *g.* Unfortunately *G.M.* does not give verb forms but *G.M.C.(2)* (which has become available since the first printing of this book) gives *osta/o'ta*, [§64(3)] so I have decided for this printing to standardise on *o'ta* in all cases though it seems clear that the use of *t* or *s* in the MS depends to some extent on harmony with the adjacent sounds. Maybe a rule should be formulated to govern this. It has been suggested that "osta" is so well established in revived spoken Cornish that it would be very difficult to replace it with "o'ta" in everyday speech.

Lemmyn. Somewhat surprisingly *G.M.* tells us that the word *lemen* in fairly common use especially in Unified Cornish to mean 'but, except', is the same word as *lemmyn* meaning 'now'. This is confirmed by the fourteen examples in our Poem where *lemen* is used in the Unified versions. In nine cases the MS word ends in *-yn* with one *m* or two in the middle, so I have used *lemmyn* in every case, but it has to be admitted it does not aid comprehension as one has to decide whether the meaning is 'now' or 'but'.

Onan/honan. This is the *G.M.* spelling though in only one case in our Poem do we find *honan* rhyming with a word ending in *-an.* Ken George has come to the conclusion that these words were written with *-yn, -an* or *-on* endings depending on the words with which they were set to rhyme. In almost every case the rhyming words in the Poem end in *-on* so that *onon/honon* do likewise in the MS, implying, I would think, that these final rhyming syllables are just neutral vowels. Williams confirms this (§13.33) Out of the three, the ending

-an was chosen in imitation of Welsh and Breton forms with the unfortunate result for this Poem that these syllables will appear not to rhyme and the reader will have to treat them as neutral vowels for them to do so. The MS seems to use *e* most commonly to indicate a neutral vowel as does modern French.

Krist. Murdoch quotes William Camden in his *Britannia*, 1586, as saying that one MS of the Poem always has *Chrest* for *Christ* in accordance with some Latin authors, and that the Cornish pronounce it *Chrest*. This would suggest, perhaps, that the K.K. spelling should be *Krest* or *Kryst*. However, the modern English pronunciation with the long *i* indicates that this vowel was long in Middle English which would support the likelihood of it being long in Cornish also, so I feel more evidence is needed before a change is seriously considered. The spelling is always *Crist* or *Cryst* in our present MS.

Other biblical names. Other names in our Poem in the K.K. spelling which I have used are as follows:

Yesus, Yerusalem, Yosep, Yowann, Yudas, Edhow.

In April 1989 I circulated a paper which concluded that most biblical names beginning with *J* in English should begin with *Y* in Cornish. No one opposed this and Wella Brown indicated to me his agreement. I was told that the Bishop of Truro's Advisory Group on services in Cornish came to the same conclusion in 1977. It seems likely that this initial sound survived right through from Hebrew through Greek, Latin and British into Middle Cornish. However, in a few cases the initial semi-vowel in Latin lengthened to become a full vowel *i.* The case in which we are interested is 'Jew', *Iudaeus* in its Latin form which became *Iddew* in Welsh and seems to have had a dual development in Cornish as we find the spelling *Ethow* in the MS of our Poem, but *Yedhow* in the *Ordinalia*. However, it may be that *Ethow* was the earlier development and the initial *y* sound was put back in imitation of the Latin used in the Mass. This opinion finds some support in Richard Gendall's *A Students' Dictionary of Modern Cornish* which gives the following spellings from late Cornish writers: *Ethow*, *Ethowan*, *Ethohan* (Gwavas); *Ethewan* (Rowe) and *Edheuan*, *Idheuon* (Lhuyd). None of these starts with Y. I have kept *Edhow* in the K.K. version.

Of the above names, only the spellings *Jowann, Yowann* and *Yedhow* are given in *G.M.* It points out that *Jowann* correponds to the late pronunciation *Dzhûan* found in Lhuyd and that *Yowann* is preferable

However Nicholas Williams (§8.20) makes a case that *Yesus* and *Yowann* should have initial *J (Jesus/Jowann)* basing his argument partly on the belief that these names were lost in native Cornish and reintroduced from Breton or French after the Norman invasion. He seems to make a similar case for many other biblical names beginning with J (but excluding "Jew") though in these cases the reasoning is not explicit.

References to *Cornish Simplified Part II*

Cornish Simplified Part Two by A. S. D. Smith, edited by E. G. R. Hooper, and formerly known as the *Supplements to Cornish Simplified* provides a wealth of examples from the Cornish texts to illustrate points of Cornish Grammar, many of them quite elementary, some more advanced and some rare or exceptional. The following list gives all those taken from Passhyon agan Arloedh. The list should be used in conjunction with the book where more details will be found than in the very brief notes below. In the book the Poem is given the abbreviation "M.C." (*Mount Calvary*), and for that reason the references in the first column have this heading. Verse and line numbers are quoted.

The references to *Cornish Simplified Part II* under the heading *C.S.II* are by the page and the sub-section number appearing on the page but omitting chapter and main section references for simplicity.

The quotations from the poem are in Kernewek Kemmyn. They are printed in Unified Cornish in *C.S.II*.

The notes are copied or summarised from *C.S.II* except where I have added my own comments in brackets.

M.C.	C.S.II	Extract	Notes
4/5-7	23-24/13	May fynnas diyskynna Yn gwyrghes ha bos genys Gans y gig agan prena...	Three verbs dependent on *fynnas.*
7/1	58/40	War-lergh mabden dhe begha.	*War-lergh = "after."*
9/2	35/4	Oll y sorr may fe gevys	*oll* preceding noun.
10/1-2	24/13	Y vamm pan y'n drehevis Ha'y vos devedhys dhe oes.	Two verbs depending on *pan;* *drehevis,* a finite verb, and bos, a verb-noun.
10/4	8/b	Henna ganso nyns o poes	Short form imp. *bos (o)* with *gans* and adjective; [cf. *G.M.C.* §147(5); *G.M.C.(2)* §147(5)]
14/3	86/b	Ahanas yth yw skrifys Bos eledh orth dha witha	*yth yw* linking prepositional phrase to complement.
15/3	28/21	Yn neb eghenn a servis	*eghenn* followed by *a* and noun.
15/4	60/50	Lemmyn prest y enora.	*lemmyn* = "but" (See page 13, *lemmyn.*)
17/8	49/v	Dha vaystri a vydh lehes Nevra war an enevow.	*war* = "over."
19/8	59/46	Ma na allo an tebel Ogas dhis bones treylys.	*ogas dhis* = "near (to) you."
21/1-2	66/c	............prest yma A-dro dhyn ni.	*yma* with prepositional phrase.
22/2	42/E	Anodho na ro demma. = "Don't give a halfpenny for him."	*a* in idiomatic phrase.

M.C.	C.S.II	Extract	Notes
24/2	56/26	dres pub tra..	*dres* = "beyond."
24/7-8	20/8 37/9/i	Oll an da ha'n drog kepar, Dhe Yesu bedhes grassys.	*grassys* followed *dhe* governing person being thanked.
25	40/B	Whole verse.	Use of Habitual Imperfect.
26/4	42/B	Hag anedha na wre vri. "...and did not take heed of them."	*a* in idiomatic phrase.
29/3	56/28	Meur a dus ha benynes A Yerusalem y 'n dre Erbynn Krist, rag y weles I eth	*mos erbynn* = *"to meet."*
32/5/6	7/14	Rag an laghys dhyn ni eus A vynn hy dampnya porres	*eus* with *dhe* in relative clauses.
32/7	71/15	Fordh nyns eus.	*nyns eus* following subject.
33/3	9/20	Yth esa an venyn gansa.	*esa* indicating place.
33/6	51/i	Yesus y'n dor a skrifas.	*yn* = "on."
36/4	55/b	awos Dew (*as in C.S.II*)	*awos* = "for the sake of." (*C.S.II* reads *awos Dew.* Hooper and Pennaod read *awos den*, but this does not affect the meaning of *awos* which is the point being made by *C.S.II.* However, both my MS readings have *a vos den* which I have followed. See note on text, and translation.)
39/2-3	45/e	Ha my a wra dhywgh spedya Ow kavoes Krist yredi.	*spedya* used with present participle.
40/5	48/ii	Orth Yesu ev a fekla	*fekla orth* = *" to fawn upon."*
43/2	65/5	Ow tybri genen yma.	Present participle preceding *yma.*
43/4	79/31	......yw my henna?	*C.S. II* suggests "'Is it I (who am) that man?' or 'Am I that man?' Both versions are possible. In the first, 'it' is the subject (contained in the verb), with *my* as the complement. In the second, *my* is the subject with pronoun *henna* as complement.'" (I prefer the second explanation.)
44/2	54/20	Dherag y abesteli	*dherag* = "in the presence of."
45/2	59/42	Ha'n gwin esa war an voes Ev a rannas yntredha.	*ynter/yntra* = *"among."*
45/4	58/34	par cheryta	*par* = "out of."
49/3	52/vii	Yn nos haneth. = "This very night."	Idiom using *yn.*
49/7	58/37	Tann ow fydh = "By my faith."	*tann* = "by." (in oath)
51/2	57/31	....res yw porres Batalyas kyns es koska.	*kyns es* = *"rather than."*
51/3-4	34	an geffo pows as gwyrzyns ha zozo pernas cleze (MS)	Older form of 3rd sing. imperative.

(In line 4 there is a hand written amendment of *pernas* to *pernans* in my copy of the *Kernow* MS. Line 3 shows *gwyrzyns*, an imperative with the *n* but K.K. has standardised on the form without *n*. See note on text.)

M.C.	C.S.II	Extract	Notes
53/7	77/26	....pysi may halla Dh'y Das hwath usi a-vann.	*usi* used in relative clause.
59/6	49/vi	Na leverel war anow.	*war anow* = "by word of mouth."
59/8	57/31	Kyns es bones marow	*kyns es* = "before."
62/3	51/i	Yudas eth yn y negys.	*yn y negys* = "on his business."
65/1	55/a	Pan dhodhyens bys y'n tyller.	*bys yn* = "to."
67/6	40/ii	Yesus yw, a'n kaffen ni.	*C.S.II* seems to suggest that this is a potential (i.e. imperf. subj.) with pluperfect meaning, but see text note.
68/1	55/25	drefenn an vertu.	*Drefenn* = "because of."
69/3	83/35	Agas negys, pyth ywa?	Complement preceding *yw* in interrogative sentence.
71/3	58/35	.....ryb an penn	*ryb* = "close to."
72/3	39/12/vi	rag dre gleze a veughe (MS)	*C.S.II* says *-gh-* is an ancient sign of the subjunctive. (The Unified versions have *vewo* which I have followed with *vywo* in K.K.)
72/5	52/vii	yn unn rew	Idiom with *yn.* = "one after another."
75/1-2	18/4	Yn agas mysk pan esen Laghys Duw dhywgh ow tyski.	Object preceding present participle.
79/8	53/15	A-dryv tus.	*a-dryv tus* = "behind people."
80/1-2	43/vii	Pandra a wovynn'ta sy Dhiworthiv vy a'm laghys?	*a* = "about."
85/3	86/b	Dre dha gows yth yw prevys Dha vos den a Galila.	*yth yw* linking prepositional phrase to complement.
88/2	53/14	Yesus a veu dannvenys A-dhiworth an pryns Annas.	*a-dhiworth* = *"away from."*
88/5	13/4	Dredho Krist may fe breusys.	(*C.S.II* queries whether there is any difference between *dre* and *gans* in such sentences. *G.M.C.* §142(3); *G.M.C.(2)* §142(5) suggests that with a noun denoting an animate being *dre* means 'through the medium of', whilst *gans* means 'by', with the animate being acting as the agent. This seems to apply here, implying that Christ was judged by Caiaphas acting *on behalf of* the authorities rather than in his own name. However, cf. 142/6 where Pilate says "Let him be killed by you," and *dre* is used, although 'through the medium of' hardly applies as the Jews are being addressed.)
89/2	53/9	a-berth y'n wlas.	*a-berth yn* = " in."
91/6	51/i	Y'n tressa dydh.	*yn* = "on."
94/8	55/d	Awos dampnya an den ma	*awos* = "in order to."
98/2	55/a	I eth....... Bys yn Pilat.	*Bys yn* = "to."

M.C.	C.S.II	Extract	Notes:
99/2	50/xi	Yn-medh Pilat, "Pana dra A ynniowgh hwi warnodho?"	*war* = "against."
99/3-4	40/iii	Na ve bos fals an den ma Ny'n drossen ni bys dhiso.	Conditional sentence.
99/4	55/a	bys dhiso.	*bys dhe* = "to."
100/5-6	28/21	Pilat orto govynnas Y'n keth maner ma govynn.	*govynn* appositional genitive after *maner*; "in this same manner of question." (It seems more reasonable to take *govynn* as the direct object of *govynnas* and *yn keth maner* as an adverbial phrase; "asked a question in this same way.")
102/1-2	76/25	.....Nyns usi Ow mestrynsys y'n bys ma.	*usi* with definite noun subject.
104/3-4	18/4	Fest yn krev my re beghas Yesus dhy'hwi ow kwertha.	*ow kwertha* = "by selling." (*C.S.II* calls this English construction "preposition with particle." This should probably read "preposition with *participle*" but, in fact, as the Cornish phrase does not use a preposition, it is more closely parallel to the Latin ablative of the gerund or the Spanish present participle without a preposition , *vendendo* and *vendiendo* respectively. Both words could translate as 'by selling' in the appropriate context. See Language Notes, page 11.)
105/3	53/14	Ni a'n prenas dhiworthis.	*dhiworth* = "from."
105/3-4	35/1	Ni a'n prenas dhiworthis Hag a'th pes pur yredi.	*ha* joining two finite verbs.
110/1-2	9/19	Dhe Herodes yth esa Pur wir orth Pilat sorr bras.	*yth esa* with prepositional phrase preceding.
111/4	43/iii	Ma'n jeva marth a henna.	*marth a* = "wonder at."
113/5-8	15/1	Ha leverewgh bos gevys Oll ow sorr, bedhes lowen, Ha'm galloes y vos grontys Dhodho dhe vreusi an den.	Two kinds of indirect statement with *bos,* after *leverewgh.*
114/6	45/iii	Pilat o justis dhedha. = "Pilate was their magistrate."	*dhe* showing possession.
114/8	49/v	War Yesus Krist....	*war* = "over."
117/3-4	16-7/2	Rag Yesus Krist dhe'n mernans I a vynna porres dri.	Unusual omission of poss. adj. before *dri*, probably to fit length of line.
117/3-4	22/10	Rag Yesus Krist dhe'n mernans I a vynna porres dri.	Use of *porres* with *mynnes.*
117/5	49/ix	...Orth an myns	*orth* = "according to."
118/1-2	22/10	An Edhewon a vynna Porres y vones ledhys.	*porres* used with *mynnes.*
121/2	9/18	Dhe'n traytour esa ganso.	*esa* used with *gans.*

M.C.	C.S.II	Extract	Notes
121/6	74/20	Laghys eus y'n pow a-dro.	*eus* used instead of *yma,* and following subject to emphasise it.
122/7-8	41/vi	War hy mester venjans krev Y to, Yesus mar lattha.	*C.S.II* says "..a complete conditional sentence in indirect narration; instead of direct 'war hy mester venyons cref *a dhothya*, Jhesus mar latha,' the conditional '*a dhothya*' has to give way to the Imperfect Indicative '*y to*.'" (See note on text.)
123/1-2	43/vii	Dh'y gour hi a dhannvonas A Krist kepar dell welsa.	*a* = "about."
123/4	81/33	Nyns yw ragos sy ladha Krist.	Prepositional phrase as complement to *yw*.
124/5	8/a	Maner o dhe'n Edhewon.	Imperfect *o* with *dhe* preceding a noun. [cf. *G.M.C.* §237; *G.M.C.(2)* §253(2a)]
124/7	48/iii	A'n pryson govynn onan.	*govynn* without *orth* meaning "to demand; claim."
126/6	43/vii	A Yesus pyth a vydh gwrys?	*a* = "about."
127/4	57/d	Gwitha Krist heb vileni	*gwitha heb* = "to protect from."
128/2/6	51/i	y'n grows.	*yn* = "on." [The MS has *yn crows* ("on a cross = crucified") and I have followed this along with Hooper and Pennaod. (See Language notes, page 10). However, this does not affect the point that *yn* means "on" in this context.]
130/3	48/ii	Hag orth post fast a'n kolmas	*kelmi orth* = *"to tie to."*
131/3	48/ii	Hag yn fast kelmys dhedha.	*kelmi dhe* refers to things bound to sticks, not personal.
131/6	54/20	Hag a-rag gwrys kolmennow.	*a-rag* = "in the front", (i.e. at the ends of the whips.)
135/5	53/10	Meur o an payn adar ken.	*adar* = "beyond."
137/7	8/a	Henn o dhodho meur a bayn.	*o* used with *dhe* and a noun.
138/7	53/16	a-dro dh'y dhiwen.	*a-dro dhe* = "about."
142/4	43/vi	Merwens a'n grows. = "Let Him die by the cross."	*a* = "by." (MS has *mernans* and Hooper gives a note, "Formerly thought to be *merwens* by Mordon." I have taken it as *mernans* which would now mean "death of the cross.")
142/6	13/2	Dredhowgh hwi bedhes ledhys.	*dredhowgh* = "by you." (but cf. 88/5)
146/4	60/50	Kerensa Sesar, ytho Ny dheu lemmyn bylini.	*lemmyn* = " but" (See Spelling Notes, page 13)
147/6	67/7	Awotta....... Agas myghtern ple'mava!	*ple'ma* = "where is." (*ma* used after *ple.*)
148/3	63	Meth yw dhyn.	Complement preceding *yw.*

M.C.	C.S.II	Extract	Notes
152/8	35/2	Dredhi Adam may peghsa. = "Through which Adam had sinned."	*may* used as oblique relative pronoun.
153/7	35/2	May teuth frut may fen kellys	ditto.
154/1	8/a	Hwath kentrow dhedha nyns o.	*o* used with *dhe* im-mediately followed by a noun. (This does not agree with the rule given in *G.M.C.* §237; *G.M.C. (2)* §253(1) which states that the long form of *bos* should be used if the subject is indefinite. This would require *Hwath kentrow dhodho nyns esa*, which would upset the line length and also the rhyme, so maybe this is the reason for the *o.)*
154/1	9/20	Hwath kentrow dhedha nyns o.	(In this section *C.S.II* includes this line in a list of examples of the use of *esa*, realising, presumably that it ought to be *esa* and not noticing that it was not!)
155/5	55/d	Mar omwreth klav..... Awos guthyl hwel mar skav...= "If you pretend to be ill over doing such a light job..."	*awos guthyl* = "through doing/ because of doing."
155/6	51/iv	Yn edhomm	*yn* = "at." [*C.S.II* quotes this as an example of *yn* meaning "at." Hooper has "If thou failest us at need," but it is rather quaint English. The context suggests "in (our) need."]
156/6	51/i	. ".....Kleves bras Eus y'm diwla devedhys."	*yn* = "to."
160/6	43/vii	A'n grows, piw ella dh'y doen.	*a* = "about."
162/3	54/22	A-ves dhe'n dre yth esa.	*a-ves dhe* = "outside."
163/1	38/v	Dew lader dreus o dempnys.	soft mutation after a dual.
166/3	90/46	Nyns yw ow faynys byghan.	*Nyns yw* with plural noun subject. *Nyns yns* can also follow a plural subject and is a stronger negative.
166/5	59/c	Ow holonn yntra mil rann...	*yntra* = "into;" indicating a division; [cf. *G.M.C.* §180(4b); *G.M.C.(2)* §178(4b)].
171/3	56/28	May halla dos er y bynn.	*dos erbynn* = "to meet."
172/2	59/42	Ena hi a veu sevys Yn-bann ynter benynes.	*ynter* = "among."
172/4	5/6	Ow holonn yma genes.	*genes* = "with you."
173/8	50/iv	......rag y wannder.	*rag* = "because of."
174/2	43/vi	Simon o a'y ewn hanow.	*a* = "by "(name)
175/2	44/xiii	.......a'y anvodh. =	Idiomatic use of *a. ".....against his will."*
175/2	82/33	.......henn o a'y anvodh = "....that was against his will."	Prepositional phrase as complement of *o*
178/4	57/e	hepken = wantonly	Idiomatic use of *ken.* (*C.S.II.* seems to take the phrase to mean that the two holes were drilled carelessly, i.e. without being properly measured. I have followed Hooper and Pennaod who take *ken* as meaning "another" so that *hepken* means "without another," or "one only." We read in v.180 how the one hole was in the wrong place)

M.C.	C.S.II	Extract	Notes
179/1	50/xi	Gansa Krist a veu tewlys War an grows dhe wrowedha	*war* = "on." The cross was lying flat. Otherwise, "On the cross" = *Y'n grows.*
181/5	43/v	Gans re a gemmys kolonn.	*a* = "with."
182/1	49/v	......war an toll.	*war* = "over."
182/2	35/2	Dre an nerth may tennsons i	*may*, oblique relative pronoun = "with which."
182/2	60/51	Dre an nerth may tennsons i.	*may* = "with which."
182/7	45/ii	Ha na vo gesys dhe goll An laghys a wrug dhyn ni.	*gesys dhe goll* = "wasted."
184/2	51/i	Ha Yesus festys ynni	*yn* = "on." (the cross)
186/2	43/viii} 52/8 }	Lader dhe Krist a'n barth kledh.	*A* = "on" (the left)
186/2	45/iii	Lader dhe Krist a'n barth kledh = "A thief on the left side of Christ."	*dhe* = "of," showing possession.
188/4	45/iii	Y vones myghtern dhyn ni. = ."..that He is our King."	ditto.
192/5	63	Den glan yw a begh.	Complement preceding *yw.*
194/6	51/vi	Ragon ny woer omwitha	*gwitha rag* = "to guard against."
200/4	56/26	dres oll an bys	*dres* = "over."
204/8	59/c	yntra dha dhiwla.	*yntra* = "into."
205/1	50/iv	Rag gwan spern....	*rag* = "because of."
205/5	43/viii	Mar poessa'n eyl tenewen.	*a'n eyl tenewen* = "on the one side."
207/5	58/39	Wor'tu ha'y vamm.	*wor'tu ha* = "towards."
208/1	58/35	Ryb Krows Yesus.	*ryb* = "by."

208/3 44/ix A vernans Krist...... *a* = "at;" a rare meaning. (Hooper has "At Christ's death," but the translation does not really fit the context and I have taken it with the following clause to mean "of" or "about Christ's death.")

209/2	73/17	.....dell yma skrifys.	*dell* used with *yma.* An exceptional example.
209/6	59/c	Vayl an tempel a skwardyas Yntra dew.	*Yntra* = "into."

211/3 44/ix A Krist ow kodhav mernans *a* = "at," a rare meaning. (As in 208/3, Hooper has "at Christ suffering death." I feel "from" is more appropriate.)

M.C.	C.S.II	Extract	Notes:
214/3	51/i	Yn mernans Krist	*yn* = "on."
214/7	8/b	Yesus ganso o kerys	*o* used with *gans* and past participle. [cf. *G.M.C.* §147(6); *G.M.C(2)* §147(6)].
214/8	45/ii	Ha nyns o hardh dh'y notya.	*hardh dhe* = "so bold as to." (There are several examples of this usage. See Language Notes, page 10.)
216/3	48/viii	Dhe vires orth Krist i eth.	*vires orth* = "to look at." *Orth* indicates the exact spot.
217/1	52/vii	Y'ga herwydh.	An idiom = "with them; in their company."
218/1	43/viii	Longys sur a'n barth deghow Dhe grows Yesus yth esa.	*a'n barth.* = "on the" (left/right).
218/3	48/viii	.......orth y hanow.	*orth hanow* = "by name."
218/7	60/49	Pur ewn yn-dann an asow.	*yn-dann* = "under."
219/3	58/35	......ryb an guw.	= "along the spear."
222/5&840/ii & iv		Ha'y holonn hweg a ranna .....Na's gwittha an Spyrys Sans.	Exceptional example of the imperfect subjunctive (called "Potential" in *C.S.II*) used in both clauses of a conditional sentence. Normally the main clause is conditional and the *if* clause is imperfect subjunctive. [Cf. *G.M.C.*§328(3) though this note is omitted in *G.M.C.(2)*]
229/3	8/a	rag Pask o dhedha	*o* used with *dhe* and noun subject. [Cf. *G.M.C.*§238; *G.M.C.(2)* §253(2a)]
230/1	56/28	Erbynn bones henna gwrys.	= "by the time that was done."
234/6-7	9/18	Ev eth dhe'n korf o marow Gans unyent dhodho esa.	*esa* used with a prepositional phrase.
234/7	7/15	Gans unyent dhodho esa.	*esa dhodho* = "which he had."
235/4	57/c	heb pedri.	= "uncorrupted."
236/3-4	43/viii	Dhe Krist a bub tenewen Hag a dheghow hag a gledh.	*a* = "on." (three examples)
237/5	56/26	Ganso dres nos y hwoelyas	*dres nos* ="through-out the night."
242/7-8	41/vi	Bost a wrens, tynn ha diveth, Y'n gwithens orth y eghenn!	Indirect statement.
243/4	52/vii	yn le may fynna	*yn le may* = "wherever."
245/4	43/vii	A Yesus fatell via.	*a* = "about, concerning."
247/8	58/b	war-lergh y arghadow	*war-lergh* = "according to."
248/4-5	19/5	Ha dhodho a leveris Re savsa Krist heb strivya.	*re* instead of *y* introducing indirect statement.

M.C.	C.S.II.	Extract.	Notes
249/6	59/46	a-ogas hag a-bell	= "near and far."
251/8	52/7	Yn le mayth ens	*Yn le mayth* = "wherever."
252/1	51/i	Y'n keth jydh na.	*yn* = "on."
254/3-4	45/iii	Orth an penn i a welas Dhe'n bedh yw leverys kyns.	*dhe* "showing possession."
254/8	38/i	Rag an marthus re welsens.	The noun *marthus*.

The adjective is *marthys*. (The noun ends in *-us* in the MS, K.U. and K.K.)

255/8	82/34	Omma nyns yw ev trigys.	*yw* with *nyns* and expressed pronoun.
256/3-4	56/28	....dos yn skon Er y bynn...	*dos erbynn* = "to meet."

The Poem and its Sources

Like the plays of the *Ordinalia* the *Passion Poem* is based on the Four Gospels and other biblical material, with some episodes drawn from other sources, stories that were no doubt well known at the time of the Poem. It starts with the Genesis story of Adam eating the forbidden fruit which caused, or at least symbolised, the Fall of Man, and goes on to portray the Divine Plan of Salvation by which Jesus Christ as *Mab Duw ha den keffrys* begged God to let him offer himself as Redeemer *gans y gorf dre baynys bras*. We see him tempted by the Devil and the narrative moves swiftly on, to his Triumphal Entry into Jerusalem on Palm Sunday with only four verses devoted to his three year Ministry. The Jews grow angry with him and Judas arranges to betray him. The story of the Last Supper, Trial, Crucifixion and Resurrection follow closely the Gospel narratives except for the horrificly realistic description of the Scourging and Crucifixion. These details are also found in the *Passio Christi* and other medieval plays such as the *York Crucifixion.* A particularly gruesome detail is the stretching of the arms with a rope to meet the holes which have been drilled too far apart. Cawley suggests that this is because cords had to be used in the plays to secure to the cross the actor who was playing the part of Jesus.

Most of the following non-biblical details seem to stem from medieval legend though one or two go back to the *Gospel of Nicodemus*, dated about A.D. 600 and one to the *Gospel of Peter*, about A.D. 150. All except one also occur in the *Passio Christi.* References to the Bible and the Cornish Texts are given to the right of the K.K. text, but other non-biblical sources are mentioned below only.

Verse 106 The soul of Judas could not escape through his mouth after he had hanged himself. This is in *P.C.*, and a medieval poem in the Northern English dialect, the *Cursor Mundi*, says his soul went out through his belly because it might not come out at the mouth which had kissed Christ (Mardon).

Verse 152 The Tree from which the Cross is made is found in water where the sun had never shone. This is linked with the *Legend of the Rood* which runs through the *Origo Mundi*. The tree is descended from the tree from which Adam took the apple. In *P.C.* the water is the Brook Cedron. Another version of the legend in the *Cursor Mundi* has the tree made into a bridge over the Pool of Siloam (Halliday).Our Poem contrasts the Fruit taken from the Tree which caused Adam's fall with the Fruit now to be borne by it which will save Mankind (*Adam* is Hebrew for 'Man.') *Verses 154 - 60* This is the story of the smith who refused to make nails to crucify Jesus, and his wife who agreed to do so. One cannot help but detect an element of male chauvinism. Throughout the narrative, apart from this insertion, it is the men who do evil things and the women who do good!

The story is in *P.C.*, the *Northern English Passion Play* and nearly all the French Passion Plays (Longsworth). It appears in the *Legend of the Holy Rood*, *Queen Mary's Psalter*, and the *Holkham Bible Picture Book* (Anderson). There is a miniature of the scene by Jean Fouquet (Mâle). Note how the executioners are the first to suggest his excuse of having leprous hands. It is not made by the smith himself. Maybe this indicates how well known the story was.

The Poem and its Sources

Verse 177 Here a woman wraps a garment around Jesus, One wonders whether this corresponds with the legend of Veronica still known nowadays. She figures in the sixth Station of the Cross (Kim), where she is shown as receiving the imprint of Christ's face on a cloth. Her name is not mentioned in our Poem, and in *P.C.* there is no more than a stage direction indicating that she speaks, but no lines are given for her to say or any act for her to perform. The *Gospel of Nicodemus* which goes back to about A.D. 600 identifies her with the woman who had an issue of blood (Mt 9 v.20). She has an important part in *The Death of Pilate*, a non-biblical episode at the end of the *Resurrexio Domini*. Also see below, verse 252.

Verse 186 The Poem is more scriptural than *P.C.* in *not* naming the two thieves who were crucified with Jesus. Their names are given as Dismas and Jesmas in *P.C.*, and Dismas and Gestas in the *Gospel of Nicodemus*.

Verses 212-3 The Harrowing of Hell. This is a popular medieval theme. Kim quotes seventeen biblical references which, he suggests, refer to a visit made by the Spirit of Jesus to Hell after his death, but there is no mention of it in any Gospel as part of the main narrative. This is made up for by a long account in the *Gospel of Nicodemus*. It is also in the *Resurrexio Domini*. The clause, "He descended into Hell" is included in the Apostles' Creed in the Book of Common Prayer though it is omitted from the Nicene Creed. The account in the Poem is much shorter and less detailed than other accounts.

Verse 217 John's Gospel tells us that a soldier pierced the side of Jesus with a spear. It does not say his name or that he was blind. The *Gospel of Nicodemus* gives his name as "Longinus" and Kim suggests that this might derive from the Greek word for spear used in John, `lo,gch|` *(lonche*; or *longkhe*, as Kim transliterates it) from which also "lance" is derived. Mr Thornton Edwards, a Welsh K.D.L. student living in Greece tells me the word is still used as part of the Liturgy and the first syllable is pronounced "long", so this would support Kim's suggestion. There is no mention that the soldier was blind but the story is in *P.C.* and a number of other accounts including the York play *Mortificacio Christi* and Jacobus de Voragine's *Golden Legend* (Davidson).

Verse 225 I do not have any source for the story of Mary's three tears of blood. It is not mentioned even in *P.C.* though Murdoch says: *The reaction of the Virgin at the cross occupies six stanzas, and refers not only to her tears but to the motif of an arrow striking her heart, causing her to weep tears of blood something she does also in a number of other medieval works, part of the extensive tradition of the sorrows of the Virgin.* See "Further Reading" below.

Verse 230 There is no mention of the three Marys in the Gospels, *P.C.* or other sources at the time when Jesus was laid in the Tomb. Mark mentions Joseph of Arimathaea, Mary Magdalene, Mary the mother of Joses (or Joseph) and James, and Salome. Luke and John mention Joseph only. *P.C.* says Joseph, Nicodemus, Mary the Mother of Jesus, Mary Magdalene, John, and others.

Verses 241-51 This story of the four soldiers keeping watch at the Tomb gives far greater detail than the brief account of the setting of the watch in Matthew. There is some degree of elaboration in the *Gospel of Peter*, dated about A.D. 150, where we are told there were four soldiers keeping watch two by two, and in the *Gospel of Nicodemus*. It occurs in many medieval plays and poems. Woolf says the most highly developed treatment is in the Chester and Coventry plays. It is in *R.D.* and there, as in our Poem, it is the fourth soldier who overcomes the panic of his colleagues and persuades them they should tell Pilate the truth about the Resurrection of Jesus. All the accounts make the soldiers responsible to Pilate although Matthew makes it clear that they were the men of the chief priests.

.

Verse 252 At the empty tomb the Three Marys are again mentioned as in other medieval versions including *R.D.* and also the Coptic *Book of Bartholomew* which dates from the fifth, sixth, or seventh century (James). This names Mary Magdalene, Mary the mother of James, Salome who tempted him, Mary who ministered to him, and Martha her sister, Joanna (or Susanna), the wife of Chuza, Berenice who was healed of an issue of blood, Leah, the widow whose son was raised at Nain, and the woman to whom he said, "Thy sins which are many are forgiven thee." But further on it seems to confuse Mary Magdalene with Mary the Mother of Jesus. It seems too, that the woman with the issue of blood was called Berenice which must be another form of Veronica as mentioned under verse 177. Biblical references are as follows: Matthew mentions Mary Magdalene and 'the other Mary'; Mark mentions Mary Magdalene and Mary the mother of James, and Salome; Luke mentions Mary Magdalene, Joanna and Mary the Mother of James. John mentions only Mary Magdalene and Peter, so, again, the *Three* Marys are not fully biblical.

Versification

In the present edition, as in those of Hooper and Pennaod, the Poem consists of 258 verses of eight lines, and one (208) of ten, though the arrangement is different in the MS. See page 7. Each line has seven syllables, often with an alternating stress pattern, but not always so. In some verses every line ends in a stressed syllable; e.g. verse 1. In others it ends in an unstressed syllable; e.g. verse 4, and in some verses stressed and unstressed syllable alternate; e.g. verse 3. Alternate lines usually rhyme, though sometimes rhymes are missed or are assonances rather than rhymes; e.g. verse 4. Sometimes, differing unstressed final vowels seem to be intended to rhyme, suggesting that these were neutral vowels rather than having the value indicated; e.g. verse 12. According to Zeuss it resembles old Irish verse. The result is a steady rhythm which carries the verse along, yet is to some extent irregular so that it does not get monotonous. This is essentially the same as the verse pattern used in the Cornish plays and it has been imitated in modern Cornish verse, notably Caradar's epic *Tristan hag Ysolt* and *Devedhyans Sen Pawl yn Bro Leon*. In this latter poem Ken George deliberately set out to imitate the versification of *Passhyon agan Arloedh*.

Whilst Talek considers that "the Passion Poem is a Cornish treasure and equivalent to good poetry in any language," Goulven Pennaod disagrees fundamentally with this opinion, saying that the rhymes are very limited and the natural order of the sentences is contorted. Henry Jenner "was clearly unimpressed with the literary quality of the work" (Murdoch). The reader may be inclined to agree with Jenner, but be that as it may, we who study the Cornish language owe it to what literature has come down to us to try to understand it, appreciate it, and maybe even apply a little "positive discrimination".

The English Translation With the comfort of Talek's translation as a starting point, and some help from Pennaod, the aim has been to produce a version as close as possible to the original which is at the same time good modern English. These aims are often mutually incompatible so that the result may not be always completely satisfactory.

Presentation The Poem is printed using a two-page spread with the MS version and the English on the left-hand page. Opposite the MS on the right is the new Kernewek Kemmyn version. Under this are notes on the text, grammar, translation and verse pattern. To the right of the K.K. text are references to the Bible and the Cornish texts. Other non-biblical sources are discussed above.

Further Reading Since writing the above and publishing the Fourth Print I have read the chapter on "The Poem of the Passion" in "Cornish Literature" by Brian Murdoch. In it he mentions a dissertation by Mark Herniman (1984). I have not yet seen this and I understand it is unpublished but I gather from Harry Woodhouse who has seen it that it is a very full treatment of the Poem and may be obtainable from the University of Exeter. Murdoch also makes reference to an article written by him called "*Pascon agan Arluth*: the literary position of the Cornish Poem of the Passion" in *Studi Medievali*, 22 (1981) and "The Virgin's Tears of Blood" by Andrew Breeze in *Celtica* 20 (1988). Lauran Toorians has also sent me a long essay he has written on the Poem. This was published in the Dutch magazine *Kruispunt* in 1990. Unfortunately it is in Dutch so needs someone to translate it. Perhaps the Cornish Language Board should take steps to make such writings as these more available to students of Cornish.

PASCON AGAN ARLUTH

1 Tays ha mab han speris sans
wy abys a levn golon
Re wronte zeugh gras ha whans
ze wolsowas y basconn
Ha zymmo gras ha skyans
the zerevas par lauarow
may fo ze thu ze worthyans
ha sylwans zen enevow

2 Suel a vynno bos sylwys
golsowens ow lauarow
a ihesu del ve helheys
war an bys avel carow
Ragon menough rebekis
ha dyspresijs yn harow
yn growys gans kentrow fastis
peynys bys pan ve marow

1 *May Father, Son, and the Holy Ghost grant to you who pray with a full heart, grace and a desire to hear his Passion, and to me grace and knowledge to tell it in words that it may be to the glory of God and for the salvation of souls.*

2 *Let all who wish to be saved listen to my words about how Jesus was hunted on earth like a stag; for us often rebuked and cruelly despised; to the cross secured with nails; tortured till he was dead.*

PASSHYON AGAN ARLOEDH

1 Tas ha Mab ha'n Spyrys Sans,
Hwi a bys a leun golonn,
Re wrontyo dhywgh gras ha hwans
Dhe woslowes y Basshyon;
Ha dhymmo gras ha skians
Dh'y dherivas par lavarow,
May fo dhe Dhuw dh'y wordhyans,
Ha selwyans dhe'n enevow.

2 Seul a vynno bos selwys
Goslowes ow lavarow
A Yesu dell veu helghys
War an bys avel karow;
Ragon menowgh rebekys Isa 53 v.3
Ha dispresys yn harow,
Y'n grows gans kentrow festys,
Paynys bys pan veu marow.

1/6 & 8 **par lavarow....dhe'n enevow**. Hooper, following Nance, emended these lines to:

Dh'y dheryvas par del won,
May fo dhe Dhew dh'y wordhyans,
Ha sylwans dhe Grystonyon.

to preserve the *ab ab ab ab* rhyme scheme. This is also printed in the Pennaod edition, but, following a suggestion from Wella Brown, I am keeping to the MS, though 1/6 now has eight syllables. The rhyme scheme is now *ab ab ac ac,* similar to verse 44 which Nance also queried.

1/4 & 2/2 **Dhe woslowes....**; **Goslowes....** Two examples of this verb used with a direct object. Usually it is followed by *orth* [*G.M.C.* §153(3); *G.M.C.(2)* §152(4)].

1/6 **par lavarow**. *par* is the French word for 'by' rather than the Cornish word meaning 'equal'; cf. 45/4.

1/7 The repeated *dhe* suggests an imitation of the Latin predicative dative construction.

2/2 **Goslowes**. See Language Notes, page 12, 3rd singular imperative.

2/7 **festys.** The Unified versions have *fastys* in agreement with *fastis* in the MS but the *a* regularly changes to *e* by vowel affection [*G.M.C.* §194; *G.M.C.(2)* §189]. This now assonances better with *helghys* and *rebekys*. The Unified spelling *rebukys* is also normal in K.K. but the *e* of the MS is retained for the sake of the rhyme.

3 Du sur dre virtu an tas
zynny a zyttyas gweras
En mab dre y skyans bras
pan gemert kyg a werhas
han sperys sans leun a ras
dre y zadder may fe guris
Gozaff paynys pan vynnas
neb na ylly gull peghes

4 An dus vas a zeserya
zeze gulas nef o kyllys
gans aga garm hag olua
ihesus crist a ve mevijs
may fynnas dijskynna
yn gwerhas ha bos genys
gans y gyk agan perna
arluth du gwyn agan bys

5 Ihesu crist mur gerense
ze vab den a zyswezas
an vghelder may zese
zen bys pan deyskynnas
Pehadoryon rag perna
o desevijs dre satnas
rag henna gorzyn neffra
ihesus neb agan pernas

3 *Indeed, God, through the power of the Father, the Son through his great wisdom when he accepted a Virgin's flesh, and the Holy Ghost full of grace, through his goodness by which he who could do no sin willingly suffered torture, prepared help for us.*

4 *The good people wanted for themselves the Kingdom of Heaven which had been lost. Jesus Christ was moved by their cries and lamentations so that his will was to come down into a Virgin and be born to redeem us with his flesh. Lord God, how happy we are!*

5 *Jesus Christ showed great love to mankind when he came down to earth from the height where he was, to redeem sinners who had been deceived by Satan. Therefore let us always praise Jesus who redeemed us.*

3 Duw, sur dre vertu an Tas
Dhyn ni a dhyghtyas gweres:
An Mab, dre y skians bras
Pan gemmer's kig a wyrghes
Ha'n Spyrys Sans leun a ras,
Dre y dhader, may feu gwrys
Godhav paynys, pan vynnas,
Neb na ylli gul peghes.

4 An dus 'vas a dhesirya
Dhedha gwlas nev, o kellys.
Gans aga garm hag oelva
Yesus Krist a veu mevys
May fynnas diyskynna
Yn gwyrghes ha bos genys
Gans y gig agan prena.
Arloedh Duw, gwynn agan bys!

5 Yesu Krist meur gerensa
Dhe vab-den a dhiskwedhas,
A'n ughelder mayth esa
Dhe'n bys pan dhiyskynnas
Peghadoryon rag prena
O dessevys dre Satnas.
Rag henna gordhyn nevra
Yesus neb a'gan prenas.

3 It is very difficult to translate this verse literally.

3/2 **dhyghtyas**. I have taken *Duw* in line 1, *An Mab* in line 3, and *an Spyrys Sans* in line 5 as being joint subjects of this verb.

3/4 **gemert** in the MS has an Old Cornish preterite ending (Hooper). The normal *-as* ending brings in an extra syllable, making the apostrophe necessary.

3/6-7 **may feu gwrys godhav paynys.** Literally, 'by which a suffering of torture was done.' Maybe it should be understood as *may feu gwrys (dhodho) godhav paynys* = 'by which he was made to suffer torture.'

4/2 **Dhedha** = 'for themselves.'

4/2 **o kellys**. Best translated as 'which <u>had been</u> lost.' See Language Notes, page 11.

5/1 **meur gerensa.** *meur* meaning 'great' comes directly before the noun and causes mutation [*G.M.C.* §54(2a); *G.M.C.*(2) §57(2a)].

5/4 **pan dhiyskynnas.** The mutation is missed in the MS and Unified versions.

5/6 **O desevys**. Best translated as 'who <u>had been deceived</u>'. See Language Notes, page 11. *desevijs* (MS) is taken by Stokes, Hooper and Pennaod as the p.p. of *disevel* = "to cause to fall". However I can find no other verb of the *-el* type with a p.p. in *-ijs* (MS) which usually corresponds with verbal nouns in *-ya,* having a p.p. in *-ys or -yes*. I am therefore accepting a suggestion from Nicholas Williams that the verb is *desevya* = "to deceive" which does not appear in G.M. or Nance but is in Tregear and is given in the mini-dictionary in "Cornish Today".

6 A(n) peynys a wotheuys
ny ve ragtho y honan
lemmyn rag pobyll an bys
pan vons y kefis mar wan
an ioull ze adam kewsys
an aval te kemer tam
a vell du y fethyth gurys
pan yn provas nyn io mam

7 War lyrgh mab den ze begha
reson prag y fe prynnys
yw ihesus crist ze ord(na)
yn neff y vonas tregys
y vos kyllys ny vynna
y doull ganso o tewlys
rag henna ze bob dyzgthtya
forth a rug the vos sylwys

8 Kyn na goff den skentyll pur
par del won lauaraff zys
yn tre du ha pehadur
acord del ve kemerys
rag bonas gonn pegh mar vur
mayn yn treze a ve gurys
eff o crist a theth dhen leur
mab du ha den yw kyffris

6 *The tortures he suffered were not for himself alone but for the people of the world as they were found (to be) so frail. The devil spoke to Adam: "The apple, you take a bit! You will become like God !" When he tried it, in no way was it so!*

7 *After mankind had sinned, the reason he was redeemed is that Jesus Christ ordained that he should dwell in Heaven. He did not intend that he should be lost. By him his plan was made. Therefore he prepared a way for everyone to be saved.*

8 *Although I am not a very learned man, I will tell you what I know: how an accord was made between God and sinner. Because our sin was so great, an intermediary was made between them. He was Christ who came down to earth. He was the son of God and Man alike.*

6 An paynys a wodhevis
Ny veu ragdho y honan,
Lemmyn rag pobel an bys
Pan vons i kevys mar wann.
An jowl dhe Adam gewsis, Ge 3 v.1-6
“An aval ty kemmer tamm; O.M. 149-256
Avel Duw y fydhydh gwrys!” C.W. 542-864
Pan y’n provas, nyns o mann.

7 War-lergh mab-den dhe begha,
Reson prag y feu prenys
Yw Yesus Krist dhe ord’na
Yn nev y vones trigys.
Y vos kellys ny vynna,
Y dowl ganso o tewlys.
Rakhenna, dhe bub, dyghtya
Fordh a wrug dhe vos selwys.

8 Kyn nag ov den skentyl pur,
Par dell wonn, lavarav dhis,
Yntra Duw ha peghador
Akord dell veu kemmerys,
Rag bones ’gan pegh mar veur
Mayn yntredha a veu gwrys.
Ev o Krist, a dheuth dhe’n leur.
Mab Duw ha den yw, keffrys.

6/2 **honan**. See Spelling Notes, page 13.

6/5 **gewsis.** The preceding particle *a* is omitted, presumably to fit the metre. There seems no reason why the mutation which should result should not be observed and I have therefore emended the *kewsys* which is found in the MS.

6/6-7 **aval....Avel**. Is a pun intended so that 6/7 could seem to mean ‘You will be made the apple of God(’s eye)’ when read aloud?

6/6 **ty kemmer tamm**. Read as *ty kemmer, tan* by Hooper and Pennaod. Stokes take it as *tamm.*

6/8 **nyn io mam** (MS) I have followed Hooper and Pennaod in reading as *mann*. Stokes translates *mam* as “good” following Keigwin

8/4 **....dell veu kemmerys.** I have taken this as a noun clause being the object of *lavarav*. See Language Notes, page 10.

8/1/3/5/7 **pur; -or; veur; leur.** These rhymes seem suspect although the first three are spelled *-ur* in the MS. Ken George suggests they are not intended to rhyme, but this makes the verse rather irregular.

9 Ragon y pesys y das
oll y sor may fe gevys
gans y gorff dre beynys bras
agan pegh may fo prennys
mab marea leun a ras
oll y voth a ve clewys
ha kemmys a theseryas
zozo eff a ve grontis

10 I vam pan yn drehevys
hay vos deuezis ze oys
gull penans ef a pesys
henna ganso nyn io poys
(d)evguans dyth ow penys
y speynas y gyk hay woys
ha woteweth rag densys
eff an geue awell boys

11 Han ioull henna pan glewas
y demptye a brederys
ha zozo y tysquezas
cals meyn hay leuerys
Mars sos mab du leun a ras
an veyn ma gura bara zis
ihesus crist par del vynnas
zozo ef a worthebys

9 *He begged his Father for us that all his wrath should be remitted, that our sin should be redeemed with his body through extreme torture. Mary's Son, full of grace - all his will was heard and all he desired was granted to him.*

10 *When his Mother brought him up, and when he was come of age, he continued to do penance. That was no hardship for him. For forty days he spent his flesh and blood in fasting, and eventually, because he was human, he had a craving for food.*

11 *And when the devil heard this, he thought he would tempt him and he showed him a heap of stones and said, "If you are God's Beloved Son, make these stones bread for yourself." Jesus Christ answered him exactly as he intended:*

9 Ragon y pysis y Das
Oll y sorr may fe gevys
Gans y gorf, dre baynys bras,
Agan pegh may fe prenys.
Mab Maria, leun a ras,
Oll y vodh a veu klywys,
Ha kemmys a dhesiryas
Dhodho ev a veu grontys.

10 Y vamm pan y'n drehevis
Ha'y vos devedhys dhe oes
Gul penans ev a besis,
Henna ganso nyns o poes.
Dew ugens dydh ow penys Mt 4 v.1-10
Y spenas y gig ha'y woes Mk 1 v.12-13
Ha wor'tiwedh rag denses Lk 4 v.1-13
Ev a'n jeva awell boes. P.C. 43-168

11 Ha'n jowl henna pan glywas
Y demptya a brederis
Ha dhodho y tyskwedhas
Kals meyn hag y leveris:
"Mars os Mab Duw, leun a ras,
A'n veyn ma gwra bara dhis."
Yesus Krist, par dell vynnas,
Dhodho ev a worthybis:

9/4 **may fe prenys.** Emended from the present subjunctive of MS. See Language Notes, page 9.

10/3 **besis.** Emended from normal *besyas* to conform with the MS and for the sake of the rhyme.

10/7 **rag denses.** Hooper has 'out of manhood'. Wella Brown suggests 'because of His mortal nature' and takes *rag* as causal [*G.M.C.* §155(2a); *G.M.C.(2)* §154(2a)].

10/8 **awell**. Given as *ewl* in *G.M.* with note that *awell* is an earlier form. It is kept here as two syllables are needed.

12 Mab den heb ken ys bara
nyn geuas ol y vewnans
lemmen yn lauarow da
a the ze worth an dremas
dre worzyp crist yn urna
lemmyn ny a yll gwelas
lauar du maga del wra
neb a vynno y glewas

13 Gans gloteny ef pan welas
cam na ylly y dolla
en tebell el a vynnas
yn ken maner y demptye
war penakyll yn goras
dyantell ze eseza
a vgh eglos tek yn wlas
an yset(h)va y zesa

14 An ioul ze grist a gewsys
yn delma rag y demptya
a hanas y thew scrifys
bos eleth worth ze wyze
rag own yw zom desevys
ze droys worth meyn ze dochye
mar sos mab du a vur brys
dijskyn ha zen dor ke

12 "*Man does not find all his life in bread alone, but in the good words that come from God.*" *Now we can see by Christ's answer at that time how the Word of God feeds whoever will hear it.*

13 *When he saw that he could not trick him at all with gluttony, the evil angel decided to tempt him in another way. He put him to sit dangerously on a pinnacle. The seat was above a beautiful church in the land.*

14 *The devil spoke to Christ thus to tempt him: "It is written of you that angels are guarding you for fear you were going to stumble by catching your foot on a stone. If you are God's Son of great worth, come and drop down to the ground."*

12 “Mab-den hepken es bara — Dt 8 v.3
Ny’n jeves oll y vywna’s, — P.C. 65-72
Lemmyn yn lavarow da
A dheu dhiworth an dremas.”
Dre worthyp Krist y’n eur na
Lemmyn ni a yll gweles
Lavar Duw maga dell wra
Neb a vynno y glywes.

13 Gans glotni ev pan welas
Kamm na ylli y doella,
An tebel el a vynnas
Yn ken maner y demptya.
War bynakyl y’n gorras
Deantell dhe esedha.
A-ugh eglos teg y’n wlas
An esedhva yth esa.

14 An jowl dhe Krist a gewsis
Yndellma, rag y demptya:
“Ahanas yth yw skrifys — Ps 91 v.11-12
Bos eledh orth dha witha,
Rag own yth omdhisevys
Dha droes orth men dh’y dochya.
Mars os Mab Duw a veur bris
Diyskynn ha dhe’n dor ke.”

12 Murdoch points out that this verse corresponds closely with *P.C.* 65-72 where Jesus addresses the first four lines to Satan and the last four to the disciples though Jesus should have been alone with Satan. Murdoch suggests that this ‘moral summary’ was taken from the poem and thus used awkwardly in the play, proving the poem was written before the play, but see v. 17 note.

12/4 **dhiworth**. Presumably understood as *a-dhiworth*, hence the mutation; cf. 29/6.

12/4 **dremas**. Usually translates as ‘goodman’ or ‘saint.’ Hooper has ‘supremely-good’.

12/6/7 **gweles....maga dell wra ....** See Language Notes on *dell* etc., page 10.

The rhyme pattern of the lines in verse 12 ending in unstressed *-a, -a(n)s, -, -es,* and *ke* suggests these rhyme together as neutral vowels. *Vywnans* (12/2) is spelt *vewnas* in Hooper’s Unified and I have followed a suggestion by Ken George to write *vywna’s* to indicate the frequent omission of *n* in such words and to improve the rhyme with *dremas.*

14/5 **Rag own yth omdhisevys.** *G.M.C.(2)* §274(10) gives this line as *rag own yth omdhisaves* as an example of a subordinate clause introduced by *y*. I have taken the verb to be an imperfect indicative which should be spelled as shown according to *G.M.C.* (2) §191 which also agrees with the MS. I am grateful to Nicholas Williams for pointing out that the note which appeared in previous prints was incorrect.

15 Ihesus crist a leueris
ze thu ny goth thys temptye
yn neb ehan a seruys
lemmyn prest y honore
Ha whath an Ioul a dewlys
towll ken maner mar calle
dre neb forth a govaytis
guzyll zy gowsys tryle

16 A lene yn hombronkyas
vghell war ben vn meneth
ha zozo y tysquethas
owr hag arghans gwels ha gweth
ha kymmys yn bys vs vas
yn meth an ioul te a feth
ha me ad wra arluth bras
ow honore mar mynnyth

17 Ihesus crist a leueris
y vos scryfys yn lyffrow
yn pub gwythres ycoth thys
gorzye ze zu hay hanow
Ke ze ves omscumvnys
ze zyveyth veth yn tewolgow
the vestry a vyth lezys
neffre war an enevow

15 *Jesus Christ said, "You must not tempt your God into any kind of enthralment, but always honour him". And again the devil cast a plan of another kind to see if, in some way involving greed, he could make him change his mind.*

16 *From there, he led him high up to the top of a mountain, and showed him gold and silver, grass and trees, and the devil said, "You shall have all there is of value in the world, and I will make you a great Lord if you are willing to honour me."*

17 *Jesus Christ said that it was written in the Scriptures, "In everything that is done you must worship your God and his Name. Go away, accursed one, to a desert in darkness. Your dominion over souls will be destroyed for ever".*

15 Yesus Krist a leveris, Dt 6 v.16
"Dha Dhuw ny goedh dhis temptya
Yn neb eghenn a servis,
Lemmyn prest y enora."
Ha hwath an jowl a dewlis
Towl ken maner, mar kalla,
Dre neb fordh a govaytys
Guthyl dh'y gowses treylya.

16 Alena y'n hembronkyas
Ughel war benn unn menydh,
Ha dhodho y tiskwedhas
Owr hag arghans, gwels ha gwydh,
Ha "Kemmys y'n bys eus 'vas",
Yn-medh an jowl, "ty a' fydh,
Ha my a'th wra arloedh bras
Ow enora mar mynnydh."

17 Yesus Krist a leveris
Y vos skrifys y'n Lyvrow: Dt 6 v.13
"Yn pub gweythres y koedh dhis P.C. 137-44
Gordhya dha Dhuw ha'y hanow -
Ke dhe ves, emskemunys
Dhe dhifeyth yn tewolgow,
Dha vaystri a vydh ledhys
Nevra war an enevow."

16/2 **unn menydh.** I am following Hooper in taking the *unn* as a simple indefinite article. None of the Gospel accounts refers to a *certain* mountain. See Language Notes, page 9.

17/3-8 Crysten Fudge points out the similarity of these lines to *P.C.* 139-44, saying it is not known which came first, but see v. 12 note.

17/6 **veth** in the MS is omitted in the Unified versions. Its inclusion represents an extra syllable, unless *tewolgow* is pronounced *tew'lgow* as in later Cornish.

17/7 **lezys** (MS). Read by Hooper and Pennaod as *lehes* = 'diminished'. *Lezys* occurs many times in the MS where it is read as *ledhys* = 'killed'.

18 An ioul a trylyas sperys
hag eth zy tyller tythy
tergweyth y fe convyctijs
evn yw zyn y voleythy
ze ihesu may fons parys
zy gomfortye yredy
an neff y fe danvenys
ze worth an tas eleth dy

19 Ha satnas gans y antell
hay scherewneth hay goyntis
crist mab an arluth vghell
y demptye pan prederis
besy yw zyz bos vuell
ha seruabyll yth seruys
manno allo an tebell
ogas zys bonas trylys

20 Rag y hyller ervyre
hay welas yn suredy
y vos prest worth ze vetye
ze veth zys ha belyny
te na yllyth omweze
vn pres yn geyth na peghy
pan omsettyas ze demptye
guzyll pegh neb na ylly

18 *The devil turned angrily and went home to his lair. Three times he was overcome. It is right for us to curse him. To Jesus were sent heavenly angels from the Father to be ready indeed to support him there.*

19 *And since Satan thought he would tempt Christ, Son of the Supreme Lord, with his treachery, malice and cunning, it is important for you to be humble and diligent in your service so that the evil one cannot be turned upon you.*

20 *For you may be sure, and see indeed that he is always waylaying you to your shame and disgrace, you who cannot keep yourself from sinning for a single moment in the day! After all, he undertook to tempt him who could not commit sin!*

18 An jowl a drelyas, serrys,
Hag eth dh'y dyller teythi.
Teyrgweyth y feu konviktys.
Ewn yw dhyn y vollethi.
Dhe Yesu may fens parys
Dh'y gonfortya yredi,
A'n nev y feu dannvenys
Dhiworth an Tas, eledh di.

19 Ha Satnas gans y antell,
Ha'y sherewneth ha'y goyntis,
Krist, Mab an Arloedh Ughel,
Y demptya pan brederis,
Bysi yw dhis bos uvel
Ha servabyl y'th servis,
Ma na allo an tebel
Ogas dhis bones treylys.

20 Rag y hyllir ervira,
Ha'y weles yn surredi,
Y vos prest orth dha vetya
Dhe veth dhis ha bileni,
Ty, na yllydh omwitha
Unn prys y'n jydh na beghi,
Pan omsettyas dhe demptya
Guthyl pegh neb na ylli.

18/1 **sperys** (MS). I have followed Hooper and Pennaod in taking this as *serrys*. Stokes translates *trylyas sperys* as "lost heart".

18/2 **dyller**. It seems necessary to translate this rather colourless word in sympathy with the context; cf. 77/5.

18/2 **teythi**. All the dictionaries give this as a noun though it appears to be used here as an adjective

18/5 **may fens parys**. Emended from the present subjunctive of the MS. See Language Notes, page 9.

19/2 **sherewneth.** The meaning of *roguery* given in G.M. seems hardly strong enough to fit the context here and in 52/8. *wickedness*, *malice*, as given in Nance seem better.

19/5 **uvel.** The spelling *vuell* in the MS supports the unexpected absence of *h* in the K.K. spelling.

21 Del yw scrifys prest yma
adro zynny ganso try
mara kyll ze worth an da
ze wezyll drok agan dry
folle yn ta y whela
ys del wra lyon y pray
drey den yn peyn a calla
neffre ny vnsa moy ioy

22 Gans ioul kyn fy temptijs
anozo na ro dymme
rag comfort yw henna zys
scrifys yw yn leas le
yt allos y vos gorrys
kyffris seuell ha cothe
ha ganso kynfes tewlys
te a yll seuell arte

23 Ihesu crist yn pow a dro
pub eroll pregoth a wre
han virtu an pregoth o
mab den ze ase peghe
ha gevys may fe zozo
kyffrys y begh hay fyltye
degis na ve ze worto
gulas nef (h)a roys ze gen re

21 *As it is written, he is always round about us with violence in case he can bring us from the good to do evil. Much more furiously he seeks us than does a lion his prey. If he could bring a man to woe, never would he desire more joy.*

22 *Though you are tempted by the devil, do not give a halfpenny for him! For it is written in many places that it is put into your power both to stand and to fall, and though you are cast down by him, you may rise again. That is a comfort for you !*

23 *Jesus Christ preached in the country round about all the time, and the substance of the preaching was that mankind should cease from sinning so that his sin as well as his evil might be forgiven him, lest the Kingdom of Heaven be taken away from him and given to others.*

21 Dell yw skrifys, prest yma 1 Pe 5 v.8
A-dro dhyn ni, gans otri/outray,
Mara kyll dhiworth an da
Dhe wuthyl drog agan dri.
Folla yn ta y hwila
Es dell wra lion y bray.
Dri den yn payn: a kalla,
Nevra ny yeunsa moy joy.

22 Gans an jowl kyn fi temptys,
Anodho na ro demma!
Rag (konfort yw henna dhis)
Skrifys yw yn lies le,
Y'th halloes y vos gorrys
Keffrys sevel ha koedha,
Ha ganso kyn fes tewlys,
Ty a yll sevel arta.

23 Yesu Krist y'n pow a-dro Mt 4 v.17
Pub eur oll pregoth a wre, Mk 1 v.14-15
Ha'n vertu a'n pregoth o
Mabden dhe asa pegha
Ha gevys may fe dhodho
Keffrys y begh ha'y vilta,
Degys na ve dhiworto
Gwlas nev ha res dhe gen re.

21/2 **otri/outray.** The Unified versions have *gans otry* though both Nance and *G.M* have *outray,* The *G.M.* authentication code gives it as a neologism not attested so maybe it is regarded there as a different word. However, I have followed this meaning (*outrage*) in the translation. If *ganso tri* ('three with him') is the meaning intended by the writer, it must imply a diabolical equivalent of the Holy Trinity. *Otri* rhymes with *dri* whilst *outray* rhymes, according to the K.K. spelling, with *bray but* Nicholas Williams (§3.5) asserts that final stressed *-i* tended to diphthongise to an *ey* or *ay* sound making it possible for *outray/dri/bray/joy* to rhyme together. It is not entirely clear how the *joy* fits in but it seems to me more likely that this all embracing diphthong tended to be a neutral one, that is shwa plus yod, something like the French word *oeil* bordering on *oy.*

21 Based, presumably on 1 Pe 5 v.8: '....your adversary the devil, as a roaring lion, walketh about, seeking whom he may devour.' (*A.V.*)

23/5 **gevys**. The MS supports the K.K. amendment from *gyvys* in Unified, which assumes a double vowel affection, from *a* to *e* and then *e* to *i.*

The even numbered lines of 22 and 23 seem to rhyme with neutral vowels spelled *-a* or *-e* in K.K. though *-e* is used throughout in the MS. However, Ken George is doubtful whether they are neutral vowels. Nicholas Williams (§7.7) asserts that vowels in final unstresed syllables are usually neutral

24 Benegas yw neb a gar
du dris pub tra vs yn bys
hag a wozaffo yn whar
zozo kymmys vs ordnys
bo clevas bo peth kescar
po dre breson presonys
ol en da han drok kepar
ze ihesu bezens grassys

25 Ihesu crist yn pow may the
ef a sawye an glevyon
dal na bozar ny ase
nag omlanar na gonon
na claff vyth ow crowethe
mar pesy a leun golon
whare sawijs y feze
del vynna crist y honon

26 Pan welas en ethewon
bos crist au cuthyll meystry
ow care ezomogyon
hag a neze na wre vry
rag henna an vuscogyon
orto a borzas avy
dre vraster bras yn golon
y chungfyons y zestrewy

24 *Blessed is he who loves God beyond everything there is in the world, and who will meekly suffer all that is ordained for him, whether it is illness or dispersion of wealth, or being shut up in prison. For all good and bad alike, let Jesus be thanked.*

25 *Wherever he went in the country, Jesus Christ healed the sick. He did not abaondon the blind or deaf or any dumb person, nor any bedridden invalid. If he prayed with a full heart, straight away he would be cured in accordance with the will of Christ himself.*

26 *When the Jews saw that Jesus Christ was exercising power, caring for people in need and that he paid no heed to them, for that reason the crazy ones bore him malice. Because of arrogance in their hearts they attempted to destroy him.*

24 Bennigys yw neb a gar
Duw dres pub tra eus y'n bys
Hag a wodhaffo yn hwar
Dhodho kemmys eus ord'nys;
Po klevys po pyth-keskar
Po dre bryson prysonys.
Oll an da ha'n drog kepar,
Dhe Yesu bedhes grassys.

25 Yesu Krist y'n pow mayth e — Mt 4 v.23
Ev a sawya an glevyon. — Mk 1 v.34
Dal na bodhar ny asa, — Lk 4 v.40
Nag omlavar, nagonan, — Jn 9 v.7-15
Na klav vydh ow krowedha. — P.C. 393-418
Mar pysi a leun golonn
Hware sawys y fedha,
Dell vynna Krist y honan.

26 Pan welas an Edhewon — Mk 3 v.6
Bos Krist ow kuthyl maystri, — Lk 20 v.19
Ow kara edhommogyon, — Jn 5 v.16
Hag anedha na wre vri, — Jn 7 v.1
Rakhenna an vuskogyon — Jn 7 v.32
Orto a borthas avi. — Jn 8 v.40
Dre vraster bras y'n golonn — Jn 8 v.59
Y chonsyons y dhistrui. — Jn 10 v.31
Jn 10 v.39
Jn 11 v.50-53

24/3 **Hag a wodhaffo.** The subjunctive contrasts with indicative *gar* in the first line though both depend on the same indefinite antecedent, *neb*. Maybe the suffering is portrayed as doubtful or less than essential, but the loving as vital.

24/8 **bedhes.** See Language Notes, page 12, 3rd singular imperative.

25/4 **omlavar.** This was thought to be a mistake for *avlavar* until it was found again in the *Tregear Homilies.* (Nance writing in *Old Cornwall,* Summer 1951)

25/4 **nagonan**. See Spelling Notes, page 13. Although *nagonan* is normally a pronoun it occurs as an adjective at PC 1336, 2435 and PAA 187/6 and is taken as such here also.

25/8 **honan.** See Spelling Notes, page 13.

26/8 **chungfyons** (MS) Stokes and Nance insist that this is *chungfyons* not *chonsyons* as is read by Hooper and Pennaod. Stokes suggests *thugtyons* which would give *dhyghtyons*, = "prepare". I have followed Hooper and Pennaod.

27 Dewsull blegyow pan ese
yn mysc y abestely
y wreg ze re a neze
mos zen dre ha degylmy
an asen ha dry ganse
ha leuerell yredy
mar teffa tus ha gweze
bos ze zu ze wull gynsy

28 Del yrghys ihesus zeze
y a rug a zesympys
ol y voth ef del vynne
an asen a ve kerghys
war nezy rag eseze
dyllas pan a ve gorrys
rag morogeth a vynne
zen Cyte ze vos gorthijs

29 Mur a dus ha benenas
a ierusalem yn dre
erbyn crist rag y welas
y eth ha rag y worzye
war an fordh dyllas a les
a ve gurris ze ragthe
palm ha floris kekyffris
er y byn degis a ve

27 *When he was among his apostles on Palm Sunday, he made some of them go to the town and untie the ass and bring it with them, and if any man came to prevent it, to say indeed that it was on God*'s *business.*

28 *Straight away they did as Jesus instructed; all his will as he intended. The ass was fetched. A cloth garment was placed upon it for sitting on, because he wanted to ride to the city to be honoured.*

29 *Many men and women of Jerusalem came into the town towards Christ in order to see him and honour him. On the road clothes were spread out before him. Palms and flowers also were carried to meet him.*

27 Dy' Sul Bleujyow, pan esa
Yn mysk y abesteli,
Y hwrug dhe re anedha
Mos dhe'n dre ha digelmi
An asyn ha dri gansa
Ha leverel yredi,
Mar teffa tus ha gwitha,
Bos dhe Dhuw dhe wul gensi.

Mt 21 v.1-9
Mk 11 v.1-11
Lk 19 v.29-38
P.C. 173-312

28 Dell erghis Yesus dhedha,
I a wrug a-dhesempis,
Oll y vodh, ev dell vynna.
An asyn a veu kyrghys.
Warnedhi rag esedha
Dillas pan a veu gorrys,
Rag marghogeth a vynna
Dhe'n sita, dhe vos gordhys.

29 Meur a dus ha benynes
A Yerusalem y'n dre
Erbynn Krist, rag y weles,
I eth, ha rag y wordhya.
War an fordh dillas a-les
A veu gorrys dheragdho
Palm ha flourys kekeffrys
Er y bynn degys a veu.

27/5 **An asyn ha dri.** Wella Brown points out that one would expect ...*ha'y dri. G.M.* gives *asyn* as masculine, from Latin *asinus*, but there is also as fem. form *asina* in Latin. Nance gives the word as masculine or feminine. *warnedhi* in 28/5 makes it clear that it is feminine in this case.

28/7 **marghogeth.** See Spelling Notes, page 12.

29/6 **dheragdo**. Understood as *a-dheragdho*, hence the mutation; cf. 12/4.

29/8 **degys a veu**. The use of the particle *a* between a complement and a part of the verb *bos* is abnormal; see Language Notes, page 9. Here it is needed to make up the syllable count.

30 I helwys a leun golon
gans mur ioy ha lowene
yn hanow du yn trezon
benegas yw neb a the
crist a gafas gorkorian
yn templys a berth yn dre
ef a rug zeze yn scon
monas yn mes a lene

31 En scherewys a sorras
rag bonas crist honoris
ha bos y ober mar vras
ha dris an bys ol notijs
grussons cusyll na go vas
rag may fo ihesus dyswris
ha kymmys y an cablas
may fe an dre (crehe)lys

32 En gusyl o may fe dris
ze rag crist pehadur(es)
ol zy voth may rollo bres
a nezy del ve ze gres
rag an lahys zynny es
a vyn y dampnye porres
ym mezens y forth nyn ges
may hallo bos deflam guris

30 *There was a wholehearted cry with much joy and gladness: "Blessed is he who comes among us in the name of God!" Christ found traders in the temples inside the town. He made them go away from there quickly.*

31 *The wicked were angry because Christ was honoured and because his work was so great and known throughout all the world. They made a plan which was not any good to destroy Jesus and they accused him so much that the town was in an uproar.*

32 *The plan was that a sinful woman should be brought before Christ so that he might give a decision of his own accord as to what was to be done in her case. "For the laws which we have will condemn her outright," they said. "There is no way in which she may be made blameless."*

30 Y helwis a leun golonn
Gans meur joy ha lowena,
"Yn hanow Duw yntredhon
Bennygys yw neb a dheu!"
Krist a gavas gwikoryon Mt 21 v.12-13
Y'n templys a-berth y'n dre. Mk 11 v.15-17
Ev a wrug dhedha yn skon Lk 19 v.45-46
Mones yn-mes alena. Jn 2 v.14-15
P.C. 313-54

31 An sherewys a sorras Mt 21 v. 15
Rag bones Krist enorys
Ha bos y ober mar vras,
Ha dres an bys oll notys.
Gwrussons kusul nag o 'vas
Rag may fe Yesus diswrys,
Ha kemmys i a'n kablas
May feu an dre kryghyllys.

32 An gusul o may fe dres Jn 8 v.3-11
Dherag Krist peghadores,
Oll dh'y vodh may rolla breus
Anedhi dell vedha gwrys:
"Rag an laghys dhyn ni eus
A vynn hy dampnya porres,"
Yn-medhons i. "Fordh nyns eus
May hallo bos diflamm gwrys."

30/1 **Y helwis.** Impersonal imperfect: 'There was a calling.' See *G.M.C.* §181; *G.M.C.(2)* §179(1)

31/5 **'vas.** Permanently mutated from *mas*, presumably = *a vas* or *dhe vas*. See *G.M.C.* §81(2note); *G.M.C.(2)* §83(2d)

31/6 **may fe Yesus diswrys**. Both versions of the MS have *fo*. Hooper reads *fe* which is more logical and which I have followed. See Language Notes, page 9.

31/8 The *Kernow* MS has *....lys* for the last word in the line and Pennaod has *(crehe)lys*, but both Hooper and Pennaod read *May fe an dre oll tullys* in their Unified versions and Hooper translates: 'that all the town was deluded.' Pennaod's *(crehe)lys* appears to be *kryghyllys* = 'jolted; shaken', as used in 184/7.

32/1 **dres.** "An imperfect rhyme." (Ken George).

32/3 **rolla**. Emended from *rollo* in the MS which uses the present subjunctive for the imperfect. See Language Notes, page 9

36/3 **bedhes**. See Language Notes, page 12, 3rd singular imperative.

33 Then tyller crist re dethye
han ezewon o dygnas
I zesa an venyn ganse
paris ens zy huhuzas
hedre vons y ov plentye
ihesus yn dour a scryfas
ha dre virtu an scrife
peb ze ves a omdennas

34 Pan ezons oll ze wary
ancombrys y rebea
pema yn meth crist zyzy
neb a vyn ze guhuza
denvyth nyn ges yn mezy
ihesus a gewsys arta
me nyth dampnyaf yredy
ha na wra na moy pegha

35 Benyn dyr vur cheryte
y box ryche leun a yly
a vgh crist rag y vntye
hy a vynnas y derry
corf ihesus rag comfortye
gures pur sur o yredy
Iudas scharyoth ascable
ha gans mur a falsury

33 *Christ had come to the place and the Jews were truculent. The woman was with them. They were prepared to accuse her. While they were making a charge Jesus wrote on the ground and by the power of what he wrote everyone went away.*

34 *When they all went away (they had been embarrassed) Christ said to her, "Where is he who wants to accuse you?" "There is no one," she said. Jesus spoke again: "Well then, I do not condemn you. Go and sin no more."*

35 *Out of great love a woman wanted to break her rich box of perfume over Christ to anoint him. Indeed it was quite clearly done to refresh the body of Jesus. Judas Iscariot accused her very unjustly.*

33 Dhe'n tyller Krist re dhodhya
Ha'n Edhewon o dignas.
Yth esa an venyn gansa.
Parys ens dh'y huhudhas.
Hedra vens i ow plentya
Yesus y'n dor a skrifas
Ha dre vertu an skrifa
Pub dhe ves a omdennas.

34 Pan ethons oll dhe wari,
(Ankombrys i re bia)
"Pyma", yn-medh Krist dhedhi
"Neb a vynn dha guhudha?"
"Denvydh nyns eus", yn-medh hi.
Yesus a gewsis arta,
"My ny'th tampnyav yredi.
A, na wra namoy pegha."

35 Benyn, der veur jeryta, Mt 26 v.6-13
Hy boks rych leun a eli Mk 14 v.3-9
A-ugh Krist, rag y untya Lk 7 v.36-50
Hi a vynnas y derri. Jn 12 v.1-8
Korf Yesus rag konfortya P.C. 473-552
Gwrys pur sur o, yredi.
Yudas Skaryoth a's kabla
ha gans meur a falsuri.

33/5 **Hedra vens i ow plentya.** Taken as imperfect rather than present subjunctive. See Language Notes, page 9. It is just possible that the *vons* of the MS may be preterite but this seems most unlikely in this construction with the present participle.

34/2 I have followed Pennaod in putting this line in parentheses. It seems the best way of fitting it in.

34/8 **A, na wra namoy pegha,** following Hooper's emendation of the MS version.

36 Iudas fals a leuerys
trehans dynar a vone
en box oll bezens gwerthys
a vos den rag y ranne
the vohosogyon yn bys
gwel vya ys y scolye
ihesus crist a worthebys
y gowsys ef a wozye

37 Na thegough sor yn golon
war neb a vyn ow sawye
ow thermyn a the yn scon
genough me nvm byth trege
wy a gyff bohosogyon
pub er warnough ow carme
pan vynnough agis honon
wy a yll gull da zeze

38 Wh(are) y s(or)ras Iudas
ny gewsy dre geryte
(lemen) rag cafos ran vras
an pencon mar a calle
eff (o) harlot tebel was
woteweth lader vye
zen ezewon y ponyas
crist y arluth rag gwerze

36 *False Judas said, "Let the whole box be sold for three hundred pence in cash to be shared among the poor in the world. It would be better than wasting it." Jesus Christ answered (he knew what was in his mind):*

37 *"Do not bear anger in your hearts towards the one who wants to save me. My time will soon come. I shall have no dwelling with you. You will have the poor calling upon you all the time. You yourselves can do good for them whenever you want."*

38 *At once Judas grew angry. He did not speak out of love but to get a big share of the fund if he could. He was a rogue, a villain. He had been a thief to the end. He ran to sell Christ his Lord to the Jews.*

36 Yudas fals a leveris,
"Tri hans diner a vona
An boks oll bedhes gwerthys
A vos den rag y ranna
Dhe voghosogyon yn bys;
Gwell via es y skoellya."
Yesus Krist a worthybis
(Y gowses ev a wodhya):

37 "Na dhegewgh sorr y'n golonn
War neb a vynn ow sawya.
Ow thermyn a dheu yn skon,
Genowgh my ny'm bydh triga.
Hwi a gyv boghosogyon
Pub eur warnowgh ow karma;
Pan vynnowgh, agas honan
Hwi a yll gul da dhedha."

38 Hware y sorras Yudas
Ny gewsis dre jeryta,
Lemmyn rag kavoes rann vras
An penshyon mara kalla.
Ev o harlot tebelwas.
Wor'tiwedh lader via.
Dhe'n Edhewon y poenyas Mt 26 v.14-16
Krist y Arloedh rag gwertha. P.C. 585-615

36/4 **A vos den rag y ranna.** Hooper and Pennaod take this as *Awos den rag y ranna* and Hooper translates 'in order to distribute it for man's sake.' I am taking it as *A vos rag y ranna den* = 'To be for a man (someone) to share it,' or '(for it) to be shared.' See also References to *Cornish Simplified II*; page 16.

37 David Balhatchet has drawn my attention to the close similarity between this verse and *P.C.* 539-46, five of the eight lines being identical. He particularly points out that *P.C.* has *thorment* instead of the *thermyn* in line 3. None of the Gospel accounts has either word in this context but *termyn* may be an echo of Jn 7 v.6 'My time is not yet come: but your time is always ready' (*A.V.*). So, does this suggest that the writer of the Poem 'corrected' the *P.C.* version, proving it was written later? On the other hand, see the note on verse 12.

37/2 **War**. Hooper and Pennaod print *worth* but I see no reason to alter the MS; cf. 132/2.

37/7 **honan**. See Spelling Notes, page 13.

38/3 **Lemmyn.** See Spelling Notes, page 13. Both MS readings have the word bracketed and in the Unified spelling *lemen*, so presumably it is illegible in the MS itself.

38/6 **Wor'tiwedh lader via**. Hooper takes this as a future in the past and translates 'To the end he would be a thief.' I take it as a true pluperfect. Wella Brown agrees with this and suggests it implies 'When all is said and done, he had been a thief.'

39 Eff a leveris zeze
pyth a vynnough why ze ry
ha me a ra zeugh spedye
ow cafos crist yredy
yfons vnver yn treze
kepar ha del wovyny
xxx (leg. dek warn ugens) a vone
yn vn payment y wrens ry

40 Arte Iudas ow tryle
gwan wecor nyn geve par
ny yl den vyth amontye
myns a gollas yn chyffar
worth ihesus ef a fecle
kepar ha pan ve hegar
yn deweth ny acordye
y golon gans y lauar

41 Gans iudas del o tewlys
drey ihesus sur del vynne
gans crist y tho cowethys
byth nyn gens y coweze
en gyth o deyow hablys
may fenne ihesus sopye
gans an re yn y seruys
war an bys rezewesse

39 *He said to them, "What will you give me if I do indeed make you successful in finding Christ?" They agreed among themselves that they would give him thirty in cash in payment, just as he asked.*

40 *Returning again (without equal as a bad bargainer; no one can work out how much he lost on the deal) Judas greeted Jesus falsely, as if he were being affectionate. In the end his heart did not accord with his speech.*

41 *Just as he intended, so it was plotted by Judas to bring Jesus. He was in Christ's company but they were never comrades. The day was Maundy Thursday when Jesus intended to have supper with those in his service on earth whom he had chosen.*

39 Ev a leveris dhedha,
"Pyth a vynnowgh hwi dhe ri
Ha my a wra dhywgh spedya
Ow kavoes Krist yredi?"
Y fons unnver yntredha
Kepar ha dell wovynni,
Deg warn ugens a vona
Yn unn pemont y hwrens ri.

40 Arta Yudas ow treylya
(Gwann wikor ny'n jeva par;
Ny yll den vydh amontya
Myns a gollas y'n chyffar)
Orth Yesus ev a fekla
Kepar ha pan ve hegar.
Yn diwedh ny akordya
Y golonn gans y lavar.

41 Gans Yudas dell o tewlys
Dri Yesus, sur, dell vynna.
Gans Krist yth o kowethys;
Bydh nyns ens i kowetha.
An jydh o Dy Yow Hablys
May fynna Yesus sopya
Gans an re yn y servis
War an bys re dhewissa.

39/2 **hwi dhe ri.** Hooper and Pennaod print *why dhymm ry* in their Unified versions. The reason for the change is not apparent.

39/8 **unn** used as an indefinite article. See Language Notes, page 9.

39/8 **pemont.** This spelling is not in Nance but it is in both Unified versions and also in *G.M.*

40/7 **akordya**. Hooper and Pennaod have double *c*. The MS, Nance, and Old French forms have only one *c* though double *c* is restored in the Modern French and English forms of the word as closer to the Latin form.

41/1-2 **dell o tewlys...dell vynna.** These two comparative clauses [*G.M.C.* §332; *G.M.C.(2)* §348] seem to comprise a sentence without a main clause with a meaning as suggested in the translation. Hooper has: 'By Judas so it was planned to give up Jesus surely as he would.' Are there other examples of a similar construction?

42 Dew zen crist a zanvonas
ze berna boys ha dewas
an keth rena a spedyas
han soper a ve paris
crist worth an goyn a warnyas
dre onan bos treson guris
arluth du y a armas
pv a yl henna bonas

43 Ihesus crist a worthebys
ow tybbry genen yma
pub onan ol a ylwys
arluth du yv me hena
ha ihesus a worzebys
am scudel dybbry a wra
gwef vyth pan veva genys
a dor y vam zen bysma

44 Du a sonas an bara
ze rag y abestely
ow horf a ve yw henma
yn meth crist sur ragough wy
pernys a berth yn bysma
dyspresys haneth a vyth
an deppro gans cregyans da
gober tek eff an geuyth

42 *Christ sent two men to buy food and drink. These same men made good speed and supper was prepared. At the supper Christ warned that treachery would be done by one. "Lord God," they cried. "Who can that be?"*

43 *Jesus Christ replied, "He is eating with us." Every one called out, "Lord God, am I that one?" And Jesus answered, "He is eating from my dish. Woe to him that ever he was born from his mother's womb into this world."*

44 *God blessed the bread in the presence of his apostles. "This is my Body," said Christ. "This night, it will surely be despised for you who are redeemed in this world. He who eats it in good faith will receive a fair reward."*

42 Dew dhen Krist a dhannvonas — Mt 26 v.17-25
Dhe brena boes ha diwes. — Mk 14 v.12-20
An keth re na a spedyas — Lk 22 v.8-21
Ha'n soper a veu parys. — P.C. 617-764
Krist orth an goen a warnyas
Dre onan bos trayson gwrys.
"Arloedh Duw," i a armas,
"Piw a yll henna bones?"

43 Yesus Krist a worthybis,
"Ow tybri genen yma."
Pubonan oll a ylwis,
"Arloedh Duw, yw my henna?"
Ha Yesus a worthybis,
"A'm skudell dybri a wra.
Go-ev bydh pan veva genys — Mt 26 v.24
A dorr y vamm dhe'n bys ma." — Mk 14 v.21
Lk 22 v.22

44 Duw a soenas an bara — Mt 26 v.26-28
Dherag y abesteli. — Mk 14 v.22-24
"Ow horf evy yw hemma," — Lk 22 v.17
Yn-medh Krist. "Sur ragowgh hwi — P.C. 765-72
Prenys a-berth y'n bys ma
Dispresys haneth a vydh.
A'n deppro gans kryjyans dha
Gober teg ev a'n jevydh."

42/6 **onan.** See Spelling Notes, page 13.

43/3 **Pubonan**. See Spelling Notes, page 13.

43/6 **A'm skudell dybri a wra**. The Gospel accounts refer to 'the dish'. Evidently it was one common dish shared by all. I remember eating a paella with Spanish friends in a similar manner on the beach at Valencia some years ago. Clearly this Mediterranean custom was unknown to the writers of the Passion Poem and the *Passio Christi.*

44/6 **a vydh.** The insertion of *a* between a complement *dispresys* and a part of *bos* is unusual; cf. 29/8. See Language Notes, page 9.

44 The rhyme scheme in this verse has changed from *ab ab ab ab* to *ab ab ac ac*; cf. verse 1. Hooper gives a note from Nance suggesting that it has been 'tampered with' and that *abesteleth* probably rhymes with *yn-meth* in line 4 although the MS spelling is *abestely.*

45 Han gwyn esa war en foys
ef a rannas yn treza
yn meth crist hema yw goys
evough why par cheryta
gans dour gorris yn bazon
y wolhas aga garrow
hysseas ys guregh pur wyn
dell vynna du caradow

46 Henna pedyr a sconyas
ihesus ze wolhy y dreys
taw pedyr te ny wozas
yn meth crist pan dra raf zys
mar nyth wolhaff dre ow gras
yn nef ny vezyth tregis
ynmeth pedyr zym na as
troys na leyff vo golhys

47 Ihesus crist leun a bete
a leueris zen dowzek
wy yv glan a bup fylte
mas nyn iough ol da na whek
bos Iudas ef a wozye
pur hager ha molozek
an ioul ynno re drecse
may zo gweth agis cronek

45 *And the wine which was on the table he shared among them. "This is (my) Blood," said Christ. "Drink out of love." With water put into a basin he washed their legs. He made them pure white from end to end as was the will of a loving God.*

46 *Then Peter refused that Jesus should wash his feet. "Quiet, Peter," said Christ. "You do not know what I am doing for you. If I do not wash you by my grace you will not dwell in Heaven." Peter said, "Leave neither my foot nor my hand unwashed."*

47 *Jesus Christ, full of pity, said to the twelve, "You are innocent of all vileness, but you are not all good or sweet." He knew that Judas was quite hideous and accursed. The devil had dwelt in him so that he was worse than a toad.*

45 Ha'n gwin esa war an voes P.C. 823-32
Ev a rannas yntredha.
Yn-medh Krist, "Hemm yw ow goes,
Evewgh hwi par cheryta."
Gans dowr gorrys yn bason Jn 13 v.2-17
Y wolghas aga garrow. P.C. 833-64
Hys-ha-hys y's gwrug pur wynn
Dell vynna Duw karadow.

46 Ena Peder a skonyas
Yesus dhe wolghi y dreys:
"Taw, Peder, ty ny wodhes,"
Yn-medh Krist, "pandr'a wrav dhis;
Mar ny'th wolghav dre ow gras,
Yn nev ny vydhydh trigys."
Yn-medh Peder, "Dhymm na as
Troes na leuv na vo golghys."

47 Yesus Krist, leun a bita,
A leveris dhe'n dewdhek,
"Hwi yw glan a bub vilta,
Mes nyns owgh oll da na hweg."
Bos Yudas ev a wodhya
Pur hager ha mollothek.
An jowl ynno re drygsa
Mayth o gweth ages kroenek.

45/3 **Hemm yw ow goes.** Strangely the MS omits the all-important *ow* but I have followed Hooper and Pennaod in reinstating it in accordance with Scripture and tradition. The *-a* of *hema*, which in any case is irregular before *yw,* is dropped to fit the syllable count. Hooper and Pennaod have printed *hen* instead of *hem* but I do not see any reason for this.

45/4 **par cheryta.** Stokes and Nance read *par* though Hooper and Pennaod take this as *pour* in their Unified versions. Either French word could be appropriate. See also References to *C.S.II*, p. 23.

45/5 **bason.** The *-on* appears to be meant to rhyme with *wynn,* presumably as a neutral vowel. This suggests that the *y* of *wynn* could be neutral which is a little difficult to imagine, though there is no trouble with the *-on* of *bason.* This verse now rhymes *ab ab cd cd;* see the Versification Note on page 30.

46/1 **Ena.** Hooper and Pennaod follow the MS and read *Henna* but 'then' makes more sense than 'that' in the context; cf. 103/1.

48 In delma crist pan wresse
ze iudas y leueris
te ke yn vn fystene
ze voth may fo colenwys
rag an termyn re deve
may fyth an begel kyllys
ha chechys yn tre dewle
han deves ze ves fijs

49 Kyn fallens ol me a veth
yn meth pedyr yth seruys
yn meth crist yn nos haneth
kyns ys boys colyek clewys
pedyr te am nagh tergweth
bythqueth arluth na vef zys
yn meth pedyr tan ow feth
nyth nahaff kyn fen lezys

50 In meth crist a ban rug zeugh
ternoth fernoth ow holye
daver vyth wy ny zecsyugh
ze worre trevyth ynne
betegyns wy ny wozough
pan dra ezom agan be
arluth guyr aleuersough
y a gowsys yn treze

48 *When Christ had done this he said to Judas, "Hurry away so that your purpose may be fulfilled, for the time has come when the shepherd will be forfeit and taken into custody and the sheep will run away."*

49 *"Though all fail," said Peter, "I shall be in your service." Christ said, "This very night, before the cock is heard, Peter, you will deny me three times that I was ever Lord unto you." Peter said, "Upon my faith, I will not deny you even though I am slain."*

50 *Christ said, "Since I made you follow me, ill-clad and barelegged, you have not carried any holder to put anything into. Nevertheless you do not know what need we had." "Lord, you have spoken the truth," they said among themselves.*

48 Yndellma Krist pan wrussa, Jn 13 v.27
Dhe Yudas y leveris,
"Ty, ke yn unn fistena
Dha vodh may fo kollenwys,
Rag an termyn re dheuva Mt 26 v.31
May fydh an bugel kellys, Mk 14 v.27-31
Ha kechys yntra diwla Lk 22 v.33-34
Ha'n deves dhe-ves fiys." Jn 13 v.37-38
P.C. 887-910

49 "Kyn fallons oll, my a vydh,"
Yn-medh Peder, "y'th servys."
Yn-medh Krist, "Yn nos haneth,
Kyns es bos kulyek klywys,
Peder, ty a'm nagh teyrgweyth,
Bythkweyth Arloedh na veuv dhis."
Yn-medh Peder, "Tann ow fydh,
Ny'th naghav kyn fiv ledhys."

50 Yn-medh Krist, "A-ban wrug dhywgh Lk 22 v.35
Ternoeth, fernoeth ow holya, P.C. 911-18
Daffar vydh ny dhegsewgh
Dhe worra travydh ynna,
Byttegyns hwi ny wodhowgh
Pandra edhomm a'gan beu."
"Arloedh, gwir a leversowgh."
I a gewsis yntredha.

48/2 **yn unn fistena.** See *G.M.C.* §228(2); *G.M.C.(2)* §243(5).

48/5 **re dheuva.** Perfect of *dos;* see *G.M.C.* §204(2); *G.M.C.(2)* §206.

48/6 **kellys.** Read and translated as *kefys* by Hooper. Pennaod reads *kellys* which I have followed.

48/7 **kechys.** Read (or misprinted) *jychys* by Pennaod and Hooper but corrected by Hooper to *kychys* on an errata sheet.

49/1 **Kyn fallons**.

49/8 **kyn fiv.** Hooper and Pennaod follow the MS with *kyn fallens and kyn fen*, but these are examples of the imperfect subjunctive being used where the context calls for a present; see Language Notes, page 10.

50 Obscure, though apparently based on Lk 22 v.35 "And He said unto them, 'When I sent you without purse and scrip and shoes, lacked ye anything?' and they said, 'Nothing.'" (*A.V.*).

51 Mas lemmyn rys yv porris
batayles kyns ys coske
an geffo pows as gwyrzyns
ha zozo pernas cleze
sur yma dew zyn parys
y a leueris whare
hen yw lour na moy ny rys
du a leueris arte

52 Mab marya leun a ras
zen meneth olyff y zeth
hay zyscyplys an sewyas
yn meth crist yn nos haneth
golyough ha pesough ow zas
may hallough mos zy aseth
na vezough temtijs dygnas
gans gow ha gans scherewneth

53 Pedyr androw ha Iowan
yn meth crist deugh holyough ve
bys yn meneth ha me gwan
trystyns vs worth ow bluzye
ze worte vn lam beghan
y zeth pesy may halle
zy zas yn weth vgy a van
hag ef rag own ow crenne

51 "*But it is now very important to do battle rather than sleep. Let him who has a cloak sell it and buy himself a sword.*" "*Indeed we have two ready,*" *they said at once.* "*That is enough. No more are needed,*" *God said once more.*

52 *Mary's Son, full of grace, went to the Mount of Olives and his disciples followed him. Christ said,* "*This night keep watch and pray to my Father that you may go to his seat and so you will not be tempted beyond nature by falsehood and wickedness.*"

53 *"Peter, Andrew and John," said Christ, "come, follow me to the mountain. Because I am weak, sorrow is sapping my strength." He went a little way from them so that he could pray to his Father who is ever above, although he was shaking with fear.*

51 “Mes lemmyn res yw porres Lk 22 v.36-38
Batalyas kyns es koska; P.C. 919-27
A’n jeffo pows a’s gwerthes
Ha dhodho prenes kledha.”
“Sur, yma dew dhyn parys,”
I a leveris hware.
“Henn yw lowr, namoy ny res,”
Duw a leveris arta.

52 Mab Maria. leun a ras Mt 26 v.30
Dhe’n Menydh Oliv yth eth, Mk 14 v.26
Ha’y dhyssiplys a’n sywyas. Lk 22 v.39
Yn-medh Krist, “Y’n nos haneth P.C. 1011-30
Golyewgh ha pysewgh ow Thas
May hallowgh mos dh’y esedh,
Na vydhowgh temptys dignas
Gans gow ha gans sherewneth.”

53 “Peder, Androw ha Yowann,” Mt 26 v.37
Yn-medh Krist, “dewgh, holyewgh vy Mk 14 v.33-35
Bys y’n Menydh. Ha my gwann, Lk 22 v.40-41
Trystyns eus orth ow bludhya.”
Dhiworta unn lamm byghan
Yth eth, pysi may halla
Dh’y Das hwath usi a-vann,
Hag ev rag own ow krena.

51/3/4 **gwerthes**; **prenes**. See Language Notes, page 13; 3rd singular imperative. The K.K. third person singular imperative in *-es* improves the rhyme with *porres* in 51/1 but notice the MS spelling *gwyrzyns*. *Pernas,* on the other hand is only example in this poem that supports the “restoration” of *-es* as a 3s. imperative as mentioned in *G.M.C. (2)* §183(3)

52/3 **dhyssiplys**. This is the *G.M.* spelling. Presumably the *sc* spelling of the MS could indicate the sound *ss*. *G.M.* recognises *dyskybel (-blon)* and *dyssipel* (*-plys)* as the latter occurs in Tregear’s *Homilies*. Evidently it also occurs here.

52/7 **Na vydhowgh**. Hooper and Pennaod print *vedh<u>eu</u>gh* in spite of the *vez<u>ou</u>gh* of the MS. Hooper takes this as a subjunctive in a negative final clause, ‘lest you be tempted.’ It seems better to take it as a present/future indicative tense to form a consecutive clause, ‘and so you will not be tempted.’ See *G.M.C.* §334; *G.M.C.(2)* §350

53/5 **unn lamm.** *Unn* is used as an indefinite article. See Language Notes, page 10.

53/7 **hwath.** I have followed Hooper and Pennaod against the *yn weth* of the MS which creates an excess syllable.

54 Mab marya mur a beyn
a wozevy yn vrna
rag ef a wozya yn feyn
han kyg ny vynna henna
mes y zenzys o mar feyn
pub vr an trylya zeza
may zeth war ben y zewleyn
ha pesy yn ketelma

55 Mara sew ze voth ow zas
gura zen payn ma ow gasa
mes bezens guris ze vynnas
arluth du ze voth del ve
zy zyscyplys y trylyas
yscafas ol ow coske
ynmeth crist vn pols golyas
ny yllough zum comfortye

56 Ena crist sur as gasas
hag eth arta ze besy
war ben gleyn ze worth y das
del lauarsa ragon ny
y beynys o cref ha bras
warnozo heb y dylly
reson o rag ol an wlas
ef a wozye y verwy

54 *Mary's Son was suffering much pain at that time for he was perfectly aware (of his fate) and the flesh did not want that, but his Manhood which was so perfect turned him all the time to these things, so that he went down on his knees and prayed thus:*

55 *"If it is your will, my Father, make this pain leave me, but let your will be done, Lord God, whatever it may be." He returned to his disciples. He found them all sleeping. Christ said, "Can you not stay awake one moment to give me strength?"*

56 *Then Christ definitely left them and went again to pray for us on his knees to his Father as he had said. His pains were strong and great upon him without being deserved. The reason was that he knew he was gong to die for all the land.*

54 Mab Maria meur a bayn
A wodhevi y'n eur na,
Rag ev a wodhya yn fin,
Ha'n kig ny vynna henna;
Mes y Dhenses o mar fin
Pub eur a'n treylya dhedha,
Mayth eth war benn y dhewlin
Ha pysi yn kettellma:

55 "Maras yw dha vodh, ow Thas, Mt 26 v.39-40
Gwra dhe'n payn ma ow gasa, Mk 14 v.36-37
Mes bedhes gwrys dha vynnas Lk 22 v.42-45
Arloedh Duw, dha vodh dell vo." P.C. 1013-68
Dh'y dhyssiplys y treylyas:
Y's kavas oll ow koska.
Yn-medh Krist, "Unn pols goelyas
Ny yllowgh, dhe'm konfortya?"

56 Ena Krist sur a's gasas, Mt 26 v.42
Hag eth arta dhe bysi, Mk 14 v.39
War benn-glin, dhiworth y Das, P.C. 1019-74
Dell lavarsa, ragon ni.
Y baynys o krev ha bras
Warnodho, heb y dylli.
Reson o, rag oll an wlas
Ev a wodhya y ferwi.

54/3 **rag ef a wozya yn feyn** (MS). Hooper has 'for He was able to, strongly.' I have taken *feyn* as *fin* as in 54/5 and 'perfect(ly)' seems appropriate in both cases; cf. 57/3 where *yn fen* is *yn ven* in the MS.

54/4 **Dhenses**. Hooper and Pennaod read this as *Dhuwses* (*zewsys*) = "Divinity".

54/4 **ny vynna henna**. Normally *mynnes* is an auxiliary verb followed by a verb-noun. See Language Notes, page 13.

54/6 **pub vr an trylya zeza** (MS). Hooper and Pennaod have turned this to *Pub ur dhodho a'n trelya.*

55/3 **bedhes**. See Language Notes, page 13; 3rd singular imperative.

55/4 **dell vo**. Emended from the imperfect subjunctive of the MS. See Language Notes, page 10.

55/5 **dhyssiplys**. See 52/3.

55/8 **ny yllough zum comfortye** (MS). Read by Hooper and Pennaod as *ylleugh* - imperfect. I do not see any difficulty in reading it as a present tense, though vowel confusion cannot be ruled out.

56/3 **dhiworth** used with *pysi* = 'to request from'; see *G.M.C.* §154(2); *G.M.C.(2)* §153(2)

56/8 **Ev a wodhya y ferwi.** Imperfect showing future in the past; see *G.M.C.* §215(4); *G.M.C.(2)* §228(4)

57 In meth crist o du ha den
arte zy abestely
golyough ha pesough yn ven
rag own an ioul hay vestry
tresse gwyth hag ef yn cren
y pesys du delyr vy
arluth mar ny yl bos ken
bezens kepar del vynny

58 Ihesus crist dygonfortys
war ben dewlyn pan ese
an nef y fe danuenys
el zozo zy gomfortye
mab du o kymmys grevijs
rag tomder ef a wese
dowr ha goys yn kemyskys
weys crist rag ze gerense

59 Cryst kymmys payn yn geve
angus tyn ha galarow
mateth angoys ha dropye
war y fas an caradow
den vyth ny yl amontye
na leuerell war anow
oll myns peynys an geve
kyns ys y vonas marow

57 *Christ, who was God and Man, said again to his apostles, "Stay awake and pray earnestly for fear of the devil and his domination." A third time, as he was trembling, he prayed, "God, deliver me! Lord, if it cannot be otherwise, let it be as you will."*

58 *When Jesus Christ was on his knees in distress, an angel was sent to him from Heaven to give him strength. The Son of God was so oppressed because of the heat that he was sweating water and blood mixed together - the sweat of Christ for your sake.*

59 *Christ had so much pain, cruel anguish and suffering that the blood came and dropped on his face, the Beloved. No man can reckon nor say in words all the torment which he had before he was dead.*

57 Yn-medh Krist, o Duw ha Den, Mt 26 v.44
Arta dh'y abesteli, Mk 14 v.41
"Golyewgh ha pysewgh yn fen P.C 1075-80.
Rag own an jowl ha'y vaystri."
Tressa gweyth, hag ev yn kren,
Y pysis, "Duw, delirv vy!
Arloedh, mar ny yll bos ken,
Bedhes kepar dell vynni."

58 Yesus Krist, digonfortys
War benn dewlin pan esa,
A'n nev y feu dannvenys
El dhodho dh'y gonfortya. Lk 22 v.43-44
Mab Duw o kemmys grevys P.C. 1041-53
Rag toemmder ev a hwysa
Dowr ha goes yn kemmyskys -
Hwys Krist rag dha gerensa.

59 Krist kemmys payn a'n jeva
Angus tynn ha galarow,
May teuth an goes ha droppya
War y fas, an Karadow.
Denvydh ny yll amontya,
Na leverel war anow,
Oll myns paynys a'n jeva
Kyns es y vones marow.

57/8 **bedhes**. See Language Notes, page 13; 3rd singular imperative.

60 Lemmyn ny a yl gwelas
hag ervyre fest yn ta
cryst ze wozaff dre zensys
mur a benans yn bysma
ef ny ylly dre zewsys
gozaff na nyll drok na da
rag mester o war an bys
hag ol myns vs ef a ra

61 Pan o y besadow guris
zen dowzek y leuerys
koscough lemmyn mar sew prys
powesough wy yv grevijs
tus vs zym ow tevones
yv gans ow thraytor dyskis
fatel dons thov hemeres
ha del vezaff hombronkis

62 Kepar du del leuerys
pan esa crist ow pesy
Iudas eth yn y negis
en ioul yv en hombronky
zen ezewan dyrryvys
del o y fynas synsy
syndis ve dre govaytis
yn della yw leas huny

60 *Now we can see and be quite convinced that Christ, as Man, suffered much penance in this world. He could not, as God, experience either evil or good, because he was Master over the world, and everything there is, he makes.*

61 *When his prayers were done he said to the twelve, "Sleep now if it is time; rest, you are worn out. Men are coming to me who have been told by my betrayer how they are to come and take me and how I shall be led (away)."*

62 *Just as God said, when Christ was praying Judas went off on his business. It is the devil who was leading him. He intended to continue as he was, an informer to the Jews. He was destroyed by greed. So it is with many a one.*

60 Lemmyn ni a yll gweles
Hag ervira fest yn ta
Krist dhe wodhav dre Dhenses
Meur a benans y'n bys ma.
Ev ny ylli dre Dhuwses
Godhav naneyl drog na da,
Rag Mester o war an bys,
Hag oll myns eus, ev a wra.

61 Pan o y bysadow gwrys,
Dhe'n dewdhek y leveris
"Koskewgh lemmyn mars yw prys. Mt 26 v.45
Powesewgh, hwi yw grevys. Mk 14 v.41
Tus eus dhymm ow tevones P.C.1093-98
Yw gans ow thraytour dyskys
Fatell dhons dh'ow hemmeres
Ha dell vydhav hembrenkys."

62 Kepar Duw dell leveris,
Pan esa Krist ow pysi
Yudas eth yn y negys,
An jowl yw a'n hembrenki.
Dhe'n Edhewon derivys
Dell o, y fynnas synsi.
Shyndys veu dre govaytys.
Yndella yw lies huni.

60/3/5 **Dhenses....Dhuwses**. These two contrast well positioned at the ends of the lines.

61/3 **mars yw prys**. Hooper points out that 'if there is time' would be *mars eus prys*. Presumably the meaning is 'the hour is come' as in Mk 14 v41 and Mt 26 v.45.

61/6-8 **dyskys fatell dhons....ha dell vydhav.** See Language Notes, pages 15-16.

61/8 **hembrenkys**. The first *o* in the MS *hombronkis* is not recognised by Nance or the *G.M.* so presumably it is an error or irregular. The second *o* becomes *e* by vowel affection [*G.M.C.* §12(2c); *G.M.C.(2)* §14-16]. The word now echoes *hemmeres* in the previous line and the two words reinforce each other. Hooper and Pennaod have *hembrynkys* but this assumes a double vowel affection; cf. 23/5.

62/4 **hembrenki.** This is similar. The amendment of the second *o* to *e* improves the assonances. Hooper and Pennaod have *hembrynky.*

62/5 **derivys.** I have taken this as a past participle, literally 'informed to the Jews as he was.' Hooper takes it as a preterite and translates 'To the Jews he declared that, as it was, he wished to hold it.' This assumes the omission of particle *a* and the resultant mutation.

63 Then ezewon pan dozye
y leuerys hag y ow tos
me a gris yn ta spedye
om negis haneth yn nos
deugh geneff ha holyough ve
gothvezough na rellough tros
ha me a ra the crist amme
may hallough y asswonvos

64 An princis esa yn pow
gans Iudas a thanvonas
tus ven gweskis yn arvow
kepar ha del ens zen gas
ganse y a thuk golow
nos o ny welons yn fas
bys yn Ihesus caradow
y eth del dyskas Iudas

65 Pan dozyans bys yn tyller
may zese crist ow pesy
lowene zys a vester
yn meth Iudas an brathky
zozo y rug fekyl cher
hag y amme trewesy
ef a vynne yn ober
gul ken ys del dywyzy

63 *When he had come to the Jews, he said, as they were coming, "I look forward to succeeding well in my business tonight. Come with me and follow me. Be sure you do not make a noise, and I will kiss Christ so that you may recognise him."*

64 *The princes who were in the land with Judas sent strong men clad in armour as if they were going to battle . They carried a light with them. It was night. They could not see very well. They went up to beloved Jesus as Judas directed.*

65 *When they had come to the place where Christ was praying, the savage cur Judas said, "Joy to you, Master." He greeted him falsely and kissed him gravely. He intended, in fact, to do otherwise than as he showed.*

63 Dhe'n Edhewon pan dhodhya
'Leveris, hag i ow tos,
"My a grys yn ta spedya
Y'm negys haneth yn nos.
Dewgh genev ha holyewgh vy,
Godhvedhewgh na wrellowgh tros,
Ha my a wra dhe Krist amma Mt 26 v.48
May hallowgh y aswonnvos." Mk 14 v.44
P.C.1081-86

64 An prynsys esa y'n pow
Gans Yudas a dhannvonas
Tus ven, gwiskys yn arvow
Kepar ha dell ens dhe'n gas.
Gansa i a dhug golow.
Nos o. Ny welens yn fas.
Bys yn Yesus karadow
I eth, dell dhyskas Yudas.

65 Pan dhodhyens bys y'n tyller Mt 26 v.49
Mayth esa Krist ow pysi, Mk 14 v.45
"Lowena dhis, a Vester!" Lk 22 v.47
Yn-medh Yudas, an brathki. P.C. 1104 and
Dhodho y hwrug fekyl cher, stage direction
Hag y amma truesi.
Ev a vynna yn ober
Gul ken es dell dhyskwedhi.

63/2 **'Leveris**. I have followed Hooper and Pennaod in replacing the particle *y* at the beginning of the line with an apostrophe to correct the syllable count. Wella Brown points out that this particle is often omitted.

64/1 **prynsys**. Wella Brown points out that English words are not always mutated.

64/6 **Ny welens**: 'They could not see.' See Language Notes, pages 14-15.

65/6 **Hag y amma.** Usually *amma* <u>*dhe*</u> as in 63/7. See *G.M.C.* §141(14a); *G.M.C.(2)* §141(15a)

66 Ihesus a gewsis pur dek
Iudas ow ry ty avyn
dre ze vay a reyth mar whek
ze neb am tormont mar dyn
moll(o)z den ha gour ha gwrek
a ze poran erzebyn
peynys ad wra morezek
yn yffarn down pub termyn

67 Ihesus crist a wovynnys
worth anbobyll a zeth dy
gans an fals yn y seruys
pandra yw a vynnough wy
en rena a worzebys
Ihesus yw an caffans ny
en arluth a worzebys
me yw henna yredy

68 Pur wyr drefen an virtu
an lauar crist pan gowsas
neb a wheleugh why me yw
ze ves y a omdennas
rag own y a gangyes lyw
rag gwander y a gozas
yn trevyth y nyn gens gyw
ze wezyll dris y vynnas

66 *Jesus spoke very courteously: "Judas, by your kiss which you give so sweetly you intend to deliver me to those who will torture me cruelly. The curse of mankind, both male and female, will come directly upon you. Tortures will make you sorrowful in deep hell for all time."*

67 *Jesus Christ asked the people who came there with the traitor in his service, "What is it that you want?" They replied, "It is Jesus, if only we could find him." The Lord replied, "I am he indeed."*

68 *Truly, because of the power of Christ's words when he said, "I am he whom you seek," they fell back. Through fear they changed colour. Through weakness they fell. In no way were they in a fit state to act beyond his will!*

66 Yesus a gewsis pur deg: Lk 22 v.48
"Yudas, ow ri ty a vynn P.C. 1105-8
Dre dha vay a reth mar hweg
Dhe neb a'm torment mar dynn.
Molleth den, ha gour ha gwreg,
A dheu poran er dha bynn.
Paynys a'th wra morethek
Yn ifarn down pub termyn."

67 Yesus Krist a wovynnis
Orth an bobel a dheuth di
Gans an fals yn y servis,
"Pandra yw a vynnowgh hwi?" Jn 18 v.4-5
An re na a worthybis, P.C.1109-14
"Yesus yw, a'n kaffen ni."
An Arloedh a worthybis,
"My yw henna yredi."

68 Pur wir drefenn an vertu
A'n lavar Krist pan gowsas,
"Neb a hwilowgh hwi my yw,"
Dhe-ves i a omdennas Jn 18 v.6
Rag own i a janjyas liw, P.C. 1113
Rag gwannder i a goedhas. Stage direction
Yn travydh i nyns ens gwiw
Dhe wuthyl dres y vynnas.

66/5 ....**den, ha gour ha gwreg.** A good illustration of the fact that the basic meaning of *den* is 'human being' rather than 'man' in the sense of 'male person'.

67/1 **wovynnis**. The third singular preterite usually ends in *-as*; see *G.M.C.* §183; *G.M.C.(2)* §180. Nance gives it as the first of two alternatives. Here, *-is* is better for the rhyme. Cf. also 69/1 where the same ending occurs in the MS.

67/4 **vynnowgh**. Used without the usual following verb-noun. See Language Notes, page 13.

67/6 This line is quoted in *C.S.II* as an example of a conditional sentence and I have followed this; see References to *C.S.II,* page 20. Stokes and Hooper have 'It is Jesus whom we would take,' but this would be *a gaffen ni.* The literal meaning would be 'if we (had) found Him,' but Wella Brown suggests, more idiomatically, 'if only we could find Him.' This does not explain why there is an *s* at the end of the verb in the MS, making it seem to be a third person, unless we should understand 'if <u>they</u> found Him (for) us,' but this seems unlikely. Strictly speaking, the main clause should be *Yesus <u>via</u>,* but this irregularity is common in the texts as in Modern English, so that I have translated it literally rather than 'correcting' it.

68/2 **gowsas**. This is from *kows*, not *kewsel. Kows* is more common in the Poem and the ending *-as* is better for the rhyme in this case.

68/7 **i nyns ens gwiw**. A striking example of a pronoun subject preceding *nyns* for emphasis. I have followed Hooper in underlining 'they'.

69 Cryst a wovynys arte
orth an ezewon woky
agis negis pyth ywe
pv yw neb a weleugh wy
ihesus crist an nazare
an rena a worzeby
yn meth ihesus me ywe
lemmyn gureugh agis meystry

70 Whare y an kemeres
hag an sensys yn treze
gans lauarow an scornyas
gallus o grontis zeze
ze wezyll aga mynnas
yn della ef a vynne
may halle dre baynys bras
merwel rag ze gerenze

71 Pedyr an neyl tenewen
yn mes a dennas cleze
hag a drohas ryb an pen
scovern onan aneze
crist a settyas yn tyen
an scovern arte ze dre
hag an dyzgthtyas pur lowen
maga tek del rebye

69 *Christ asked the foolish Jews again, "What is your business? Who is it that you seek?" "Jesus Christ of Nazareth," they answered. Jesus said, "I am he. Now exercise your authority."*

70 *Straight away they arrested him and held him between them. They mocked him with words. Power was granted to them to do as they wished. In this way he willed it to be possible for him to die with great pains for your sake.*

71 *Peter on the one side drew out a sword and cut off the ear of one of them close to the head. Christ set the ear completely back in its place and restored it very comfortably, as handsomely as it had been.*

69 Krist a wovynnas arta — Jn 18 v.7-8
Orth an Edhewon wokki, — P.C. 1113-24
"Agas negys, pyth ywa?
Piw yw neb a hwilowgh hwi?"
"Yesus Krist a Nasara,"
An re na a worthybi.
Yn-medh Yesus, "My ywa.
Lemmyn gwrewgh agas maystri."

70 Hware i a'n kemmeras — P.C. 1131-35
Hag a'n synsis yntredha
Gans lavarow y'n skornyas.
Galloes o grontys dhedha
Dhe wuthyl aga mynnas.
Yndella ev a vynna
May halla dre baynys bras
Merwel rag dha gerensa.

71 Peder a'n eyl tenewen — Mt 25 v.51-52
Yn-mes a dennas kledha, — Mk 14 v.47
Hag a droghas ryb an penn — Lk 22 v.50-52
Skovarn onan anedha. — Jn 18 v.10-11
Krist a settyas yn tien — P.C. 1137-54
An skovarn arta dhe dre
Hag a'n dyghtyas pur lowen,
Maga teg dell re bia.

70/7 **May halla.** Hooper prints *May hallas* but this appears to be a misprint as he translates 'that he might, through great pains, die for thy sake,' thus indicating a purpose rather than a result clause and agreeing with the imperfect subjunctive as read by Pennaod.

71/7 **pur lowen**. Although Hooper translates 'right gladly,' any such sentiment seems incongruous. Nance and *G.M.*.give 'comfort' as a meaning of *lowenhe*, and with this support, I feel 'very comfortably' is more appropriate.

71/8 **dell re bia**. See *G.M.C.* §265(6); *G.M.C.(2)* §279(8) and G.M.C. §332; *G.M.C.(2)* §348(1).

72 Gor ze gleze yn y goyn
ze pedyr crist a yrghys
rag dre gleze a veughe
dre gleze yfyth lezys
dewzek lygyon yn vn ro
vye an nef danuenys
ha moy a mynnen zymmo
pesy ow zas pur barys

73 Hag a pe yn della ve
neffre ny vean fethys
yn vrna fatell vye
am bewnans del yw scrifys
yn lyffrow yn leas le
dre brofusy leuerys
reys yw porris heb strevye
both ow zas ze vos sewijs

74 Ihesus a gewsys arte
why a theth zym yn arvow
dre dreyson yn un scolchye
gans boclers ha clezyzyow
thom kemeres zom syndye
zom peynye bys yn crow
kepar ha del vena ve
an purra lader yn pow

72 *"Put your sword into its sheath," Christ commanded Peter, "for he who lives by the sword shall be slain by the sword. Twelve legions of angels and more would be sent from heaven one after another with great readiness if I wished to pray to my Father for myself.*

73 *"And if it were thus, I would never be defeated. How would the story of my life then be? It is written in the Scriptures (and) told by the Prophets in many places: 'It is entirely necessary that My Father's will be followed without dispute.'"*

74 *Jesus spoke again. "You have come to me armed, treacherously, furtively, with shields and swords to arrest me, to harm me, to torture me to death, just as if I were the most arrant thief in the land.*

72 "Gorr dha gledha yn y woen," P.C. 1155-70
Dhe Beder Krist a erghis,
"Rag dre gledha a vywo,
Dre gledha a fydh ledhys.
Dewdhek lyjyon yn unn rew Mt 26 v.53
Via a'n nev dannvenys,
Ha moy, a mynnen dhymmo
Pysi ow Thas, pur barys.

73 "Hag a pe yndella, my
Nevra ny vien fethys.
Y'n eur na, fatell via
A'm bywnans? - dell yw skrifys
Y'n lyvrow yn lies le,
Dre brofusi leverys:
'Res yw porres, heb strivya,
Bodh ow Thas dhe vos sywys.'"

74 Yesus a gewsis arta, Mt 26 v.55
"Hwi a dheuth dhymm yn arvow, Mk 14 v.48-49
Dre dreyson yn unn skolkya Lk 22 v.52-53
Gans boklers ha kledhedhyow P.C. 1171-76
Dhe'm kemmeres, dhe'm shyndya,
Dhe'm paynia bys yn krow,
Kepar ha dell vena vy
An purra lader y'n pow.

72/1 Hooper and Pennaod have altered this to: *Yn y woen dha gledha dro*, presumably to correct the rhyme.

72/6 **Via.** Normal grammar requires *a via*, as *Dewdhek lyjyon* in 72/5 is a preceding subject. The reverse occurs in 29/8 and 44/6 where particle *a* is abnormally inserted. Evidently these irregularities are to correct the syllable count.

72/8 **pur barys.** Hooper takes this with *Pysi ow Thas* and translates 'should I wish for myself to pray to my Father, very readily.'

73 This verse is tricky to translate. Presumably the sense is that if Jesus called for supernatural angelic help he would not fulfil Scripture or the will of his Father.

73/1-2 **ve neffre ny vean fethys** (MS) Hooper takes the *ve* as part of *bos*, but I feel it more likely to be *my* with the *m* either misread or mutated under the influence of the preceding *a,* and giving a negative sentence with a stressed pronoun subject.

73/4 The question mark is inserted in this line for the sake of clarity. Grammatically it should be at the end of the sentence in 73/8.

74/2 **Yn unn skolkya.** See *G.M.C.* §228(2); *G.M.C.(2)* §243(5).

74/6 **paynia.** One would expect *paynya* as in G.M. or *payna* as in Nance but this would leave the line a syllable short as both are only two syllables. Maybe *paynia* resulted from the influence of French *punir* or Latin *punire/poenire,* and it is spelt here with *y* to complete the syllable count. Cf. 90/3 where the two syllable spelling is used.

75 In agis mysk pan esen
la(h)ys du zeugh ow tysky
gallus nyn gese kemmen
zom cara na zom sensy
lemmyn deve ken termyn
ow thas rom growntyas zewy
leun a beghas ny won ken
ze wezyll agis meystry

76 In vrna y a colmas
y zefregh fast gans cronow
en goys yn mes may tarzas
del fastsens en colmennow
gansa y an hombronkyas
yn prys hanter nos heb wow
bys yn aga fryns annas
o vn Iucter bras yn pow

77 Tus crist ze ves a fyas
pep aydu pur vorezek
saw pedyr crist a holyas
abell avel vn ownek
ze dyller an prins annas
ene y zese sethek
orto ef y a sethas
may clewo leff ihesus whek

75 *"When I was among you, teaching you God's laws, there was no power at all to fetter or hold me. Now another time has come. My Father has granted me to you, full of sin for aught I know, to exercise your supremacy."*

76 *Then they tied his arms tightly with thongs so that the blood gushed out as they had tightened the knots. They took him with them just at midnight, to their prince Annas who was a great magistrate in the land.*

77 *Christ's men escaped each his own way in great grief. Only Peter followed Christ some way off as one afraid, to the court of prince Annas. There, there was a seating area. He sat in it to hear the voice of gentle Jesus.*

75 "Yn agas mysk pan esen,
Laghys Duw dhywgh ow tyski,
Galloes nyns esa kammenn
Dhe'm k'ara na dhe'm synsi.
Lemmyn deuva ken termyn.
Ow thas re'm grontyas dhy'hwi
Leun a beghas, ny wonn ken,
Dhe wuthyl agas maystri."

76 Y'n eur na i a golmas — Jn 18 v.12-13
Y dhiwvregh fast gans kroenow
An goes yn-mes may tardhas,
Dell fastsens an kolmennow.
Gansa i a'n hembronkyas,
Yn prys hanter-nos, heb wow,
Bys yn aga fryns Annas
O unn juster bras y'n pow.

77 Tus Krist dhe-ves a fias — Mt 26 v.56-58
Pub a'y du pur vorethek. — Mk 14 v.53-54
Saw Peder Krist a holyas — Lk 22 v.54
A-bell, avel unn ownek, — Jn 18 v.15.
Dhe dyller an prins Annas. — P.C. 1176-77 and following
Ena yth esa sedhek. — stage direction
Orto ev a esedhas
May klywa lev Yesus hweg.

75/4 "**c'ara** for *carghara*: See Williams *Lexicon*, and Lhuyd, 1707 *carhar*" (Hooper). Lhuyd actually prints *kar□ar*, □ being his phonetic symbol for *gh.* Williams suggests *cara* (MS*)* means "to kiss" and refers to the kiss of Judas.

75/5 **deuva**. Perfect of *dos* . See *G.M.C.* §204; *G.M.C.(2)* §206.

75/7 **ny wonn ken.** I have taken *ken* as meaning 'otherwise'. Hooper takes it as 'reason' and translates 'I know not wherefore.' The words seems little more than a line filler.

76/4 **fastsens**. Hooper and Pennaod read this as *fastsons* (pret.) and Stokes translates "they fastened". I have taken it as a pluperfect though it is not really appropriate in the context. Cf. also 132/8 (hwarsa)

76/6 **heb wow**. This, again, is little more than a line filler. Hooper has 'indeed'. In translating it by 'just' I am suggesting this may be one way of expressing 'just' in Cornish. It is a notoriously difficult word to translate.

76/8; 77/4 **unn juster; unn ownek.** *Unn* used as an indefinite article. See Language Notes, page 9.

77/5 **dyller.** As in 18/2 it seems necessary to interpret this rather colourless word in accordance with the context.

77/6 "**sedhek**: if 'stool' was meant, *war* and not *orth* would normally be used" (Hooper). The use of *orth* suggests that the *sedhek* was something at which one sat, perhaps a barrier at which Peter was allowed to sit, but away from the officers of the court.

77/7 **orto ef y a sethas** (MS) As read by Stokes and Nance. The scribe seems to have reversed the *y* and the *a.*

77/8 **May klywa**.MS has present subjunctive for imperfect. See Language Notes, page 9.

78 En prins scon a leueris
te crist lauar zym plema
ze dus mar voldh re zyssys
prag na zons genas omma
an la(h)ys a bregowthys
lemmyn dyswe mar syns da
ha ihesus a worzebys
ef dell vynna yn vrna

79 Pur apert hag yn golow
y leueris ow dyskas
ow la(h)ys haw lauarow
suel a vynna y clewas
yn le may then yn trevow
yn splan me as derevas
ny gowsyn yn tewolgow
a dryff tus yn vn hanas

80 Pan dra a woventa se
ze worzaff ve ham la(h)ys
mar a mynnyth govynny
ordh en keth re as clewas
an rena a yl ze zysky
yn della y re zyskas
yn delma heb velyny
orto Ihesus a gowsas

78 *At once the prince said, "You, Christ, tell me, where are your men who are so bold and whom you have trained? Why do they not come with you here? The laws that you preached, demonstrate now whether they are good." And Jesus answered, as he intended at that time:*

79 *"Very openly and in the light I told my doctrine, my laws and my sayings. Whoever wanted to, heard. Wherever I went in the towns I declared them clearly. I did not speak in the dark, whispering behind people.*

80 *"What do you ask of me and my laws? If you will, ask those who have heard them. They can instruct you just as they have learned." Thus, without disrespect Jesus spoke to him.*

78 An pryns skon a leveris, Jn 18 v. 19-21
"Ty, Krist, lavar dhymm, ple'ma P.C. 1245-50
Dha dus mar vold re dhyssys?
Prag na dhons genes omma?
An laghys a bregowthys
Lemmyn dyskwa, mars yns da."
Ha Yesu a worthybis,
Ev dell vynna y'n eur na,

79 "Pur apert hag yn golow P.C. 1251-64
Y leveris ow dyska's,
Ow laghys ha'w lavarow.
Seul a vynna y's klywas.
Yn le mayth en y'n trevow
Yn splann my a's derivas.
Ny gowsyn yn tewolgow
A-dryv tus yn unn hanas.

80 Pandra a wovynn'ta sy
Dhiworth vy ha'm laghys?
Mara mynnydh, govynn e
Orth an keth re a's klywas.
An re na 'yll dha dhyski
Yndella i re dhyskas."
Yndellma heb vileni
Orto Yesus a gowsas.

78/3 **mar vold**. Hooper takes this with *re dhyssys*, 'Where are thy folk so boldly thou hast taught?'

78/4 "MS **na zons**. Imperfect indicative, must be for *dens* unless a variant based on 3rd singular *de*." (Hooper). I see no difficulty in taking it as a present tense.

79/4 **y's klywas**. I have followed Hooper and Pennaod in inserting the pronoun *'s*.

79/6 **derivas**. *G.M.C.*(2) §180(4b) gives *derivis* as third sing. preterite but *-as* as in the MS rhymes better.

79/8 **yn unn hanas.** See *G.M.C.* §228(2); *G.M.C.(2)* §243(5).

80/1 **Pandra a**. Normally *pandr'a* but the extra syllable is needed to complete the line.

80/2 **ha'm laghys**. Hooper and Pennaod print *a'm laghys* but Pennaod clearly reads the MS *ham* as *ha'm* in his Breton translation.

80/3 **govynny** (MS). I read this as *govynn e* = 'ask it'. Hooper and Pennaod print *gowyn y*, corrected by Hooper on errata sheet to *govyn y* = 'ask them'. See *G.M.C.* §64(5); *G.M.C.(2)* §66(3a).

80/5 **na 'yll**. The MS has an extra syllable and I have followed Hooper in eliding the particle *a* to correct this.

80/7 **heb vileni**. *G.M.* recognises *bileni* but not *vileni. G.M.C. (2)* §148 does not recognise mutation of *bileni* after *heb* so I have gone against both and followed Hooper and Pennaod.

81 Gans henna an ezewon
onan yn ban a sevys
hag a ros ryb an scovern
box ze grist a zesympys
ha dhe Ihesus y honon
an harlot a leuerys
pu a woras yt colon
cows yn delma worth iustis

82 In meth ihesus yn vrna
mara kewsys falsury
ha na blek genas henna
ha fals te dok dustuny
mes mara kewsys yn ta
han gwreoneth y synsy
prag omgwysketh yn delma
nyn gyw mernas belyny

83 Ena mur a vylyny
pedyr ze gryst a welas
y scornye hay voxscusy
trewe yn y zewlagas
hag ef rag own ny ylly
gans ihesu kewsel ger vas
henna o poynt a falsury
dezewys heb koweras

81 *Thereupon one of the Jews stood up and immediately gave Christ a blow by his ear, and to Jesus himself the villain said, "Who put it into your heart to speak thus to a magistrate?"*

82 *Jesus said then, "If I have told a lie and that is not pleasing to you and false, you produce the evidence. But if I have spoken well and held to the truth, why do you strike me thus? It is nothing but villainy."*

83 *Then Peter saw Christ (suffer) much ill-treatment; mocking him, punching him and spitting in his eyes, and because of fear, he could not speak a good word for Jesus. This was an act of falsehood, a promise that was not kept.*

81 Gans henna a'n Edhewon — Jn 18 v.22-23
Onan yn-bann a sevis — P.C. 1265-70
Hag a ros ryb an skovarn
Boks dhe Krist a-dhesempis.
Ha dhe Yesus y honan
An harlot a leveris,
"Piw a worras y'th kolonn
Kows yndellma orth justis?"

82 Yn-medh Yesus y'n eur na, — P.C. 1271-76
"Mara kewsis falsuri
Ha ny bleg genes henna,
Ha fals, ty dog dustuni.
Mes mara kewsis yn ta
Ha'n gwiryonedh y synsi,
Prag y'm gwyskydh yndellma?
Nyns yw marnas bileni."

83 Ena meur a vileni — Mt 26 v.67
Peder dhe Krist a welas, — Mk 14 v.65
Y skornya ha'y voksusi, — Lk 22 v.63-65
Trewa yn y dhewlagas,
Hag ev rag own ny ylli
Gans Yesus kewsel ger 'vas.
Henn o poynt a falsuri,
Dedhewys heb keweras.

82/3-4 **Ha ny bleg.** I have followed Hooper in taking this as a second clause depending on *Mara* in 82/2 '....and if that does not please you....' This reading calls for *na* in the MS to be emended to *ny* (which Hooper and Pennaod have not done) and reading *yw* after the *Ha* in 82/4.

Possibly *na bleg* is a relative clause: 'and which does not please'. In this case, *henna ha fals* might be for *ha henna fals* = 'that being false,' or 'because that is false' (cf. 86/8). The alternative translation would be:

'If I told a lie and (one) which does not please you because it is false, you produce the evidence.'

82/6 **synsi**. An example of a verb-noun being used as a finite verb in conjunction with *kewsis* in 82/5 [*G.M.C.* §226; *G.M.C.(2)* §241]. It is preceded by its object *gwiryonedh* and so has the object pronoun *y* inserted before it; cf. *Cornish Simplified,* §176(a).

84 Vn venyn hardh a ynnyas
war pedyr y vos tregis
gans ihesus ef a naghas
y arluth a zesympys
taw gans crist me ad welas
gurek arall a leueris
pedyr arta agowsas
bythqueth me nyn aswonys

85 Mur a dus a leuerys
ny dayl zys cam y naghe
dre ze gows y zew prevys
ze vos den a galyle
ef a doys a zesempys
maga town ty del wozye
gans crist na vye tregis
na bythqueth ef nan quelse

86 Gans hemma ef a clewas
en colyek scon ow cane
ha crist worto a wetras
an peynys bras may zese
pedyr sur a omdennas
yn vrna del rebeghse
ow nagha du leun a ras
hag ef gwarnyys del vye

84 *A woman boldly insisted to Peter that he dwelt with Jesus. Immediately he denied his Lord. "Silence, I have seen you with Christ," another woman said. Peter spoke again: "I never knew him."*

85 *Many people said, "It is no use at all your denying it. It is proved by your speech that you are a man of Galilee." Straight away he swore as great an oath as he could that he had not dwelt with Christ and that he had never seen him.*

86 *Immediately upon that he heard the cock crowing and Christ gazed upon him from the great torments he was in. Then Peter abruptly withdrew as he had sinned by denying God full of grace, although he had been warned.*

84 Unn venyn hardh 'ynnias — Mt 26 v.69-75
War Peder y vos trigys — Mk 14 v.66-72
Gans Yesus. Ev a naghas — Lk 22 v.56-62
Y Arloedh a-dhesempis. — Jn 18 v.17
"Taw! Gans Krist my a'th welas," — P.C. 1234-40
Gwreg arall a leveris.
Peder arta a gowsas,
"Bythkweyth my ny'n aswonnis!"

85 Meur a dus a leveris — Jn 18 v.25-27
"Ny dal dhis kamm y nagha. — P.C.1405-16
Dre dha gows yth yw prevys
Dha vos den a Galila."
Ev a dos a-dhesempis
Maga town ti dell wodhya
Gans Krist na via trigys,
Na bythkweyth ev na'n gwelsa.

86 Gans henna ev a glywas
An kulyek skon ow kana
Ha Krist orto a hwithras
A'n paynys bras mayth esa.
Peder, sur, a omdennas — P.C. 1417-46
Y'n eur na dell re beghsa
Ow nagha Duw, leun a ras
Hag ev gwarnys, dell via.

84/1 **Unn venyn**. *Unn* used is as indefinite article. See Language Notes, page 9.

84/1 **'ynnias.** The long *i* makes this word three syllables so that the MS and Unified versions have an excess syllable. For this reason the particle *a* is elided.

84/8 **aswonnis**. Hooper and Pennaod print *aswonsys* but this must be a misprint. The verb is first person with emphasising pronoun *my* preceding *ny*.

85/4 **Galila**. Hooper and Pennaod mutate the *G* as is normal in the Unified texts but I have followed the MS and *G.M.C.* §19(8); *G.M.C.(2)* §23(3h). Also, *Galila* is more easily recognisable.

85/6 **Maga town ti.** As oaths are not normally described as 'deep' I have taken the liberty of translating *town* by 'great'.

86/5 **omdennas**. Hooper and Pennaod have altered this to *aswonsys* without giving a reason. *Omdennas* agrees e.g. with Mt 26 v.75: 'And he went out and wept bitterly.' (*A.V.*).

86/7 **ow nagha**: *by denying.* Present participle used as gerund. See Language Notes, page 11.

86/8 **Hag ev gwarnys.** This and similar phrases of attendant circumstances (*G.M.C.* §335; *G.M.C.(2)* §351) are a close parallel to Virgil, *Aeneid,* Book II line 49: *Timeo Danaos et dona ferentes* = literally: 'I fear the Greeks and (them) bearing gifts', but usually translated, ' I fear the Greeks even when they bear gifts.' I feel the Cornish has the same concessive force here. (Virgil was a Gaul, i.e. a Celt, from Gallia Cisalpina, now part of Northern Italy.)

87 Whare yn-mes y trylyas
hay golon nam na dorre
rag y arluth leun a ras
mar zynas ef zy nahe
dybbry boys ef ny vynnas
lymmyn pub erol ole
zozo bys pan danvonas
crist y to ze galyle

88 Ihesus a ve danvenys
ha ze worth an prins annas
gans tus ven a zesempys
bys an ebscop cayphas
drezo crist may fe bresys
ol zy voth ha zy vynnas
mur a dus o cuntullys
er ybyn zy guhuzas

89 Rag y vos war bronteryon
mester bras a berth yn wlas
gurris ve yn y golon
yn delma gul may cowsas
rys yw porris ze onon
merwel rag pobyl an wlas
pobyl ihesus y honon
na vons tregis gans satnas

87 *At once he turned away and his heart was almost breaking because he had so heinously denied his Lord, full of grace. He would not eat food but wept all the time until Christ sent to him to say that he was coming to Galilee.*

88 *Jesus was sent away from prince Annas immediately with strong men to the bishop Caiaphas for Christ to be judged by him entirely at his will and pleasure. Many people had assembled against him to accuse him.*

89 *Because he was over priests, a great authority in the land, it was put into his heart to do thus, so he said, "It is entirely necessary for one to die for the people of the land, the people of Jesus himself, so that they will not dwell with Satan."*

87 Hware yn-mes y treylyas
Ha'y golonn nammna dorra
Rag y Arloedh, leun a ras,
Mar dhignas ev dh'y nagha.
Dybri boes ev ny vynnas,
Lemmyn pub eur oll oela,
Dhodho bys pan dhannvonas
Krist y to dhe Galila.

88 Yesus a veu dannvenys — Mt 26 v.57
A-dhiworth an pryns Annas — Jn 18 v.24.
Gans tus ven, a-dhesempis, — P.C. 1447-76
Bys y'n epskop Kaifas,
Dredho Krist may fe breusys
Oll dh'y vodh ha dh'y vynnas
Meur a dus o kuntellys
Er y bynn, dh'y guhudhas.

89 Rag y vos war bronteryon
Mester bras a-berth y'n wlas,
Gorrys veu yn y golonn
Yndellma gul, may kowsas,
"Res yw porres dhe onan — Jn 11 v.49-51
Merwel rag pobel an wlas,
Pobel Yesus y honan
Na vons trigys gans Satnas."

87/2 **dorra.** Hooper points out that the imperfect subjunctive is used in place of the indicative *derri.*

87/6 **Lemmyn**. See Spelling Notes, page 13.

87/7-8 **....pan dhannvonas Krist y to....** : '....when Christ sent to say that he was coming....', cf. Nance: *danvon* = 'to send to say'; cf. also 93/3. This usage is not mentioned in *G.M.* or *G.M.C.(2).*

87/8 **Galila.** Cf . 85/4.

88/4 **epskop.** I have retained the incongruous word 'bishop' in the translation. A medieval bishop was seen as much as a man of power as a Christian leader; cf. the Bishop in *Bewnans Meryasek* and Archbishop Turpin in *La Chanson de Roland.*

88/4 **Kaifas.** The metre calls for this to be three syllables, *Ka-i-fas*, so presumably the *i* will be long; cf. 93/1, 94/1 and 118/7 where the name is two syllables as is more usual.

88/5 **Dredho**. See References to *Cornish Simplified II,* page 17.

90 En ezewon yn treze
a whelas dustuneow
rag peyne crist ha syndye
ny gewsys ze blegadow
saw war thu y a vynne
dre envy leuerell gow
a dus fals y redozye
an purre laddron yn pow

91 Ha dew a thuk dustuny
yn clewsons ow leuerell
pur wyr y fenne terry
an tempel cref hay wuzell
war lyrgh henna dre vestry
yn tressa dyth heb fyllell
dre nerth bras yn drehevy
bytqueth ef na vye gwell

92 Neb o mester ha Iustis
worth ihesus ef a gowsas
myns vs omma cuntullys
pur apert y ret flamyas
ha te ger vyth ny gewsys
onweyth lemmyn mar cozas
ol Ihesus an gozevys
hay worzeby ny vynnas

90 *The Jews sought witnesses among themselves to punish Christ and destroy him. They did not speak in a proper manner but they were intent on telling lies against God through malice. They had come from false men, the very worst thieves in the land.*

91 *And two bore witness that they had heard him saying indeed that he would destroy the mighty temple and after this build it by a miracle without fail on the third day. By great power he would raise it so that it had never been better.*

92 *He who was master and magistrate spoke to Jesus: "All those who are gathered here have accused you very clearly and you have not spoken a word. Defend yourself now if you can." Jesus endured it all and would not answer him.*

90 An Edhewon yntredha — Mt 26 v.59-62
A hwilas dustuniow — Mk 14 v.55-59
Rag payna Krist ha'y shyndya.
Ny gewsens dhe blegadow,
Saw war Dhuw i a vynna — P.C. 1307-16
Dre envi leverel gow.
A dus fals i re dhodhya
An purra ladron y'n pow.

91 Ha dew a dhug dustuni
Y'n klywsons ow leverel
Pur wir y fynna terri
An tempel krev ha'y wudhyl — Jn 2 v. 19
War-lergh henna, dre vaystri
Y'n tressa dydh heb fyllel.
Dre nerth bras y'n drehevi
Bythkweyth ev na via gwell.

92 Neb o mester ha justis — P.C. 1317-34
Orth Yesus ev a gowsas,
"Myns eus omma kuntellys
Pur apert i re'th vlamyas,
Ha ty ger vydh ny gewsis.
Omwith lemmyn mar kodhes."
Oll, Yesus a'n godhevis
Ha'y worthybi ny vynnas.

90'3 **payna**. G.M. recognises *paynya* but not *payna.* Cf . 74/6. Maybe the distincton should be *paynia* and *paynya*, rather than *paynya* and *payna* as in Nance.

90/3 **ha'y shyndya**. I have followed Hooper an Pennaod in inserting *'y* which is missing in the MS.

90/5 Hooper and Pennaod have altered *war* in the MS to *worth* and omitted the pronoun *i.* I see no reason for this and have restored both.

92/4 **re'th vlamyas.** Both Hooper and Pennaod follow the MS with *re'th flamyas*. I have used the special mutation after *th* recommended by Wella Brown [*G.M.C.* §16; *G.M.C.(2)* §22] and accepted by Ken George.

92/6 **mar kodhes**. An interesting example of *godhvos* in the sense of 'can' rather than 'know'.

93 Kayphas arta a gewsys
yn hanow du te lavar
mar sos du del danvansys
me yw yn meth crist yn whar
yn nef y fezaff tregis
an barth dyghow gans am car
yn sur thu ow tevones
wy am gwylvyth heb neb mar

94 Kayphas pur wyr a sorras
hag eth pur fol yn vrna
hag a squerdyas y zyllas
pan gowsas crist yn della
ytterevys dre sor bras
dustuneow drok na da
ny reys zynny ze welas
awos dampnye an denma

95 Al ow cows why an clewas
leuerough mar pyth sawys
ol warberth y a armas
gweff yw ze vones lezys
gans mowys y anscornyas
yn y fase y a drewys
ty yv mab du leun a ras
yn ges y a leuerys

93 *Caiaphas spoke again: "In God's name, say if you are God as you asserted." "I am," said Christ gently. "I shall be dwelling in heaven on the right hand by my Father. You will see me coming as God himself, without any doubt!"*

94 *Caiaphas indeed became angry and then went quite mad and tore his clothes when Christ spoke thus. He declared in great anger, "There is no need for us to seek witnesses good or bad to condemn this man.*

95 *"Oh yes! You heard him speaking. Say whether he shall be saved!" All together they shouted, "He is worthy to be slain!" They mocked him with grimaces. They spat in his face. "You are God's Son, full of grace!" they said in mockery.*

93 Kayfas arta a gewsis; Mt 26 v.63-67
"Yn hanow Duw, ty lavar Mk 14 v.60-65
Mars os Duw dell dannvensys."
"My yw," yn-medh Krist yn hwar.
"Yn nev y fydhav trigys
A'n barth deghow gans am Kar.
Yn sur Dhuw ow tevones
Hwi a'm gwelvydh, heb neb mar."

94 Kayfas pur wir a sorras P.C. 1334-50 &
Hag eth pur fol y'n eur na, stage direction
Hag a skwardyas y dhillas
Pan gowsas Krist yndella.
Y terivis dre sorr bras,
"Dustuniow drog na da
Ny res dhyn ni dhe hwilas
Awos dampnya an den ma!

95 "Oll, ow kows hwi a'n klywas.
Leverewgh mar pydh sawys!"
Oll war-barth i a armas,
"Gwiw yw dhe vones ledhys!"
Gans mowys i a'n skornyas,
Yn y fas i a drewis.
"Ty yw Mab Duw leun a ras!"
Yn ges i a leveris.

93/1 & 94/1 **Kayfas**. This is disyllabic in these two lines, so is spelled with *y*. The name occurs several times in *Passio Christi* where it is always two syllables; cf. 88/4 where it is three syllables.

93/6 **gans am Kar**; 'with my Father'. *am* is not used in this way in Revived Cornish. See *G.M.C.*§48(2); *G.M.C.(2)* §51(2). Hooper says "Identical expression in Bodenar's letter, 1770," but the words there are *gen carra vee* (Ellis, page 119).

93/7 **Yn sur Dhuw.** *sur* is an adjective preceding the noun and so causing soft mutation. See *Cornish Simplified,* §6.

95/1 **A ow cows** (MS) Stokes seems to take the *A* as an interrogative particle although it is not followed by a verb. *A* is amended to *Oll* by hand in the *Kernow* copy of the MS which Mr. Hooper sent me and this is how he reads it. Pennaod takes it as an interjection and reads *A! ow kows....* I have followed Pennaod. (In P.C. Caiaphas says "Re'm fay" at this point)

95/4 **Gwiw.** This word is one syllable as indicated by the syllable count and the MS spelling. Or is it: *Go-ev! Yw dhe vones ledhys!* = 'Woe to him! He is to be slain!'? (cf. 43/7) *Gwiw* is spelled *gyw* in 68/7, MS.

96 Gans queth y ben y quezens
guelas banna na ylly
ze ihesus crist betegyns
ow kuzyll drok ha belyny
avel brathken aga dyns
orto y a theskerny
eraga fyn betegyns
crist vn ger ny leuery

97 Hag y worth y dormontye
y cuzens y ben gans queth
han dus esa ol yn dre
ha pryncis yn pow yn weth
ha mur a bobyll ganse
a zyghow sur hag a gleth
the gryst y tons zy syndye
ha ze dry zen dor gans meth

98 I eth ha Ihesus ganse
bys yn pylat o Iustis
a nozo bres may rolle
dre y vres may fo lezys
lavarsons y heb pyte
agan traytour yw kefys
rys yw zeso y zamnye
zen mernans a zesempys

96 *They were covering his head with a cloth so that he could not see a thing, but nevertheless wreaking injury and evil upon Jesus Christ, gnashing their teeth at him like savage curs. But Christ said not one word against them.*

97 *While tormenting him they covered his head with a cloth, and all the people who were in the town, and the princes in the land also and many people with them on the right indeed and on the left came to Christ to destroy him and bring him shamefully to the ground.*

98 *They went with Jesus to Pilate who was a magistrate for him to give judgement about him so that he could be slain through his verdict. They said without pity, "Our traitor is found. He must be condemned to death by you at once."*

96 Gans kweth y benn y kwethens — P.C. 1369-1404
Gweles banna na ylli,
Dhe Yesus Krist byttegyns
Ow kul drog ha bileni
Avel brathkeun aga dyns
Orto i a dheskerni.
Er aga fynn, byttegyns,
Krist unn ger ny leveri.

97 Hag i orth y dormentya
Y kudhens y benn gans kweth,
Ha'n dus esa oll y'n dre,
Ha prynsys y'n pow ynwedh,
Ha meur a bobel gansa
A dheghow sur hag a gledh
Dhe Krist y tens dh'y shyndya
Ha dh'y dhri dhe'n dor gans meth.

98 I eth, ha Yesus gansa — Mt 27 v.2
Bys yn Pilat o justis, — Mk 15 v.1
Anodho breus may rolla — Lk 23 v.1-2
Dre y vreus may fe ledhys. — Jn 18 v.28
'Lavarsons i heb pita, — P.C. 1567-79
"Agan traytour yw kevys.
Res yw dhiso y dhampnya
Dhe'n mernans a-dhesempis."

96 & 97 All the verbs in these two verses are in the imperfect tense. Does this suggest that all this brutal activity was going on as a background to the trial proper, or is it just to fit in with the verse and rhyme pattern? The normal narrative preterite tense is resumed in 98 when Jesus is taken to Pilate.

96/4 **kuzyll** (MS). With this spelling the line has an excess syllable but this is corrected by the more usual shorter form used in the Unified and K.K. spellings. Maybe this suggests it was pronounced as one syllable even though spelt as two.

97/7 **tens**. I have followed Hooper and Pennaod in taking this as a past tense even though the MS suggests a present.

98/4 **may fe ledhys.** Present subjunctive used in the MS for imperfect. See Language Notes, page 9.

98/5 **'Lavarsons**. The normal verbal particle *y* is omitted; cf. 63/2.

99 In meth pylat pan adra
a ynnyough wy warnozo
na ve bos fals an denma
nyn drossen ny bys deso
y leuerys dre laha
ha why dampnowgha yzo
yn mezens y ny a wra
dampnye den lader kyn fo

100 Henna pylat pan welas
kymmys cawsys er y byn
rowtors ha tus kyche yn wlas
resons mar fol ha mar dyn
pylat orto govynnas
yn keth vaner ma govyn
ose mab du leun a ras
lemyn gwyr (te) lauar zyn

101 In meth crist an kveff colon
pur wyr te re leuerys
te a wozye ze honon
pe dre gen re ves guarnys
pylat a gewsys yn scon
te a ve zym danvenys
lauar zymme ze honon
pyth yw en drok rewrussys

99 *Pilate said, "What charge do you press against him?" "If it were not that this man is false, we would not have brought him to you." He said, "Then you also condemn him by means of law." They said, "We condemn a man even though he is a thief?!"*

100 *When Pilate saw this; so much opposition to him; rulers and rich men in the land; such foolish and cruel reasons, Pilate asked him a question of this sort, "Are you the Son of God, full of grace? Now tell us the truth."*

101 *Christ the Beloved said, "You have spoken very truly. Did you know this yourself or were you told by others?" Pilate spoke at once: "You were sent to me. Tell me yourself what is the bad thing you have done!"*

99 Yn-medh Pilat, "Pana dra
'Ynniowgh hwi warnodho?"
"Na ve bos fals an den ma
Ny'n drossen ni bys dhiso."
Y leveris, "Dre lagha
Ha hwi dampnyewgh e ytho."
Yn-medhons i, "Ni a wra
Dampnya den, lader kyn fo?!" Jn 18 v.29-31

100 Henna Pilat pan welas
Kemmys kowses er y bynn;
Routers ha tus rych y'n wlas;
Resons mar fol ha mar dynn,
Pilat orto govynnas
Y'n keth vaner ma govynn, Mt 27 v.11
"O'ta Mab Duw, leun a ras? Mk 15 v.2
Lemmyn gwir ty lavar dhyn." Lk 23 v.3 Jn 18 v.34

101 Yn-medh Krist, an kuv kolonn, P.C.1582-88
"Pur wir ty re leveris.
Ty, a wodhyes dha honan,
Py dre gen re 'veus gwarnys? Jn 18 v.34
Pilat a gewsis yn skon,
"Ty a veu dhymm dannvenys.
Lavar dhymmo dha honan
Pyth yw an drog re wrussys."

99/2 **'Ynniowgh**. cf. 84/1.

99/6 **Ha hwi**. Taken by Hooper as the imperative of *mos* = 'Go you'; cf *G.M.C.* §203(2); *G.M.C.(2)* §205. Pennaod omits it. I have taken it as 'and' or 'also'.

99/7 Both Hooper and Pennaod emend this line to: *Yn medhans, 'Yedhow ny wra'*. Presumably the *y* in the MS is taken as an abbreviation of Yedhow (Jews). This is the spelling in the *Ordinalia* (See Spelling Notes, page 14) but in this Poem the name invariably starts with *E*. Taken literally as a statement, the MS version: *ny a wra dampnye den lader kyn fo*, contradicts Jn 18 v.31 'It is not lawful for us to put any man to death' (*A.V.*), so it seems likely to be an expression of disbelief that Pilate should suggest an illegal procedure.

100/3 **kyche** (MS). Both the *Kernow* and Pennaod MS transcripts have this but Hooper and Pennaod both read *rych* which I have followed.

100/7 **O'ta**. See Spelling Notes, page 13.

101/1 **kuv kolonn**. According to *G.M.C.* §81(4); *G.M.C.(2)* §83(4a) the *k* of *kolonn* should soften after *kuv*, but the phrase is given complete without mutation in Nance and *G.M.* so it must be an exception.

101/3 **te a wozye** (MS). Hooper emends to T*y, a wodhyes* and I have followed this.

102 In meth Ihesus nyn gvgy
ow mesternges yn bysma
hag a pe ow thus zewy
nym delyrfsens yn delma
ytho mygtern ote se
yn meth pylat yn erna
gwyr re gwesys yredy
yn meth crist mygtern oma

103 Henna Iudas pan welas
crist an bewnans na sawye
an arghans a gemeras
rag corf crist ze rysseve
ef astewlys dre sor bras
zen ezewon yn treze
dremas yw ef leun a ras
neb re werzys yn meze

104 Iudas scaryoth a gewsys
yn keth manerma arte
fest yn creff me re beghas
ihesus ze wy ow querze
da y won y vos a ras
gevyons me nvm byth neffre
moy pegh o pan dyspresyas
ys delo pan yn guerze

102 *Jesus said, "My dominion is not in this world, and if it were my men would not have delivered me to you in this way." "So you are a king?" said Pilate then. "You have spoken the truth indeed," said Christ. "I am a king."*

103 *Then, when Judas saw that Christ would not save his life, the money which he took in payment for Christ's body, he threw in great anger among the Jews. "He is a holy man, full of grace whom I have sold," he said.*

104 *Judas Iscariot spoke again in the same way. "I have sinned most mightily in selling Jesus to you. Well I know that he is worthy. I shall never have forgiveness!" It was a greater sin when he scorned him than when he sold him.*

102 Yn-medh Yesus, "Nyns usi
Ow mestrynsys y'n bys ma,
Hag a pe, ow thus dhy'hwi
Ny'm delyrvsens yndellma."
"Ytho, myghtern o'ta sy?" Mt 27 v.11
Yn-medh Pilat y'n eur na. Mk 15 v.2
"Gwir re gewssys yredi," Lk 23 v.3
Yn-medh Krist, "Myghtern oma." Jn 18 v.33-37

103 Ena Yudas pan welas Mt 27 v.3-6
Krist an bywnans na sawya P.C. 1505-15
An arghans a gemmeras
Rag korf Krist dhe resseva,
Ev a'n tewlis dre sorr bras
Dhe'n Edhewon yntredha.
"Dremas yw ev, leun a ras,
Neb re werthis," yn medh e.

104 Yudas Skaryoth a gowsas
Y'n keth vaner ma arta.
"Fest yn krev my re beghas
Yesus dhy'hwi ow kwertha.
Da y hwonn y vos a ras.
Gevyans my ny'm beus nevra!"
Moy pegh o pa'n dispresyas
Es dell o pan y'n gwertha.

102/2 **mesternges**. (MS) Stokes reads this as *mygternes* (*myghtenses*) which does correspond better with *myghtern* in 102/5 and 102/8. The usual word for "kingdom" is *gwlas* or *gwlaskor*. I have followed Hooper and Pennaod.

102/5 **o'ta**. See Spelling Notes, page 13.

103/1 **Ena**. Hooper and Pennaod read *Henna* as in the MS; cf. 46/1.

103/2-3 Literally, 'the money he took to receive for the body of Christ.'

104/1 **a gowsas**. Although the MS has *gewsys*, *gowsas* is better for the rhyme and is the more usual of the two verbs in this Poem.

104/2 See Notes on the Manuscript, page 7.

104/4 **ow kwertha**: 'by selling'. See Language Notes, page 11.

104/7 "**pa'n dyspresyas** in full is *pan y'n dyspresyas*" (Hooper).

104/8 "The imperfect is used for rhyme, and in 112/5" (Hooper). It could also reinforce the statement by portraying the selling as an ongoing background action subservient to the 'greater sin' of despising Jesus, which was its root cause.

105 Han ezewon a gewsys
pan drew henna zynny ny
ny an pernas ze worzys
ha ad pes pur yredy
Iudas eth a zensympys
a neyl tu ze omgregy
cafas daffar pur parys
lovan cryff rag y sensy

106 Eneff iudas ny allas
dos yn mes war y anow
rag y anow y ammas
ze ihesu leun a rasow
dywolow yfarn a squerdyas
corf iudas ol ze zarnow
hag a notho a gerhas
y eneff ze dewolgow

107 En ethewon dre envy
a gewsys crist rag syndye
pylat Iustis otese
Ihesus gorweyth y dampnye
a ierusalem thynny
ef a thueth a galyle
la(h)ys nowyth ov tesky
leas ganso ov tryle

105 *And the Jews said, "What is that to us? We bought him from you and paid you promptly." Immediately Judas went away to hang himself. He found the means all ready; a rope strong enough to hold him.*

106 *The soul of Judas could not come out of his mouth because his mouth kissed Jesus full of grace. The devils in hell tore the body of Judas all to pieces, and from it carried his soul into darkness.*

107 *To destroy Christ the Jews said spitefully, "Pilate, you are a magistrate. Be sure to condemn Jesus. He came to us of Jerusalem from Galilee, teaching new laws, converting many to him."*

105 Ha'n Edhewon a gewsis, Mt 27 v.4-5
"Pandr'yw henna dhyn nyni? P.C. 1509-30
Ni a'n prenas dhiworthis,
Hag a'th pes pur yredi."
Yudas eth a-dhesempis
An eyl tu dhe omgregi.
Kavas daffar pur barys,
Lovan krev rag y synsi.

106 Enev Yudas ny allas P.C. 1535-36
Dos yn-mes war y anow,
Rag y anow a ammas
Dhe Yesu, leun a rasow.
Dyowlow ifarn a skwardyas
Korf Yudas oll dhe dharnow
Hag anodho a gyrghas
Y enev dhe dewolgow.

107 An Edhewon dre envi Lk 23 v.5
A gewsis, Krist rag shyndya, P.C. 1593-98
"Pilat, justis o'ta sy,
Yesus gorwith y dhampnya.
A Yerusalem dhyn ni
Ev a dheuth a Galila,
Laghys nowydh ow tyski,
Lies ganso ow treylya."

105/8 **....krev rag y synsi**. See Language Notes, page 10.

107/3 **o'ta sy**. See Spelling Notes, page 13.

107/4 **dhampnya**. The MS, Hooper and Pennaod all miss this mutation.

107/6 **Galila**. See 85/4 note.

108 Ganse pylat pan glewas
bos Ihesus a galyle
bos herodes war an wlas
mygtern pylat a wozye
Rag henna y tanvonas
crist zozo ef mayn dempne
ruth veyr a dus an sewyas
pub eyr paris zy vlamye

109 I eth bys yn herodes
ha crist ganse fast kylmys
ef a gara crist gwelas
rag kymmys y zo praysys
ganso mar callo clewas
whelth nowyth a vo coyntis
mar callo trylye ze hes
lauar crist pan vo clewys

110 The herodes y thesa
pur wyr worth pylat sor bras
y welas ef ny gara
na boys yn y gowezas
zozo Ihesus zy thampnye
pylat bys pan danvonas
yn vrna keskeweza
y a ve ha specyall bras

108 *When Pilate heard from them that Jesus was from Galilee (Pilate knew that Herod was king over the land) for that reason he sent Christ to him for him to condemn him. A great crowd of people followed, ready to revile him all the time.*

109 *They went to Herod and Christ with them securely bound. He was anxious to see Christ because he was so highly acclaimed, in case he could hear from him some strange new tale, and eventually twist round what Christ had to say when it had been heard.*

110 *Indeed, Herod bore Pilate a serious grudge. He did not want to see him or be on terms of friendship with him, until Pilate sent Jesus to him to condemn him. At that moment they became especially good friends.*

108 Gansa Pilat pan glywas — Lk 23 v.6-7
Bos Yesus a Galila, — P.C. 1599-1616
Bos Herodes war an wlas
Myghtern, Pilat a wodhya,
Rakhenna y tannvonas
Krist dhodho ma'n dampnya.
Routh veur a dus a'n sywyas,
Pub eur parys dh'y vlamya.

109 I eth bys yn Herodes, — Lk 23 v.8
Ha Krist gansa fast kelmys. — P.C. 1699-1704
Ev a gara Krist gweles
Rag kemmys yth o praysys,
Ganso mar kalla klywes
Hweldh nowydh a ve koyntys
Mar kalla treylya dhe-hys
Lavar Krist pan ve klywys.

110 Dhe Herodes yth esa — Lk 23 v.12
Pur wir orth Pilat sorr bras. — P.C. 1699-1704
Y weles ev ny gara, — P.C. 1845-49
Na bos yn y gowethas,
Dhodho Yesus dh'y dhampnya
Pilat bys pan dhannvonas.
Y'n eur na keskowetha
I a veu, ha speshyal bras.

108/1; 109/5. **Gansa** = 'from them'; **Ganso** = 'from him'. See *G.M.C.* §147(7); *G.M.C.(2)* §147(7).

108/2 **Galila**. See 85/4 note.

109/5/6/7/8 **mar kalla**; **a ve**; **Mar kalla**; **pan ve**. These imperfect subjunctives have the form of the present subjunctive in the MS. See Language Notes, page 9.

109/6 **whelth** (MS). Hooper points out that this is *whethel* (Unified spelling) and prints *whelth* in his Unified version whilst Pennaod has *whethl*. This is unpronounceable as one syllable as required by the syllable count so I have followed Hooper with *Hweldh,* and retained the metathesis.

109/8 **pan ve klywys**. Imperfect subjunctive of *bos* translated by 'had been'. See Language Notes, pages 9 (confusion of present and imperfect subjunctive) and page 11 (*o* plus past participle).

110/2 **orth**. The MS and both Unified versions have *worth*.

111 Herodes a wovynnys
orth Ihesus crist leas tra
ha trevyth ny worzebys
man geve marth a henna
an ezewon a gewsys
doyn thyn dustuny a wra
mygtern yfyn bos synsys
ha mester bras yn bysma

112 Kymmys tra a lavarsa
ena y an rebukyas
the rag an try may zesa
annas pylat ha cay(p)has
pur vylen y an pyltye
hag yn spytis an scornyas
moygha zozo drok a wre
henna veza an guella gwas

113 Herodes a leuerys
zen ezewon eugh yn fen
ze bylat agis Iustis
rag me an syns pur zen len
ha leuerough bos gevys
ol ow sor bezens lowen
ham gallus y vos grontijs
zozo ze urusy an den

111 *Herod asked Jesus Christ many things and he answered nothing so that he was amazed at that. The Jews said, "He bears us witness that he wants to be held up as a king and a great master in this world."*

112 *Whatever he had said they then rebuked him for it when he was before the three, Annas, Pilate and Caiaphas. Very wickedly they beat him and mocked him spitefully. Whoever did him the most harm, he would be the best fellow.*

113 *Herod said to the Jews, "Go in haste to Pilate your magistrate, for I consider him a true honest man, and tell him that all my wrath is abated; let him be happy, and my authority is granted to him to judge the man."*

111 Herodes a wovynnis Lk 23 v.9
Orth Yesus Krist lies tra, P.C. 1735-38
Ha travydh ny worthybis P.C. 1757-62
Ma'n jeva marth a henna.
An Edhewon a gewsis,
"Doen dhyn dustuni a wra
Myghtern y fynn bos synsys
Ha mester bras y'n bys ma."

112 Kemmys tra a lavarsa
Ena i a'n rebukyas
Dherak an tri mayth esa,
Annas, Pilat ha Kayfas.
Pur vilen i a'n pyltya,
Hag yn spitus a'n skornyas.
Moyha dhodho drog a wre
Henna 'vedha 'n gwella gwas.

113 Herodes a leveris Lk 23 v.15
Dhe'n Edhewon, "Ewgh yn fen P.C. 1793-98
Dhe Pilat agas justis,
Rag my a'n syns pur dhen len,
Ha leverewgh bos gevys
Oll ow sorr, bedhes lowen,
Ha'm galloes y vos grontys
Dhodho dhe vreusi an den."

111/1 **wovynnis**. The normal ending is *-as* but I have followed the MS and Unified versions for the sake of the rhyme.

112/3 **mayth esa**. I have followed Hooper in taking this as 'when he was', which would correspond with the pluperfect *lavarsa* in 112/1. Wella Brown suggests it should be 'where he was'. The *mayth* does not have a proper antecedent.

112/4 **Kayfas**. See 93/1 note.

113/4 **pur dhen len**. Hooper has 'a most upright man', but the rather unusual word order makes it clear that both *pur* and *len* are adjectives qualifying *den*; cf. *G.M.C.* §81(4); *G.M.C.(2)* §83(4). *Pur* is not an adverb modifying *len.* It is not entirely clear whether Herod is referring to Jesus or to Pilate. Either would be consistent with Lk 23 vv. 12 and 15. The other Gospels do not mention the referral to Herod.

113/6 **bedhes**. See Language Notes, page 12; 3rd singular imperative.

114 I a wyskis cryst gans gwyn
avel fol y an scornye
hag an gweska fest yn tyn
betegyns ger ny gewsy
hag an hombronkyas bys yn
pylat o Iustis zeze
may caffons y aga gwayn
war Ihesus crist zy laze

115 Then ioul mur neb o tus keth
ze belat a leueris
lowenna gwelha ze feth
herodes reth tenyrghys
yn y golen fast regeth
mur a gerense worzys
hag ef a dalvyth zis wheth
y honore del wrussys

116 Ha zeso y tanvonas
y allus crist rag iudgye
ha ny ad cusyll na as
lemyn y voth heb sewye
yn meth pylat scyle vas
me ny gafe rum lewte
na byth moy ef ny gaffas
prag may fe rys y dampnye

114 *They dressed Christ in white. They mocked him like a madman and beat him most cruelly. Nevertheless he did not speak a word, and they led him to Pilate who was their magistrate in order to get the advantage over Jesus Christ to kill him.*

115 *Those who were bondsmen to the great devil said to Pilate, "Cheer up. Don't be downcast. Herod has sent you a greeting. Much love towards you has steadfastly entered his heart and he will yet repay you for honouring him as you have done.*

116 *"And he has sent you his authority to judge Christ, and we advise you, do not leave his will unfollowed." Pilate said, "Upon my word I do not find a good reason." Nor did he ever find a reason why it should be necessary to condemn him.*

114 I a wiskas Krist gans gwynn. Lk 23 v.11
Avel fol i a'n skornya P.C. 1780
Hag a'n gweska fest yn tynn. P.C.1844
Byttegyns ger ny gewsi
Hag a'n hembronkas bys yn
Pilat o justis dhedha,
May kaffens i aga gwayn
War Yesus Krist dh'y ladha.

115 Dhe'n jowl meur neb o tus keth
Dhe Pilat a leveris,
"Lowenha! Gwellha dha feth! P.C. 1841-46
Herodes re'th tynnerghis.
Yn y golonn fast res eth
Meur a gerensa orthis,
Hag ev a dalvydh dhis hwath
Y enora dell wrussys.

116 "Ha dhiso y tannvonas
Y alloes Krist rag jujya,
Ha ni a'th kusul, na as
Lemmyn y vodh heb sywya."
Yn-medh Pilat, "Skila 'vas Lk 23 v.14-16
My ny gavav, re'm lowta." P.C. 1850-64
Na bydh moy ev ny gavas
Prag may fe res y dhampnya.

114/3 **gweska**. Hooper points out that the imperfect subjunctive is used for the indicative.

114/4 **gewsi**. Hooper and Pennaod take this as a pluperfect *gowssa*. However, the MS looks very much like an imperfect and I have taken it as such to match *skornya* and *gweska* in the previous two lines, or possibly with future in the past meaning. This does not appear to rhyme as well as *gowssa* but it seems likely that any unstressed final syllable can weaken to a neutral vowel, especially if it suits the verse for it to do so.

114/7 **kaffens**. Although Hooper and Pennaod follow the MS with *caffons,* the narrative calls for an imperfect subjunctive. See Language Notes, page 9, on confusion of the present and imperfect subjunctive.

115/3 **feth**. Hooper says this is an alternative form of *fas*. *G.M.* gives a note under *fas* that *fath* is sometimes found in Middle Cornish, but it seems better here to keep *feth* which occurs several times in this poem.

115/5 **fast**. Pennaod misprints this as *fas*.

116/8 **Prag** stands as a noun meaning 'reason'; see *G.M.C.* §72(10); *G.M.C.(2)* §74(16).

117 Orth pylat ol y setsans
ha warnozo a rug cry
rag Ihesus crist zen mernans
y a vynne porrys dry
yn meth pylat worth an myns
an pegh peuas ris yv ry
me ny gafa moys kyns
reson gans gwyr zy vrvsy

118 En ezewon a vynne
porrys y vonas lezys
reson(s) y a rey ragthe
mes war fals y zens growndys
henna pylat a wozye
rag henna a zesympys
bys yn cayphas zy zey yvggye
ef a rug may fe gorrys

119 Kayphas an droys arte
ze pylat o pen Iustis
hag ef eth zy gusulye
ihesus crist may fe lezys
en ezewon a arme
treytour pur y vos keffys
hag ol drok suel awresse
ha gow bras ganso clewys

117 *They all set upon Pilate and shouted at him because they urgently wanted to bring Jesus Christ to death. Pilate said, "It is necessary to give a penalty according to the gravity of the offence. I do not find any more than before a just reason to condemn him."*

118 *The Jews urgently wanted him to be put to death. They were giving reasons for it but they were falsely based. Pilate knew that, therefore he had him sent immediately to Caiaphas to judge him.*

119 *Caiaphas brought him again to Pilate who was chief magistrate and he went and advised him that Jesus Christ should be slain. The Jews were shouting that he had been found to be an absolute traitor, that whatever he had done was completely evil, and that a great lie had been heard from him.*

117 Orth Pilat oll y settsons Mt 27 v.22-23
Ha warnodho a wrug kri, Mk 15 v.14
Rag Yesus Krist dhe'n mernans Lk 23 v.18-23
I a vynna porres dri. Jn 19 v.40
Yn-medh Pilat, "Orth an myns
A'n pegh, piwas res yw ri.
My ny gavav moy es kyns
Reson gans gwir dh'y vreusi."

118 An Edhewon a vynna
Porres y vones ledhys.
Resons i a ri ragdho
Mes war fals yth ens grondys.
Henna Pilat a wodhya.
Rag henna a-dhesempis
Bys yn Kayfas dh'y jujya Lk 23 v.11
Ev a wrug may fe gorrys.

119 Kaifas a'n dros arta
Dhe Pilat o penn justys,
Hag ev eth dh'y gusulya
Yesus Krist may fe ledhys.
An Edhewon a arma
Traytour pur y vos kevys
Hag oll drog, seul a wrussa,
Ha gow bras ganso klywys.

117/7 **moy es**. Although the *e* is elided in the MS it is necessary to retain it for the syllable count.

118/7 **Kayfas**. Two syllables; cf. 88/4 where it is three syllables.

118/7 **zy zey** (MS). One of these is clearly superfluous as the syllable count is exceeded. Maybe the scribe realised he had made an error but did not fully correct it.

118/8 An unusual form of causal clause using *gul* + *may* + subjunctive; cf. *G.M.C.* §141(6): "rarely *may* with the subjunctive"; *G.M.C.(2)* §141(7)

119/1 **Kaifas**. Three syllables; see 88/4 note.

120 In meth pylat marth am bes
kymmes drok a wothevyth
ha te reson vyth a dres
eraga fyn na gewsyth
a na wylta ol myns es
orth ze vlamye yn soweth
hag ov ry zys boxow tres
betegyns te ny sconyth

121 In meth pylat me ny won
zen trayteur esa ganso
yn crist cafos byth reson
merwell prag y reys zozo
y hylwys en ezewon
la(h)ys es yn pow a dro
may rys y laze yn scon
mygtern neb a omwrello

122 Own boys crist mab du an neff
an tebel el an geve
rag henna scon y zeth ef
ze wrek pylat may zeze
han tebel el hager bref
yn y holon a worre
war y mester venions cref
y to Ihesus mar laze.

120 *Pilate said, "I wonder that you suffer so much evil and make no counter charge against them. Do you not see all the blame they are laying upon you, alas, and giving you wicked blows? Yet you do not protest!"*

121 *Pilate said to the traitor who was with him, "I cannot find any reason in Christ why he must die." The Jews called out, "There are laws in this region by which it is necessary to slay at once anyone who makes himself a king."*

122 *The evil angel was afraid that Christ was the Son of God in Heaven. Therefore he quickly went to Pilate's wife where she was, and the evil angel, an ugly serpent put it into her heart that a mighty vengeance would come upon her lord if he slew Jesus.*

120 Yn-medh Pilat, "Marth a'm beus Mt 27 v.13-14
Kemmys drog a wodhevydh, Mk 15 v.4-5
Ha ty reson vydh a-dreus
Er aga fynn ny gewsydh.
A ny wel'ta oll myns eus
Orth dha vlamya yn sowedh,
Hag ow ri dhis boksow treus?
Byttegyns ty ny skonydh!"

121 Yn-medh Pilat, "My ny wonn,"
(Dhe'n traytour esa ganso)
"Yn Krist kavoes bydh reson
Merwel prag y res dhodho."
Y helwis an Edhewon, Jn 19 v.7
"Laghys eus y'n pow a-dro P.C. 2167-74
May res y ladha yn skon
Myghtern neb a omwrello."

122 Own bos Krist Mab Duw an Nev Mt 27 v.19
An tebel el a'n jeva, P.C. 1919-68
Rakhenna skon yth eth ev
Dhe wreg Pilat mayth esa,
Ha'n tebel el, hager bryv,
Yn hy holonn a worra
War hy mester venjans krev
Y to, Yesus mar latha.

121/2 I have put in the brackets in the hope of adding some clarity to this unusual word order.

122/7-8 A conditional sentence in the form of an indirect statement after *Yn hy holonn a worra* in 122/6. The verb of the main clause, *to* is imperfect indicative. See References to *Cornish Simplified II*, page 22, and *G.M.C.* §328(6); *G.M.C.(2)* §344(7) The latter states that the verb in the 'if' clause may be indicative or subjunctive. The MS spelling *laze* suggests *ladha,* which would be indicative, and this is what Hooper and Pennaod have printed. *C.S.II* prints *latha,* which would be subjunctive, and I have followed this. However, grammars prior to *G.M.C.* do not insist that the final stem consonant should be devoiced in the subjunctive so maybe *ladha* as printed by Hooper and Pennaod could also be taken as subjunctive.

123 Thy gour hy a zan(v)onas
a crist kepar del welse
yn kerdh delma dre gannas
nyn gew ragos se laze
Cryst yv synsys mur dremas
ze zevyth a wos plegye
rag haneth me re welas
yto ve(n)ions had laze

124 Onon esa yn preson
barabas ytho gylwys
presonys o ef dre dreyson
ha rag den lath kekyffris
maner o zen ezewon
war dyth pasch worth an Iustis
an preson govyn onon
ha bos henna delyffrys

125 Pylat a vynsse gwyze
bewnans Ihesus dre goyntis
hag a leuerys zeze
yn delma del yw skrifis
lemmyn merough pe nyle
an dus avyth delyffris
po cryst leuerough scyle
po barabas den blamys

123 *She sent to her husband by a messenger to say how she had seen (a vision) of Christ in this way (saying), "It is not for you to slay Christ who is considered to be a great holy man, to satisfy anyone, for tonight I saw that vengeance would come and slay you."*

124 *There was one in prison. He was called Barabbas. He was imprisoned for treachery and for murder also. It was the custom of the Jews on the day of the Passover to ask the magistrate for one man from the prison and for that one to be set free.*

125 *Pilate would have liked to preserve the life of Jesus by a subterfuge, and he spoke to them thus, as it is written, "Now look, which is it of the men that shall be set free, Christ - you can tell a reason - or Barabbas, a man condemned?"*

123 Dh'y gour hi a dhannvonas — Mt 27 v.19
A Krist kepar dell welsa, — P.C. 1919-68
Yn kettellma, dre gannas,
"Nyns yw ragos sy ladha
Krist yw synsys meur dhremas,
Dhe dhenvydh awos plegya,
Rag haneth my re welas
Y to venjans ha'th ladha."

124 Onan esa yn pryson, — Mt 27 v.16-18
Barabas yth o gelwys. — Mt 27 v.20-22
Prysonys o dre drayson — Mk 15 v.7-12
Ha rag denladh kekeffrys. — Lk 23 v.18-20
Maner o dhe'n Edhewon — Jn 18 v.40
War dhydh Pask orth an justis — P.C. 2365-73
A'n pryson govynn onan — P.C. 2480
Ha bos henna delivrys. — P.C. 2484

125 Pilat a vynnsa gwitha
Bywnans Yesus dre goyntys
Hag a leveris dhedha
Yndellma, dell yw skrifys,
"Lemmyn, mirewgh, pyneyl'a
A'n dus a vydh delivrys,
Po Krist (leverewgh skila)
Po Barabas, den blemys?"

123/2 **dell welsa**. See Language Notes, page 10

123/5 **meur dhremas**. I have mutated *dhremas* following *G.M.C.* §54(2a); *G.M.C.(2)* §57(2a), "*meur* used as an adjective meaning 'great'". There is no mutation in the MS, Hooper or Pennaod.

123/8 **ha'th ladha**. Hooper and Pennaod read *a'th ladha* and Hooper translates: "would come vengeance from thy slaying".

124/1 **Onan esa**. See Language Notes, page 11 (Long forms of *bos* in nominal sentences).

124/6 **War dhydh**. The MS, Hooper and Pennaod all miss this mutation.

125/5-6 Hooper and Pennaod give these two lines as: *Lemmyn, myreugh, a'n dus ma pynyl a vyth delyfrys*. This, presumably, is to avoid the difficulty of *pe nyle* in the MS. Nance suggests it is for *pyneyl yua* and I have used an apostrophe to indicate this.

125/7 **skila**. "Could be 3rd singular present = 'is there a reason?'" (Hooper). However, he translates: 'Say there is a reason'. In the context *leverewgh skila* seems to imply that a reason <u>can</u> be given for releasing Christ but not Barabbas. Cf. use of *Ty a wel* = 'You <u>can</u> see'. See Language Notes, page 9.

126 En ezewon a armas
dre bur envy me a gris
dylyver zynny barabas
ha henna ol ny a bys
Pylat arte a gowsas
a Ihesus pyth a vyth guris
y hawlsons gans golon vras
zen mernans bezens gurris

127 Pylat yn ta a wozye
y ze gusel dre envy
rag henna ef a vynse
gweze crist heb velyny
hag a leueris zeze
mar mynnough me an chasty
ol war barth yny cyte
hag an delyrf ze wary

128 I helwys en ezewon
bezens ef yn crows gorris
yn meth pylat me ny won
reson prag y fyt da(m)pnys
y hawlsons gans moy colon
bezens ef yn crows lezys
yn meth pylat byth reson
ze laze nyn ges keffys

126 *The Jews shouted in sheer malice, I believe, "Deliver us Barabbas and that is what we all request!" Pilate said again, "What shall be done about Jesus?" They called with great fervour, "Let him be put to death!"*

127 *Pilate knew well that they spoke out of malice. Because of this he would have liked to protect Christ from abuse, and he said to them, "If it is what you want, I will chastise him as one who is utterly foolish, and set him free."*

128 *The Jews called out, "Let him be crucified!" Pilate said, "I do not know any reason why he is under condemnation." They cried out with greater fervour, "Let him be crucified!" Pilate said, "No reason whatsoever can be found to slay him."*

126 An Edhewon a armas Mt 27 v.21-23
Dre bur envi, my a grys, Mk 15 v.11-15
"Delyrv dhyn ni Barabas, Lk 23 v.18 v.21
Ha henna oll ni a bys!" Jn 18 v.40
Pilat arta a gowsas, P.C. 2371-73
"A Yesus pyth a vydh gwrys?" P.C. 2480-91
Y hawlsons gans kolonn vras,
"Dhe'n mernans bedhes gorrys!"

127 Pilat yn ta a wodhya Mt 27 v.18
I dhe gewsel dre envi. Mk 15 v.10
Rakhenna ev a vynnsa Lk 23 v.16 v.22
Gwitha Krist heb vileni,
Hag a leveris dhedha,
"Mar mynnowgh, my a'n chasti
Oll war-barth yn nisyta,
Hag a'n delyrv dhe wari."

128 Y helwis an Edhewon, Mk 15 v.13-14
"Bedhes ev yn krows gorrys!"
Yn-medh Pilat, "My ny wonn
Reson prag y fydh dempnys."
Y hawlsons gans moy kolonn,
"Bedhes ev yn krows ledhys!"
Yn-medh Pilat, "Bydh reson
Dh'y ladha nyns eus kevys."

126/6 **bedhes**. See Language Notes, page 12; 3rd singular imperative.

127/4 **heb vileni**. See 80/7 note.

127/7 I have followed the rather colourful Breton translation of Pennaod: *evel foll penn-da-benn* although he places a query by it, as this seems to fit better than Hooper's 'altogether in ignorance'. Pilate feels more and more that Jesus is foolish to the point of insanity (cf. verse 120) and this is here brought to a climax. However, Wella Brown suggests 'in ignorance' means that Pilate would chastise Jesus even though he was ignorant of any justification for the punishment.

128/2/6 **bedhes**. See Language Notes, page 12; 3rd singular imperative.

128/2/6 **yn krows gorrys**; **yn krows ledhys**. Both phrases mean 'crucified'. See Language Notes, page 10.

129 Ha pylat ze war breder
a leueris ze Ihesu
ol an dusma a leuer
ze vos cregis te yw gyw
lauar gwyr zymmo vn ger
mar sota mab den ha du
cryst a gewsys dyboner
te a leuerys del yw

130 Whare y an dystryppyas
mar noyth genys del vye
hag worth post fast an colmas
vnwyth na ylly plynchye
hag ena ij an scorgyas
yn tebel gans ij scorgye
ha hager fest an dygtyas
corf ha pen treys ha dewle

131 In scorgijs prenyer esa
yn dewle an ij ethow
hag yn fast kelmys zeze
kerdyn gwezyn mesk cronow
may fons hyblyth ze gronkye
hag a rag guris colmmenow
gans pub colmen may zelle
pan wyskens yn-mes an crow

129 *And after careful thought, Pilate said to Jesus, "All these people say that you are worthy to be hanged. Tell me truly in one word if you are the Son of Man and God." Christ said courteously, "It is as you say."*

130 *At once they stripped him as naked as he had been born and bound him fast to a pillar so that he could not wriggle at all and then two whipped him wickedly with two whips and dealt with him most cruelly, body and head, hands and feet.*

131 *For whips there were sticks in the hands of the two Jews with pliant cords mixed with thongs bound tightly to them so as to be supple for beating, and the ends were made into knots so that the blood would flow out with every knot when they struck.*

129 Ha Pilat, dhe war breder
A leveris dhe Yesu,
"Oll an dus ma a lever
Dhe vos kregys ty yw gwiw.
Lavar gwir dhymmo unn ger,
Mars o'ta Mab Den ha Duw."
Krist a gewsis deboner,
"Ty a leveris dell yw."

130 Hware i a'n destryppyas — Mt 27 v.26
Mar noeth genys dell via, — Mk 15 v.15
Hag orth post fast a'n kolmas — Jn 19 v.1
Unnweyth na ylli plynchya,
Hag ena dew a'n skorjyas
Yn tebel gans dew skorjya,
Ha hager fest a'n dyghtyas,
Korf ha penn, treys ha diwla.

131 Yn skorjys, prennyer esa
Yn diwla an dhew Edhow,
Hag yn fast kelmys dhedha
Kerdyn gwedhyn 'mysk kroenow
May fons hebleth dhe gronkya,
Hag a-rag gwrys kolmennow,
Gans pub kolmenn mayth ella,
Pan weskens, yn-mes an krow.

129/1 **ze war breder** (MS). Hooper reads this as *dhe war breder*, and translates: 'at a kindly thought'. Pennaod reads *dhywar breder* and has the cognate words in his Breton translation, which Ken George interprets as 'on the spur of the moment'. This does not really fit the context so I have followed Hooper, taking the *dhe* as meaning 'in accordance with' [*G.M.C.* §141(9); *G.M.C.(2)* §141(10)], and *war* as 'careful'.

129/4 **Dhe**. Both Hooper and Pennaod have *dha* but it must be a misprint.

129/6 **o'ta**. See Spelling Notes, page 13.

129/6 **Mab Den**. It seems appropriate to take this in the biblical sense of 'Son of Man' rather than the usual Cornish sense of 'human being', in which sense *G.M.* recommends hyphenation. Hooper translates: 'human and God'. Nance gives *an Map a Dhen* for 'the Son of Man' and indicates it to be Late Cornish, but it is not given as such in Gendall's 'A Students' Dictionary of Modern Cornish' though *mab den* occurs twice in *C.W.* in the sense of 'human being'.

131/1 **Yn skorjys**. This is the instrumental use of *yn* meaning 'as whips' or 'for whips'. See *G.M.C.* §44; *G.M.C.(2)* §47(4).

131/1 **prennyer esa**. See Language Notes, page 11 (Long forms of *bos* in nominal sentences).

131/4 **'mysk**. The *Kernow* version of the MS gives *yn mysk* in full but this creates an excess syllable so I have followed Hooper in eliding the *yn*.

132 Han zewna bys pan vons squyth
war crist y fons ov cronkye
manna geve goth na leyth
na gesa worth y grevye
na war y gorff wek tam vyth
pur wyr henna o mur byte
ha whath moy wy a glewyth
a dormont crist del wharse

133 In treze avel tus fol
garlont sperne a ve dyzgthtys
ha dre aga husyll ol
war y ben a ve gorris
may zo squardijs a dro ol
ay ben y oys o scolijs
hag ynno fest luhas tol
gans an dreyn a ve tellys

134 Gans den scyntyll a wozye
me a glewas leuerell
an arlont y ze denne
war y ben gans kymmys nell
ma teth an dreyn ha cropye
zen nempynnyon dre an tell
henno payn a vur byte
esa crist ow cozevell

132 *And these two were beating upon Christ until they were tired so that he did not have a vein or a limb or any part of his sweet body that was not hurting him. Very truly this was most grievous and you will hear yet more of Christ's torture as it had happened.*

133 *A wreath of thorns was prepared between them (as they behaved) like madmen and by common accord was placed upon his head so that it was torn all around. His blood was pouring from his head and in it a great many holes were pierced by the thorns.*

134 *From a learned man who knew, I heard that they pulled the wreath over his head with such force that the thorns came and penetrated to the brains through the holes. That was a most pitiful torture that Christ was suffering.*

132 Ha'n dhew na, bys pan vons skwith
War Krist y fons ow kronkya
Ma na'n jeva goeth na lith
Nag esa orth y revya,
Na war y gorf hweg tamm vydh,
Pur wir henn o meur byta
Ha hwath moy hwi a glywvydh
A dorment Krist dell hwarsa.

133 Yntredha avel tus fol — Mt 27 v.29
Garlont spern a veu dyghtys — Mk 15 v.17
Ha dre aga husul oll — Jn 19 v.2
War y benn a veu gorrys, — P.C. 2133-50
Mayth o skwerdys a-dro oll.
A'y benn y woes o skoellys
Hag ynno fest lies toll
Gans an dreyn a veu tellys.

134 Gans den skentyl a wodhya
My a glywas leverel,
An arlont i dhe dhenna
War y benn gans kemmys nell
May teuth an dreyn ha kropya
Dhe'n ympynnyon dre an tell.
Henn o payn a veur byta
Esa Krist ow kodhevel.

132/2 **y fons ow kronkya**. The preterite of *bos* with the present participle is unusual. See *G.M.C.* §228(1); *G.M.C.(2)* §243(2). Here, the more usual *esens* would necessitate an extra syllable.

132/3 **goeth**. *G.M.* gives *goeth* as 'stream' and *gwythi* as 'veins', both developments of Old Cornish *guid*. Clearly 'vein' is intended in this context but I have followed the MS, Hooper and Pennaod and used *goeth* as *gwythi* is too long. Nance gives *goth* as 'vein' or 'stream'. *gwythi* is used in 183/7 with this same meaning

132/4. **y revya** The MS, Hooper and Pennaod all miss this mutation.

132/8 **wharse** (MS) This is the Stokes and Nance reading but it is taken as *wharfe* (pret.)by Hooper and Pennaod. I have taken it as a pluperfect but again, as in 74/4 (fastsens) the pluperfect is not really appropriate.

135 A vyne gwarze yben
war y gorff bys yn y droys
squardijs oll o y grohen
hag ef cuzys yn y woys
mur o an payn dar ken
ze vab du mur y alloys
del lever zyn an levar
kymmys payn ny ve ay oys

136 I a wyskis crist gant queth
han purpur rych o dyskis
rag y thry zen dor gans meth
yn ges y a leueris
mur a onour te afyth
te yw mygtern cvrvnys
hag yn y leff zyghow yn weth
gwelen wyn a ve gorris

137 Hag y thens ze ben dowlyn
hag y kewsens ze scornye
hag a gamma aga meyn
pub onon rag y eysye
lowene zys te yw zeyn
mygtern rys yw ze worzye
hen o zozo mur a bayn
may zezens worth y ranne

135 *From the very top of his head over his body down to his foot his skin was all torn and he was covered in his blood. Great was the pain, beyond any other of God's all-powerful Son. As the book tells us, "Never was there so much pain!"*

136 *They dressed Christ in a garment and the rich purple was taken off him to bring him to the ground with shame. They said in mockery, "You will have great honour! You are a crowned king!" - and in his right hand also a white wand was placed.*

137 *And they went on their knees and spoke to ridicule him, and pulled their faces awry, each one to mock him. "Joy to you! You are our King! You must be honoured!" What they were sharing was very painful for him.*

135 A finna gwartha y benn
War y gorf bys yn y droes,
Skwerdys oll o y groghen,
Hag ev kudhys yn y woes.
Meur o an payn a-der ken
Dhe Vab Duw meur y alloes.
Dell lever dhyn an lyver,
"Kemmys payn ny veu a'y oes!"

136 I a wiskas Krist gans kweth Mt 27 v.28-31
Ha'n purpur rych o di'skys, Mk 15 v.17-20
Rag y dhri dhe'n dor gans meth. Jn 19 v. 2-3
Yn ges i a leveris, P.C. 2127-44
"Meur a enor ty a'fydh!
Ty yw myghtern kurunys!"
Yn y leuv dheghow ynwedh
Gwelenn wynn a veu gorrys.

137 Hag yth ens dhe benn dewlin
Hag y kewsens dh'y skornya,
Hag a gamma aga min
Pub onan rag y esya.
"Lowena dhis! Ty yw dhyn
Myghtern! Res yw dha wordhya!"
Henn o dhodho meur a bayn
Mayth esens orth y ranna.

135/1 **A finna**. Hooper prints *Afyna'n* and Pennaod *A fynna* in their Unified versions. I take it as the superlative of *fin* meaning, literally, 'from the finest top', i.e. 'from the very top'. Hooper has 'From the (very) crown of His head'. Wella Brown suggests *fin* = 'last' as in *dydh fin.*

135/5 **a-der**. Hooper and Pennaod both have *ader. G.S.* gave *a-der* OR *adar* but *G.M.* gives only *a-der.* The MS *dar* needs an extra syllable to complete the count.

135/7 Hooper and Pennaod have *Del lever an Lyver dhyn*, presumably to correct the rhyme pattern. I have not used capitals for either *lyver* or 'book' as I am doubtful whether these words actually are in the Bible.

136/2 Hooper and Pennaod print *A burpur rych o dyghtys*. I have kept *dyghtys* as against *dyskis* of the MS because Hooper says *dy'sky* would be contrary to Scripture and tradition. However I am not convinced it can be completely ruled out so I have added the alternative translation in brackets.

136/2 **purpur**. In ancient times, and probably here too, purple was a deep crimson, not a mixture of blue and red as nowadays. The purple here seems to echo the blood in the previous verse.

137/4 **esya**. Hooper corrects to *jesya* but *esya* is *gesya* = 'to mock' with soft mutation after *y.*

137/8 **ranna**. The current American usage of 'to share' = 'to impart information' seems appropriate for translation here.

138 Onon gans an keth welen
yn leyff crist a ve gorris
an gwyskis lasche war an pen
bum pur gewar desezys
ha buxow leas hep ken
ha tummasow kekyffris
ze gryst a dro ze zewen
gans nerth bras a ve syttis

139 Colon den a yll crakye
a vynha prest predery
an paynys bras an geve
han dyspyth heb y dylly
hag ol rag ze gerense
ihesus crist as gozevy
lymmyn gorqvyth y gare
ha gweyth denatar na vy

140 Pylat eth yn-mes ay hell
yn vn lowarth an gevo
ogas o nyn gesa pell
hag a worras crist ganso
ena worto rag kewsell
queth esa a dro zozo
prest an ezewon debel
ze Ihesus esens a dro

138 *With the same wand that was put into Christ's hand one (man) slashed him over the head a very well-aimed blow, and many strokes without cause, and blows also were laid upon Christ about his jaws with great force.*

139 *A man's heart may break who would think all the time about the great tortures and the undeserved contempt which he had, and all for your sake Jesus Christ suffered them. Now take great care to love him and make sure you are not vilely ungrateful.*

140 *Pilate went out of his hall into a garden which he had. It was near. It was not far, and he took Christ with him to talk to him there. There was a garment about him. The wicked Jews were always around Jesus.*

138 Onan, gans an keth welenn — Mt 27 v.30
Yn leuv Krist a veu gorrys — Mk 15 v.19
A'n gwyskis lash war an penn, — P.C. 2135
Boemm pur gewar desedhys, — Stage direction
Ha boksow lies, hepken,
Ha tummasow kekeffrys
Dhe Krist, a-dro dh'y dhiwen,
Gans nerth bras a veu settys.

139 Kolonn den a yll krakkya
A vynna prest prederi
A'n paynys bras a'n jeva
Ha'n despit heb y dylli,
Hag oll rag dha gerensa
Yesus Krist a's godhevi.
Lemmyn gorwith y gara
Ha gwayt dinatur na vi.

140 Pilat eth yn-mes a'y hel
Yn unn lowarth a'n jevo.
Ogas o. Nyns esa pell,
Hag a worras Krist ganso,
Ena orto rag kewsel.
Kweth esa a-dro dhodho.
Prest an Edhewon debel
Dhe Yesus esens a-dro.

138/1 **an keth welenn**. Although it is in the MS, Hooper and Pennaod omit the mutation.

138/5 **boksow lies**. Normally *lies* precedes a singular noun; see *G.M.C.(2)* §83(5e)

138/8 **settys**. Hooper and Pennaod have *syttys* but this spelling is not in Nance or *G.M.*

139/7 **gorwith**. Ken George suggests this. Hooper and Pennaod print *gorquyth.*

139/8 **gwayt**. As read by Hooper and Pennaod, though the MS suggests *gwith* with little difference in meaning.

dinatur. Hooper translates literally 'unnatural', in the older sense of 'without natural affection; monstrous; heinous' (*Chambers*). I feel this is inappropriate for a modern translation and that 'vilely ungrateful' is a reasonable paraphrase.

140/2 **unn lowarth**. *unn* used as an indefinite article. See Language Notes, page 9.

140/3 This line is effective but *ogas* has to be taken as an adjective and *pell* as an adverb to explain the use of *o* and *esa* in accordance with *G.M.C.* §314(3); *G.M.C.(2)* §331(3) and §315(3a); *G.M.C.(2)* §332(3a). See also 200/2.

140/6 This line supports the use of *a-dro* with articles of clothing recommended on page 13 of *Notes on Spoken Cornish* by Rod Lyon and John Pengilly, and also in *A Students' Dictionary of Modern Cornish* by Richard Gendall. Edward Lhuyd gives the same usage on page 250 of his *Archaeologia Britannica* published in 1707.

140/6/8 **Kweth esa**; **esens a-dro**. See Language Notes, page 11 (Long forms of *bos* in nominal sentences).

141 Ena pylat a gewsys
yn delma zen ezewon
me ny won bonas kyfys
yn denma byth acheson
may rys y vonas lezys
gothvezough keteponon
del yw an denma dyzgtis
myrough in agis colon

142 Pan yn caffsons yn treze
ol warbarth y a ylwys
te pylat laze laze
mernans an grows desympys
pylat a gewsys arte
drezough why bezens lezys
rag ynno me ny gaffe
scyle vas may fo dampnys

143 An debel dus a gewsys
zynny sur yma laha
may rys y vonas lezys
rag mab du ef a omwra
own a gachyas an Iustis
pan glewas cows yn della
rag henna a zesympys
y trylyas thy asethva

141 *Then Pilate spoke thus to the Jews: "I do not know that any reason is found in this man for which he has to be killed. Mind, everyone, how this man is treated. Look into your hearts."*

142 *When they got him among them, they shouted altogether, "You, Pilate, kill him, kill him; the death of the cross straight away." Pilate spoke again: "Let him be slain by you, for I do not find in him any good reason why he should be condemned."*

143 *The evil people spoke: "We definitely have a law by which he must be slain because he professes to be the Son of God." Fear seized the magistrate when he heard talk of this kind so he returned immediately to his seat.*

141 Ena Pilat a gewsis — P.C.2151-60
Yndellma dhe'n Edhewon:
"My ny wonn bones kevys
Y'n den ma bydh acheson
May res y vones ledhys.
Godhvedhewgh kettep onan
Dell yw an den ma dyghtys.
Mirewgh yn agas kolonn."

142 Pan y'n kavsons yntredha — P.C. 2161-64
Oll war-barth i a elwis,
"Ty Pilat, ladh e, ladh e,
Mernans an grows desempis!"
Pilat a gewsis arta,
"Dredhowgh hwi bedhes ledhys,
Rag ynno my ny gava'
Skila 'vas may fo dempnys."

143 An debel dus a gewsis, — Jn 19 v.7-8
"Dhyn ni sur yma lagha — P.C. 2169-77 &
May res y vones ledhys — stage direction
Rag Mab Duw ev a omwra."
Own a gachyas an justis
Pan glywas kows yndella,
Rakhenna a-dhesempis
Y treylyas dh'y esedhva.

142/4 **mernans** (MS). "Formerly thought to be *merwens* by Mordon." (Hooper). This would then mean 'Let him die'.

142/6 **bedhes**. See Language Notes, page 12; 3rd singular imperative.

142/8 **dempnys**. I have assumed that the *a* of the MS will become *e* by vowel affection. See *G.M.C.* §12 & 194/1; *G.M.C.(2)* §14-16 & 189 It now rhymes or assonances better with *elwis*, *desempis*, and *ledhys* in the preceding lines.

144 Orth crist ef a wovynnys
te zen able ota gy
zy gows crist ny worzebys
ynmeth pylat yredy
gorzeby te ny vynsys
a ny wozas ow mestry
bos zymmo may fes lezys
bo delyffris ze wary

145 In meth Ihesus yn vrna
mestry vyth te ny vea
waraff ve drok vyth na da
ken onan zys nan rolla
byth moy ys ezow yn ta
a beghas orth ov zrayta
pylat pan glewas henna
a whelas y zelyffra

146 Han ezewon oll a dro
ze belat a leuery
kerense sesar ytho
ny ze lemman belyny
in ny wreth dyffry dozo
a berverth yn crows cregy
rag mygtern a omwrello
ze sesar yw contrary

144 *He asked Christ, "You, man, where are you from?" Christ did not answer his question. Without pausing Pilate said, "You would not answer. Don't you know my power which I have whereby you may be slain or set free?"*

145 *Jesus said then, "You would have no power at all over me, for evil of any kind or good, if Another did not give it to you, any more than a Jew who sinned by betraying me." When Pilate heard that, he tried to set him free.*

146 *And the Jews all around were saying to Pilate, "In that case you will not have Caesar's friendship but shame if you do not have him crucified, for anyone who makes himself a king is in opposition to Caesar."*

144 Orth Krist ev a wovynnis
"Ty dhen, a ble o'ta jy?"
Dh'y gows Krist ny worthybis.
Yn-medh Pilat yredi,
"Gorthybi ty ny vynnsys.
A ny wodhes ow maystri,
Bos dhymmo may fes ledhys
Bo delivrys dhe wari?"

Jn 19 v.9-12
P.C. 2178-86 & preceding stage direction

145 Yn-medh Yesus y'n eur na,
"Maystri vydh ty ny 'fia
Warnav vy, drog vydh na da,
Ken onan dhis na'n rolla
Bydh moy es Edhow yn ta
A beghas orth ow thrayta."
Pilat pan glywas henna
A hwilas y dhelivra.

P.C. 2187-92

146 Ha'n Edhewon oll a-dro
Dhe Pilat a leveri,
"Kerensa Sesar, ytho,
Ny dheu lemmyn bileni,
Mar ny wredh devri dhodho
A-bervedh yn krows kregi,
Rag myghtern a omwrello
Dhe Sesar yw kontrari."

144/1 **wovynnis**, following MS, Hooper and Pennaod for the sake of the rhyme. The normal ending is *-as*.

144/2 **o'ta jy**. See Spelling Notes, page 13.

144/6-7 Read as *A ny wodhes bos ow maystri dhymmo?*

144/8 **Bo**, following MS, Hooper and Pennaod. Possibly there is intentional alliteration with *bos* in 144/7. Nance gives both *po* and *bo* for 'or'.

145/5 **moy...yn ta**. Nance gives this as 'yet more' which makes Hooper's 'indeed' unnecessary.

146/4 **Ny dheu**. Hooper and Pennaod have *Ny'th o* for the *ny ze* of the MS and Hooper translates 'thou art not getting'.

146/3/8 **Sesar** (MS). The *S* must be due to English or French influence. The hard *c* sound of Latin words is usually preserved in Brythonic, cf. Welsh *Cesar* and Cornish *yskynna* = 'as<u>c</u>end'.

146/5 **in ny** (MS) All editors except Stokes take this as *mar ny* and I have followed this.

146/6 **yn krows**. See Language Notes, page 10.

147 Ena pylat pan glewas
an lauarow na ganse
Ihesus ef a zyswezas
pur evn yn cres yn treze
a watta ef a gowsas
agis mygtern ple meve
ol war barth I an naghas
hag a yrghys y laze

148 In meth pylat why a vyn
drys pub tra me zy laze
agis mygtern meth yw zyn
na vezens clewys neffre
yn mezens y nyn gorzyn
na ny goth thyn y worzye
na ken mygtern ny venyn
ys Cesar caffos neffre

149 Y thewleff pylat a wolhas
hag a leuerys zeze
glan off a wos an dremas
rag ay woys venions a ze
ol warbarth y a armas
mar te ve(n)ions ha cothe
war agan flehys yn fras
ha warnan bezans neffre

147 *Then when Pilate heard those words from them, he pointed to Jesus right in the very middle of them. "Look where your king is!" he said. All together they denied him and ordered him to be slain.*

148 *Pilate said, "You especially want me to slay him - your king! It is a disgrace to us. Never let it be heard!" They said, "We do not honour him, nor should we honour him, nor do we ever want any other king but Caesar."*

149 *Pilate washed his hands and said to them, "I am innocent of the blood of the holy man, for from his blood vengeance will come." All together they shouted, "If vengeance comes and falls heavily upon our children and upon us, let it be for ever!"*

147 Ena Pilat pan glywas
An lavarow na gansa,
Yesus ev a dhiskwedhas
Pur ewn y'n kres yntredha.
"Awotta," ev a gowsas,
"Agas myghtern ple'mava!"
Oll war-barth i a'n naghas
Hag a erghis y ladha. Jn 19 v.13-15

148 Yn-medh Pilat, "Hwi a vynn P.C. 2359-64
Dres puptra my dh'y ladha,
Agas myghtern! Meth yw dhyn.
Na vedhes klywys nevra!"
Yn-medhons i, "Ny'n gordhyn,
Na ny goedh dhyn y wordhya,
Na ken myghtern ny vynnyn
Es Sesar kavoes nevra."

149 Y dhiwla Pilat 'wolghas Mt 27 v.24-25
Hag a leveris dhedha, P.C. 2495-2500
"Glan ov a woes an dremas,
Rag a'y woes venjans a dheu."
Oll war-barth i a armas,
"Mar teu venjans ha koedha
War agan fleghes, yn fras,
Ha warnan, bedhes nevra!"

147/2 **gansa** = 'from them'. See *G.M.C.* §147(6); *G.M.C.(2)* §147/7.

148/1-2 **Hwi a vynn...my dh'y ladha**. *Mynnes* is usually followed by *orth* + noun or pronoun without *dhe.* See *G.M.C.* §292(4); *G.M.C.(2)* §306(4). Wella Brown suggests that *Hwi a vynn my dh'y ladha* puts Pilate further away from the deed as a personal act.

148/4 **na vedhes**. See Language Notes, page 12; 3rd singular imperative.

149/1 **Pilat**. Hooper and Pennaod replace this by *ef,* presumably because there is an excess syllable. But the name seems too important to omit at this climactic point so I have put an apostrophe for the particle *a* before *wolghas.*

149/3-8 The Blood Curse occurs only in Mt 27 v.25, 'His blood be on us, and on our children' (*A.V.*). The Poem adds Pilate's words, *Rag a'y woes venjans a dheu*, and *bedhes nevra* from the Jewish crowd. The words of Caiaphas in *P.C.* 2501-3 (Sandercock edition) are nearer to the Scripture:

Mar te venjyans-vyth ragtho,
warnan-ny ef re gotho
ha war oll agan fleghes.

149/8 **bedhes**. See Language Notes, page 12; 3rd singular imperative.

150 Camen pylat pan welas
na ylly crist delyffre
manan geffo ef sor bras
ze worth ol an goweze
rag henna ef a Iuggyas
Ihesus zeze zy laze
the ves y a thelyffras
barabas quyth may zelle

151 Pan o Ihesus cryst dampnys
aberth yn crows may farwe
haccra mernans byth ordnys
ze creatur ny vye
en grows whath nyn io parys
nan ezewon ny wozye
an prennyer py fens kefis
ze wuzyll crous a neze

152 Vn ethow a brederys
hag a leuerys theze
bonas pren yn dour tewlys
a vs yn houl na vye
rag an grous y zo ordnys
han huthewon ny wozye
hag an avell devezys
drezy adam may peghse

150 *When Pilate saw that there was no way he could release Christ without incurring great wrath from all the company, for that reason he awarded Jesus to them to slay him. They released Barabbas to go away free.*

151 *When Jesus Christ was condemned to die by crucifixion, a more hideous death had never been ordained for any living being. The cross was not yet ready, and the Jews did not know where timbers might be found from which to make a cross.*

152 *One Jew considered and told them there was a tree thrown into the water which had never been in the sun. It was ordained for the cross (and the Jews did not know) and derived from the apple through which Adam had sinned.*

150 Kammenn Pilat pan welas — Mt 27 v.26
Na ylli Krist delivra — Mk 15 v.15
Ma na'n jevo ev sorr bras — Lk 23 v.18-25
Dhiworth oll an gowetha, — Jn 18 v.39-40
Rakhenna ev a jujyas — P.C. 2489-91
Yesus dhedha dh'y ladha.
Dhe-ves i a dhelivras
Barabas kwit mayth ella.

151 Pan o Yesus dempnys
A-berth yn krows may farwa,
Hakkra mernans bydh ord'nys
Dhe greatur ny via,
An grows hwath nyns o parys,
Na'n Edhewon ny wodhya
An prennyer py fens kevys
Dhe wuthyl krows anedha.

152 Unn Edhow a brederis — P.C. 2543-48
Hag a leveris dhedha
Bones prenn yn dowr tewlys
A'y oes y'n howl na via.
Rag an grows yth o ord'nys
(Ha'n Edhewon ny wodhya)
Hag a'n aval devedhys
Dredhi Adam may peghsa.

151/2 **A-berth yn krows**. See Language Notes, page 10.

152/6 **huthewon** (MS). On page 231 of his *Archaeologia Britannica*, Edward Lhuyd comments that words beginning with a vowel are often prefixed with *h*, e.g. *Dhen Hydhewon* = 'To the Jews'.

152/6 Notice the effective parallel with 151/6, although it is rather forced into the syntax of the sentence.

152/8 **Dredhi**. This appears to refer to *aval* in the previous line as though it were feminine. It is marked masculine in Nance and *G.M.* Breton *aval* is masculine. Welsh *afal* is given as masculine and feminine in the *Geiriadur Mawr.*

153 An prynner a ve kerhys
en grows scon dyzgtis may fe
hag ynny bonas gorys
ragon ny cryst a vynne
ha war an pren frut degis
may fe sur zagan sawye
may teth frut may fen kellys
rag adam ze attamye

154 Whath kentrow zeze nyngo
Ihesus yn crows rag synsy
y hwalsons ol adro
mar caffons goff yredy
onan a welsons eno
hag y zezons zy besy
hag y lauarsons thozo
te gura iij kenter zynny

155 In meth an goyff me ny wraff
pur wyr kentrow zewy vyth
yn methons mar omwreyth claff
gorzewyth te an prenvyth
awos guthyll wheyll mar scaff
yn ethom zyn mar fyllyth
y worzebys ny vannaff
aga guzyll war ow fyth

153 *The timbers were fetched for the cross to be quickly prepared and on it Christ, who was willing, to be placed for us, and on the tree a fruit borne with which it was sure to save us (and) from which came the fruit through which we were lost because Adam took the first bite of it.*

(Alternative translation)

The timbers were fetched for the cross to be prepared quickly. On it Christ who was willing, would be placed for us and on the tree a fruit would be borne that was sure to save us. It was the tree which bore the fruit through which we were lost because Adam took the first bite of it.

154 *Still they had no nails to hold Jesus crucified. They called all around to see if they could indeed find a smith. They saw one there and went and asked him and said to him, "You make us three nails."*

155 *The smith said, "Very truly I will not make any nails for you." They said, "If you make out you are ill you will pay for it in the end if you fail us in our need over doing such a small job." He answered, "I will not make them, on my faith."*

153 An prennyer a veu kyrghys P.C. 2555
An grows skon dyghtys may fe,
Hag ynni bones gorrys
Ragon ni Krist, a vynna,
Ha war an prenn frut degys
May feu sur dh'agan sawya
May teuth frut may fen kellys,
Rag Adam dh'y attamya.

154 Hwath kentrow dhedha nyns o P.C. 2663-74
Yesus yn krows rag synsi.
Y hawlsons oll a-dro
Mar kaffens gov yredi.
Onan y hwelsons eno
Hag yth ethons dh'y bysi,
Hag y lavarsons dhodho,
"Ty, gwra teyr henter dhyn ni."

155 Yn-medh an gov, "My ny wrav, P.C. 2675-79
Pur wir, kentrow dhy'hwi vydh."
Yn-medhons, "Mar omwreth klav,
Gordhiwedh ty a'n prenvydh
Awos guthyl hwel mar skav
Yn edhomm dhyn mar fyllydh."
Y hworthybis, "Ny vynnav
Aga guthyl, war ow fydh!"

153 This verse is one long sentence of 'The House that Jack built' type, a long concatenation of clauses. Two translations are offered, the first as literal as possible in one sentence, and the second broken into three sentences and therefore slightly less literal, but, hopefully, easier to follow.

154/1 **nyns o**. One would expect *nyns esa*, the long form of *bos* showing possession, with an indefinite noun subject; see *G.M.C.* §237 *G.M.C.(2)* §253(1). However, this would not fit the rhyme scheme and would create an excess syllable.

154/2 **yn krows** = 'crucified'. See Language Notes, page 10.

154/3 **hwalsons** (MS). Hooper queries whether *whylsons*, 'they did seek', was intended.

155/2 Hooper and Pennaod have emended this line to *Pur wyr, dhewhy kentrow-vyth* presumably so that the *vyth* immediately follows the noun to which it refers, as is normal.

155/4 **prenvydh**. Future of *prena*. See *G.M.C.* §195(2); *G.M.C.(2)* §197(2f).

155/7 **vannaf.** (MS) Nicholas Williams (§4.9) suggests this pronunciation with *a* in the first syllable was considered as slightly substandard and marked the smith as a manual worker. This verb is commonly spelt with *a* in the stem in *Bywnans Meryasek,*

.

156 Gans mur a Iucters yn wlas
ef ave veyll rebukis
kavanskis ef a whelas
rag own y vonas lezys
yn meth angoff clevas bras
es omdewleff devezys
towyll vyth ny allaff yn fas
ynno sensy ze wonys

157 Reys o zozo dysquezas
ze pur treytours a zewle
warneze gwelsons clevas
bytegyns byth nyn gese
yn meth y wrek mur a varth bras
yv henna zym rum lewte
hezow pan ezys yn mes
cleves vyth nyth kemerse

158 In meth gurek an goff zeze
kentrow zewy why ny fyll
a wos bos claff y zewle
toche vyth gonys ef na yll
del won yn vn fystene
me as gura ny strechyaff pell
a ban na ges a wothfe
zeugh paris as guerelle gwell

156 *He was vilely rebuked by many justices in the land. He looked for a way out for fear of being killed. The smith said, "Leprosy has come to my hands. I cannot hold any tool in them properly to work."*

157 *He had to show his hands to the out-and-out traitors. They saw leprosy on them, yet there was none. His wife said, "I am very surprised at that, by my troth. When you started out today no leprosy had taken hold of you."*

158 *The smith's wife said to them, "You will not be short of nails. Because his hands are diseased he cannot do any work. I will make them as best I can in a hurry since there is no one available with the skill to make them better for you. I will not be long."*

156 Gans meur a justers y'n wlas
Ev a veu vil rebukys
Kavanskeus ev a hwilas
Rag own y vones ledhys.
Yn-medh an gov, "Kleves bras P.C. 2675-78
Eus y'm diwla devedhys.
Toul vydh ny allav yn fas
Ynna synsi dhe wonis."

157 Res o dhodho diskwedhes P.C. 2685-90
Dhe'n pur draytours y dhiwla.
Warnedha gwelsons kleves,
Byttegyns bydh nyns esa.
Yn-medh y wreg, "Meur varth bras P.C. 2679-2736
Yw henna dhymm, re'm lowta.
Hedhyw pan ythys yn-mes
Kleves vydh ny'th kemmersa."

158 Yn-medh gwreg an gov dhedha,
"Kentrow dhy'hwi hwi ny fyll.
Awos bos klav y dhiwla
Toch vydh gonis ev ny yll.
Dell wonn, yn unn fistena.
My a's gwra, ny strechyav pell,
A-ban nag eus a wodhvo
Dhywgh parys a's gwrello gwell."

156/4 **own y vones ledhys.** *own* followed by an appositional genitive without *a* is unusual. See *G.M.C.* §126(8d); *G.M.C.(2)* §126(8d). Perhaps the *y* should be read as *a.* But cf. 174/8.

156/7 **yn fas** = *yn*[5] + *mas.*

156/8 **synsi**. Hooper and Pennaod print *synsys* but this must be a misprint.

157/5 **Meur varth**. I have followed Hooper and Pennaod in omitting the *a* in the MS as this would represent an extra syllable.

158/5 **yn unn fistena.** See *G.M.C.* §228(2); *G.M.C.(2)* §243(5).

158/7/8 **wodhvo; gwrello**. The imperfect subjunctive appears to be used in the MS for the present. See Language Notes, page 9.

159 En debell wrek casadow
gans mur a doth eth yn chy
war hast ze wezyll kentrow
may fens creff ha trewesy
ij droys Ihesus caradow
hay ij leyff y a delly
rag an spykis o garow
pan vons gwyskis zy synsy

160 Pan o kentrow lemmys
hy as duk zen ezewon
crows Ihesus navnio paris
y eth zy laze yn scon
bresell cref a ve sordijs
en grows pu elle zy don
dre vur stryff y fe Iuggijs
ys degy crist y honon

161 An queth tek a ve dyskis
han purpur ryche a vsye
hay bowys yhonon gurris
a dro zozo hy a ve
gans y vam y fye guris
hag ef gensy ow tene
kepar Ihesus del devys
yn della an bows a wre

159 *The hateful evil wife went very quickly into the house to make nails hastily to be strong and cruel. They would pierce the hands and feet of beloved Jesus for the spikes were rough when they were hit to secure him.*

160 *When the nails were sharpened she brought them to the Jews. The cross of Jesus was now ready. They went to slay him quickly. A mighty quarrel arose about who was going to carry the cross. Through much contention it was decided that Christ would carry it himself.*

161 *The fair garment was taken off and the rich purple that he was wearing and his own robe was put on him. It had been made by his mother when he was still with her as a breast-fed baby. As Jesus grew, so did the robe.*

159 An debel wreg gasadow
Gans meur a doth eth y'n chi
War hast dhe wuthyl kentrow
May fens krev ha truesi.
Dewdroes Yesus karadow
Ha'y dhiwleuv i a delli
Rag an spikys o garow
Pan vons gwyskys dh'y synsi.

160 Pan o an kentrow lymmys
Hi a's dug dhe'n Edhewon.
Krows Yesus nans o parys.
I eth dh'y ladha yn skon.
Bresel grev a veu sordys P.C. 2579-90
A'n grows, piw ella dh'y doen.
Dre veur strif y feu jujys
Y's degi Krist y honan.

161 An kweth teg a veu di'skys Mt 27 v.31
Ha'n purpur rych a usya, Mk 15 v.20
Ha'y bows y honan gorrys P.C. 2531-33 & following
A-dro dhodho hi a veu. stage direction
Gans y vamm y fia gwrys
Hag ev gensi ow tenna,
Kepar Yesus dell devis
Yndella an bows a wre.

159/5 **Dewdroes**. The use of the dual with *troes* is unusual in the texts. Here it completes the syllable count and harmonises better with *dhiwleuv* in the following line. But see also *G.M.C. (1)* §41 and *G.M.C. (2)* §45

160/1 **an kentrow**. I have followed Hooper and Pennaod in inserting the *an* as it seems more appropriate and the line is a syllable short without it.

160/6 **piw ella dh'y doen** = 'who might go and carry it'. The subjunctive expressing doubt in an indirect question implied by the previous clause. See *G.M.C.* §328(5), *G.M.C.(2)* §344(5).

160/8 **degi**. The imperfect showing future in the past. See *G.M.C.* §215(4); *G.M.C.(2)* §228(4).

161/4 **A-dro dhodho**. Cf. 140/6 note.

162 Oll monas y a vynne
bys yn mont a galvary
a vest zen dre y zese
meneth vghell yredy
an grows I a rug gorre
war scoth Ihesus zy don zy
ze Ihesus crist may teffe
ol an greff han belyny

163 Dew lader drevs o dampnys
a ve dyzgtis gans Ihesu
ganso ef may fens cregis
onon zozo a bub tu
Ihesus a ve hombronkis
ha war y lyrgh mur a lu
dre volder tebel Iustis
rag y chasye kyn zo du

164 I vam whegol a welas
del esons worth y zygtye
pyteth mur askemeras
y holon nam na grakye
dre vn scochforth y ponyas
cafos y mab mar calle
I wortos hy a vynnas
guelas Ihesus a gare

162 *They all set out to go to Mount Calvary. It was outside the town, a high hill indeed. They put the cross on Jesus' shoulder to carry there, so that all the distress and shame would come to Jesus Christ.*

163 *Two arrant thieves who had been condemned were made ready with Jesus to be hanged with him, one on each side of him. Jesus was led and behind him a great mob to pursue him because of the presumption of an evil magistrate, though he was God.*

164 *His mother most dear saw how they were treating him. Great pity seized her and her heart was nearly breaking. She ran through an alley to see if she could find her son. She wanted to wait for him and see Jesus whom she loved.*

162 Oll mones i a vynna
Bys y'n Mont a Galvari.
A-ves dhe'n dre yth esa,
Menydh ughel yredi.
An grows i a wrug gorra — Jn 19 v.17
War skoedh Yesus dh'y doen dhi — P.C. 2582-84
Dhe Yesus Krist may teffa
Oll an grev ha'n bileni.

163 Dew lader dreus o dempnys — Mt 27 v.38
A veu dyghtys gans Yesu — Mk 15 v.27
Ganso ev may fens kregys, — Lk 23 v.32-33
Onan dhodho a bub tu. — Jn 19 v.18
Yesus a veu hembrynkys — P.C. 2504-5
Ha war y lergh meur a lu — P.C. 2519-24
Dre volder tebel justis
Rag y jasya, kynth o Duw.

164 Y vamm hwegoll a welas
Dell esens orth y dhyghtya.
Pyteth meur a's kemmeras;
Hy holonn nammna grakkya.
Dre unn skochfordh y poenyas — P.C. Stage direction
Kavoes hy mab mar kalla. — following 2590
Y wortos hi a vynnas
Gweles Yesus a gara.

162/1 **i a vynna**. *Mynnes* can imply the future only (see Nance, page 273) or, in this case, the future in the past.

162/2 **Galvari**. I have kept the mutation as in the MS as it is the only time the name occurs in the poem.

163/1 **dreus**. Mutation after a noun preceded by *dew*. See *G.M.C.* §93; *G.M.C.(2)* §96.

164/5 **unn skochfordh**. *unn* used as indefinite article. See Language Notes, page 9.

164/6 **mar** = 'to see if'. See *G.M.C.* §328(5); *G.M.C.(2)* §344(5) .

165 Pan welas y mab dygtis
gans an ezewon mar veyll
hay vos gans spern curunys
ha peb zozo ow cull geyll
hag yn y gorf bos gorris
goleow pals leas myll
heb cows ger y clamderis
y tethas (cothas) war bol y hyll

166 Ena pan sevys yn ban
hy a gewsys del ylly
nyn gew ow faynys beghan
vs lemyn war ow sensy
ow holon yn tre myll darn
marth yw gene na squardhy
pan welaff ow mab mar wan
ow town kemys velyny

167 Gensy prest ij venyn len
esa worth y homfortye
marya magdalenen
ha marya cleophe
y a fystena yn fen
arte zy dyerbyne
rag kerensa nyn io ken
y welas y a vynne

165 *When she saw her son treated so dreadfully by the Jews, and being crowned with thorns and everybody tricking him, and multiple wounds, many thousand being driven into his body, she swooned without saying a word and fell backwards.*

166 *Then, when she stood up, she spoke as she was able: "My torments which are gripping me now are not little ones. I am amazed my heart does not tear into a thousand pieces when I see my son so weak enduring so much atrocity."*

167 *All the time there were two faithful women with her, Mary Magdalene, and Mary (wife of) Cleophas. They hastened eagerly to meet him again. For love they wanted to see him - nothing else.*

165 Pan welas hy mab dyghtys P.C. 2591-2614
Gans an Edhewon mar vil,
Ha'y vos gans spern kurunys,
Ha pub dhodho ow kul gil,
Hag yn y gorf bos gorrys
Goliow pals, lies mil,
Heb kows ger y klamderis,
Y koedhas war boll hy hil.

166 Ena, pan sevis yn bann
Hi a gewsis dell ylli,
"Nyns yw ow faynys byghan
Eus lemmyn orth ow synsi.
Ow holonn yntra mil dharn
Marth yw genev na skward hi
Pan welav ow mab mar wann,
Ow toen kemmys vileni."

167 Gensi prest diw venyn len Mt 27 v.56
Esa orth hy honfortya, Mk 15 v.40
Maria Magdalenen Jn 19 v.25
Ha Maria Kleofa. P.C. 2627-38
I a fistena yn fen
Arta dh'y dhierbynna.
Rag kerensa, nyns o ken,
Y weles i a vynna.

165/7 **klamderis**. Retained for the sake of the rhyme; normally *klamderas*. See *G.M.C.* §183, *G.M.C.(2)* §180

165/8 **tethas (cothas)** (MS) All my editors (even Stokes!) accept the alternative reading of *koedhas* = "fell" and I have followed this. I suggest, however, that *teudhas* = "melted" is not impossible. See psalm 68 v.8. It may be a metaphor to express Mary's horrendous distress.

166/5 **dharn**. Hooper and Pennaod have improved the rhyme by reading *ran* but I have kept with the MS.

167/3 **Magdalenen**. The final *n* seems to be for the rhyme only. It would be an accusative ending in Greek but I cannot find it elsewhere in Cornish writings or in the Gospels.

167/6 **dhierbynna**. *G.M.* has *dyerbynna* but this would leave the line a syllable short. See also 174/1.

168 Benenas prest a holyas
Ihesu crist yn vn garme
Ihesus worto a veras
hag a leueris zeze
flehys mur ha benenas
a ierusalem yn dre
a wor bos ov feynys bras
ragoff na wheleugh ole

169 Olough rag agis fleghys
ha ragough agis honon
en dezyow a vyth guelys
hag a ze sur yntrezon
may fyth torrow benegis
bythqueth na allas ezon
ha benenas kekyffrys
na ve zeze denys bron

170 In erna zen menyzyow
why a ergh warnough coze
yn ketella an nanssow
wy a bys ragas cuthe
del lavare war anow
war an pren glays mar a te
yn pren seygh ha casadow
sur yn erna fatel ve

168 *Wailing women incessantly followed Jesus Christ. Jesus looked at them and said to them, "Ye many women and children of the City of Jerusalem who know that my sufferings are great, seek not to weep for me.*

169 *"Weep for your children and for yourselves. The days will be seen and will surely come upon us when wombs that could never conceive will be blessed and women also whose breast has not been sucked.*

170 *"At that time you will command the mountains to fall upon you, likewise you will beg the valleys to cover you. As I say openly, if it comes upon the green wood, how indeed will it be then upon the dry and blighted wood?"*

168 Benynes prest a holyas — Mt 27 v.55
Yesu Krist yn unn arma. — Mk 15 v.40-41
Yesus orta a viras — Lk 23 v.27-28
Hag a leveris dhedha — P.C. 2639-56
"Fleghes meur ha benynes
A Yerusalem y'n dre
A woer bos ow faynys bras,
Ragov na hwilewgh oela.

169 "Oelewgh rag agas fleghes, — Lk 23 v.28-29
Ha ragowgh agas honan:
An dydhyow a vydh gwelys
Hag a dheu, sur, yntredhon,
May fydh torrow bennigys
Bythkweyth na allas omdhon
Ha'n benynes kekeffrys,
Na ve dhedha denys bronn.

170 "Y'n eur na dhe'n menydhyow — Lk 23 v.30-31
Hwi a ergh warnowgh koedha,
Yn kettella an nansow
Hwi a bys rag 'gas kudha.
Dell lavarav war anow,
War an prenn glas mara teu
Y'n prenn sygh ha kasadow
Sur, y'n eur na, fatell veu?"

168/2 **yn unn arma.** See *G.M.C.* §228(2); *G.M.C.(2)* §243(5).

168/5 **meur**. Strictly this seems to apply to *fleghes* only, but Hooper and Pennaod have, logically, taken it also with *benynes* and I have followed this.

170/5 **war anow**. I have followed Hooper in translating this as 'openly'.

170/6/8 **mara teu...fatell veu**. Hooper and Pennaod print *mara te...fatell ve* as in the MS and I take this to be the present of *dos* and the preterite of *bos*. These forms fit the metre and rhyme scheme, but normal grammar would require *mara teu...fatell vydh* or *mara teffa...fatell via*. Hooper translates 'in the dry and hateful tree, surely then how might it be?' Cf. Lk 23 v.31 'For if they do these things in a green tree, what shall be done in the dry?' (*A.V.*). Most modern versions have 'wood' which is nearer to the Greek and *prenn* can mean both.

171 I vam whek marya wyn
pub vr fystene a wre
may halle doys war y byn
y mab kemmys a gare
Rag gwander war ben dowlyn
hy an guelas ow coze
han wlos askemeras mar dyn
may clamderas hy arte

172 Ena hy a ve seuys
yn ban ynter benenas
arluth hy a leueris
ow holon y ma genas
kepar ha te hy zew guris
yn anken worth ze welas
bytqueth den ny wozevys
payn ella zy golon nes

173 En golyas ha fowt dybbry
a wozevys Ihesus ker
han strokosow trewesy
war y gorff dris pub maner
goys ay ben ay ysely
a zroppye war y zew ver
rag dozo ef na ylly
doun an grows rag gwander

171 *His sweet mother, Blessed Mary, was hurrying all the time so that she could meet him, her son whom she loved so much. She saw him falling on his knees through weakness. Anguish seized her so sharply that she swooned again.*

172 *Then she was raised up between some women. "Lord," she said, "my heart is with you, grief-stricken today like you at the sight of you." Never did man suffer pain that went closer to his heart.*

173 *Dear Jesus suffered the lack of sleep and food and the exceedingly grievous blows upon his body. Blood was falling from his head and limbs over his legs so that he could not carry the cross any further because of his weakness.*

171 Y vamm hweg, Maria Wynn,
Pub eur fistena a wre
May halla dos er y bynn,
Hy mab, kemmys a gara.
Rag gwannder, war benn dewlin
Hi a'n gwelas ow koedha
Ha'n loes a's kemmer's mar dynn
May klamderas hi arta.

172 Ena hi a veu sevys
Yn-bann ynter benynes.
"Arloedh," hi a leveris,
"Ow holonn yma genes,
Kepar ha ty hedhyw gwrys
Yn anken, orth dha weles."
Bythkweyth den ny wodhevis
Payn ella dh'y golonn nes.

173 An goelyas ha fowt dybri
A wodhevis Yesus ker,
Ha'n strokosow truesi
War y gorf dres pub maner .
Goes a'y benn ha'y eseli
A dhroppya war y dhiwver,
Rag dhodho ev na ylli P.C. 2615-20
Doen an grows rag y wannder.

171/7 **Ha'n loes**. Hooper and Pennaod omit *Ha'n* as it brings in an extra syllable, but the sentence seems to need it so I have kept it and elided the *a* in *kemmeras;* cf. 3/4.

171/8 **klamderas**. Cf. 165/7 note.

172/6 **Yn anken**. Hooper and Pennaod take this as referring to Jesus. I have taken it as referring to Mary, or, more literally, Mary's heart.

173/1 **En golyas** (MS). Hooper and Pennaod take this as *A'n goelyas* = 'from the wakening' and treat *a wodhevis* in 173/2 as a relative instead of main clause.

173/4 **dres pub maner**. = 'exceedingly': See *G.M.C.* §144(3); *G.M.C.(2)* §144/4.

173/7/8 **Rag dhodho...Doen**. Nance (under *rak/g*) gives *don rag dhodho* = 'carry any further'. However, *G.M.C.* §155(1); *G.M.C.(2)* §154 takes *rak* as a positional prepositon governing through *dhe*, and translates: 'he would not be able to carry the cross before him', but this does not fit the context so well so I have followed Nance.

173/8 **grows rag y wannder**. I have followed Hooper and Pennaod in inserting the *y* to make up the syllable count. Maybe the *gwander* of the MS should be read as *y wander,* as *g* and *y* are often similar in MSS. Stokes reads *grows* as *grow(y)s* in the MS. The spelling *growys* is unusual but does appear at 2/7 where it does not appear to occasion an extra syllable.

174 Vn den asdyerbynnas
Symmon o ay own hanow
y leuerys zozo guas
ty a zek an grows heb wow
y don symon a sconyas
ef an geve strocosow
na moy sconye ny vynnas
rag own cafos y ancow

175 Ef a thuk an grous ganse
pur wyr henno ay anvoth
ny wrens y na hen scyle
lymyn sywye aga both
pub er te zen gura lewte
beva den yonk bo den coth
orzaff mar mynnyth cole
neffre gans an fals na soth

176 I eth yn vn fystene
zen tyller ganso o ordnys
pan dozyans zy yntreze
pows Ihesus a ve dyskis
y dysky mur an grevye
worto fast navngo glenys
whath bytqueth claff ny vee
vylle ys dello dyskis

174 *A certain man met them. He was Simon by his proper name. They said to him, "Young man, you will carry the cross won't you?" Simon refused to carry it. He received blows. He would not refuse any more for fear of being killed.*

175 *He carried the cross along with them. Most certainly this was against his will. They gave no other reason than the following of their will. Be faithful at all times, man. If you will trust me, never serve the false one, whether he is an old man or young.*

176 *They hastened to the place which had been previously arranged. When they arrived there, between them Jesus' garment was taken off. Its removal caused him great pain. It was now stuck fast to him. Not even a leper had ever been stripped more brutally than he.*

174 Unn den a's dierbynnas Mt 27 v.32
Simon o a'y ewn hanow. Mk 15 v.21
Y leveris dhodho, "Gwas, Lk 23 v.26
Ty a dheg an grows heb wow." P.C. 2615-26
A'y doen Simon a skonyas.
Ev a'n jeva strokosow.
Na moy skonya ny vynnas
Rag own kavoes y ankow.

175 Ev a dhug an grows gansa.
Pur wir henn o a'y anvodh.
Ny wrens i nahen skila
Lemmyn sywya aga bodh.
Pub eur, ty dhen, gwra lowta.
Bova den yo'nk bo den koth,
Orthiv may mynnydh koela
Nevra gans an fals na soedh.

176 I eth yn unn fistena
Dhe'n tyller kyns o ord'nys.
Pan dhodhyens dhi, yntredha
Pows Yesus a veu di'skys.
Hy dis'ki meur a'n grevya,
Orto fast nans o glenys,
Hwath bythkweyth klav ny via
Villa es dell o di'skys.

174/1 **dierbynnas**. Cf. 167/6. Again, a trisyllable would leave the line a syllable short.

174/3 **Gwas**. Hooper and Pennaod take this as the subject of *leveris*, but it seems more likely that Simon is being addressed as *Gwas* and the verb is impersonal imperfect, 'One/They said'. This also agrees with Stokes.

174/8 **kavoes y ankow**. Cf. the Welsh idiom *cael ei ladd* = 'get his killing', i.e. 'be killed'. I have translated accordingly rather than literally 'getting his death' as does Hooper.

175/3 **Ny wrens**. Hooper prints *Ny rens* and translates 'They gave'. This translation is adequate but the reading seems doubtful.

175/4 **Lemmyn**. See Spelling Notes, page 13.

175/6 **Bova**. Confusion of imperfect/present subjunctive. See Language Notes, page 9.

175/8 **an fals**. Adjective used as noun; cf. *G.M.C.* §88; *G.M.C.(2)* §90.

176/1 **yn unn fistena.** See *G.M.C.* §228(2); *G.M.C.(2)* §243(5).

176/2 **kyns**. The MS has *ganso* but this involves an additional syllable and sets the question *Piw ganso?* So I have followed Hooper.

176/7 **vee** (MS). Hooper prints *ve* and Pennaod prints *ve-a.* Both read as a preterite tense, but the pluperfect *via* fits the rhyme scheme and the sense better.

177 Vn venyn da a welas
dello Ihesus dystrippijs
pytet mur askemeras
rag y vos mar veyll dygtis
vn queth tek hy a drylyas
adro zozo desympys
ha warnans hy an quuthas
rag gwyze na ve storuys

178 Heys crist y a gemeras
an neyll lef bys yn y ben
worth an les y a dollas
ij doll yn (an) grows heb ken
may zello an kentrow bras
dre y zewleff bys yn pen
rag y dreys y a vynnas
telly zy worre yntten

179 Ganse crist a ve tewlys
war an grows ze wroweze
hay yll leff a ve tackis
ord en grows fast may zese
hay yll troys a ve gorris
poran war ben e gele
worth an grows yfons lazijs
gans kenter guyskis dreze

177 *A certain good woman saw how Jesus was stripped. She took great pity because he was treated so cruelly. She wound a beautiful cloth round him straight away and wrapped up his lower part to shield him from being killed by the cold.*

178 *They took the measure of Christ from one hand to the other. According to the width they drilled just two holes in the cross so that the great nails would go through his hands right up to the head. They would drill a hole for his feet to stretch him out.*

179 *Christ was thrown by them to lie on the cross and his one hand was nailed to the cross securely where it was, and his one foot was placed exactly on top of the other. They were fastened to the cross by a nail driven through them.*

177 Unn venyn dha a welas
Dell o Yesus destryppys
Pyteth meur a's kemmeras
Rag y vos mar vil dyghtys.
Unn kweth teg hi a drelyas
A-dro dhodho desempis
Ha warnans hi a'n kwethas
Rag gwitha na ve stervys.

178 Hys Krist i a gemmeras P.C. 2737-60
A'n eyl leuv bys yn hy ben.
Orth an les i a dollas
Dew doll yn an grows hepken
Mayth ella an kentrow bras
Dre y dhiwla bys y'n penn.
Rag y dreys i a vynnas
Telli dh'y worra yn tenn.

179 Gansa Krist a veu tewlys
War an grows dhe wrowedha
Ha'y eyl leuv a veu tekkys
Orth an grows fast mayth esa,
Ha'y eyl troes a veu gorrys
Poran war benn y gila.
Orth an grows y fons letthys
Gans kenter gwyskys dredha.

177/1 **Unn venyn**. This seems to parallel the *Unn den* in 174/1 though the man is biblical and the woman is not. See Notes on the Poem and its Sources, page 25. Hooper omits 'certain' in 177/1 though he has it in 174/1. I have included it in both verses for the sake of the parallelism, though possibly the *unn* is a simple definite article in both. See Language Notes, page 9.

177/2 **Dell o**. See Language Notes, page 10.

177/5 **Unn kweth**. See Language Notes, page 9.

177/6 **A-dro dhodho**. See 140/6 note.

178/4 **yn an grows**. *y'n* is normal but *yn an* is needed for the syllable count.

178/5 **Mayth ella**. Confusion of present and imperfect subjunctive. See Language Notes, page 9.

179/7 **lazijs** (MS). *G.M.* gives *latthya* with the meaning 'to latch'. This must be the same verb though the meaning is not very appropriate. The ending *-ijs* (MS) for past participles corresponds with verbal nouns in *-ya* having a p.p. in *-ys* or *-yes* in K.K. Here *-ys* seems better to rhyme here with *tekkys* and *gorris* above.

180 Then levff arall pan dozyans
worth an grovs rag y faste
y fylly moy es tresheys
zen tol guris hy na heze
en ezewon betegyns
gul tol arall ny vynne
lemyn an tol re wrussens
y a vyn(n)e ze seruye

181 Ganse worth levff crist loven
fast yn scon a ve kelmys
hag yn tre an ezewon
an grovs fast a ve sensys
gans re a gymmys colon
en loven a ve tennys
y iunctis keteponon
oll warbarth may zens squardis

182 Pan deth levff crist war en toll
dre an nerth may tensons hy
vn ethow avell pyth foll
a wyskis kenter ynhy
lemmyn me agis pys oll
a baynis crist predery
ha na vo gesys ze goll
an lahys a rug zynny

180 *When they came to the other hand to fasten it to the cross, there was more than a foot short so that it would not reach the hole which had been made. However, the Jews would not make another hole but they intended the hole which they had made to serve.*

181 *A rope was soon tied firmly by them to Christ's hand, and between the Jews the cross was tightly held. The rope was pulled with so much zeal by some that his joints were altogether torn, every one of them.*

182 *When Christ's hand came over the hole by the force with which they pulled, one Jew drove a nail into it like a mad thing. Now I beg you all to think of Christ's tortures, and that the laws which he made for us should not be lost.*

180 Dhe'n leuv arall pan dhodhyens P.C. 2749-73
Orth an grows rag y fasta,
Y fylli moy es troes-hys
Dhe'n toll gwrys hi na hedha.
An Edhewon, byttegyns,
Gul toll arall ny vynna,
Lemmyn an toll re wrussens
I a vynna dhe servya.

181 Gansa orth leuv Krist lovan
Fast yn-skon a veu kelmys,
Hag yntra an Edhewon
An grows fast a veu synsys.
Gans re a gemmys kolonn
An lovan a veu tennys
Y juntys kettep onan
Oll war-barth mayth ens skwerdys.

182 Pan dheuth leuv Krist war an toll
Dre an nerth may tennsons i
Unn Edhow, avel pyth fol,
A wyskis kenter ynni.
Lemmyn my a'gas pys oll
A baynys Krist prederi,
Ha na vo gesys dhe goll
An laghys a wrug dhyn ni.

180/3 **Y fylli moy es troes-hys**. Hooper says this does not rhyme. It would do if the *n* in the corresponding rhyming syllables were weakened to the point of inaudibility as often seems to be the case with such words. I have kept the MS version though Hooper and Pennaod follow Nance's suggestion of *a voy es troshes fallens*.

180/4 **hi na hedha**. It is most unusual to find a subject pronoun preceding *na* in a negative subordinate clause. Normally one would expect *na hedha hi* but this would not rhyme. David Balhatchet suggests a full stop at the end of 180/3, making 180/4 a separate sentence, by reading *ny* instead of *na*.

182/2 **may tensons hy** (MS). Hooper prints *may's* to correspond as an infixed pronoun with the *hy.* I have taken the *hy* to be the plural pronoun *i.*

183 Scrifys yw yn suredy
ha ken me nyn lauarsen
corff Ihesus hay asely
y ze denna mar velen
neb a vynna a ylly
neuera oll y yscren
hay skennys kyc ha gwyzy
pan esa yn (an) crows pren

184 Han grous a ve drehevys
ha Ihesus fasteys ynny
han pen golas delyffrys
yn tol o tellys rygthy
ena hy a ve gefys
ze goza mar ankynsy
ze crist may fe crehellys
oll y gorf hay esely

185 Ha crist yn delma peynys
a berth yn crows pan ese
yn (va)nerma y pesys
rag an keth re ren crowse
ow zas whek bezens gevys
zen rema aga nyscyte
rag me ny won py gymmys
y mons y sur ow peghe

183 *It is written quite definitely, and I would not say otherwise, that they pulled the body and limbs of Jesus so savagely that anyone who wanted could count all his bones and his sinews, flesh and veins, when he was on the cross.*

184 *And the cross was raised with Jesus fastened on it and the bottom placed in a hole which had been drilled for it. There it was dropped so brutally that all Christ's body and limbs were jolted.*

185 *While Christ was thus in pain suffering crucifixion he prayed in this manner for those who had crucified him. "My gentle father, may these be forgiven for their ignorance for even I do not know how greatly indeed they are sinning."*

183 Skrifys yw yn surredi
Ha ken my ny'n lavarsen
Korf Yesus ha'y eseli
I dhe denna mar vilen
Neb a vynna a ylli
Nivera oll y eskern Ps. 22 v.17
Ha'y skennys, kig ha'y wythi
Pan esa yn an krowsprenn.

184 Ha'n grows a veu drehevys P.C. 2811-22
Ha Yesus festys ynni.
Ha'n penn-goeles delivrys
Yn toll o tellys rygdhi.
Ena hi a veu gesys
Dhe goedha mar ankensi
Dhe Krist may feu kryghyllys
Oll y gorf ha'y eseli.

185 Ha Krist yndella paynys Lk 23 v.34
A-berth yn krows pan esa P.C. 2773-78
Y'n vaner ma y pysis
Rag an keth re re'n krowssa,
"Ow thas hweg, bedhes gevys
Dhe'n re na 'ga nisyta
Rag my ny wonn pygemmys
Ymons i sur ow pegha."

183/5 **a ylli**. I have followed Hooper in taking this as a consecutive clause depending on *mar vilen* in 183/4. *may hylli* would be normal, see *G.M.C.* §334; *G.M.C.(2)* §350. Perhaps the line should start a new sentence leaving *mar vilen* without any clause depending on it.

183/7 **ha'y wythi**. I have assumed the *g* of the MS should read as *y* following *G.M.C.* §51; *G.M.C.(2)* §54. Hooper has *has gwythy* which must be a misprint and Pennaod has *ha gwythy*.

183/8 **an krowsprenn**. I have followed Hooper. Pennaod omits the doubtful *an* of the MS and prints *esa-va* to make up the syllable count.

184/2 **festys**. Vowel affection [*G.M.C.* §194(1); *G.M.C.(2)* §189]. Hooper has *fasthes* and Pennaod *fastes*.

185/2 **yn krows**. See Language Notes, page 10.

185/6 **'ga nisyta**, I have followed Hooper and Pennaod in eliding the first *a* of *aga* which creates an excess syllable.

185/7 **my ny wonn**. Hooper says "evidently a scribal error". The line is based, presumably, on Lk 23 v.34, "Then said Jesus, 'Father forgive them; for they know not what they do.'" (*A.V.*). The change from 'they' to 'I' is certainly strange, especially as the *my ny wonn* is so emphatic. However, I have followed the MS rather than substitute *ny wodhons* as Hooper and Pennaod have done, and tried to convey the emphasis by adding 'even' to the translation.

186 An ethewon a grogas
lader ze gryst an barth cleth
hag a zyghow lader bras
cregy a russons yn weth
ha crist yn cres leun a ras
levn y golon a voreth
gans laddron y tewezas
del yw scrifys ay zeweth

187 Pylat a vynnas scrife
a vewnans (leg. vernans) crist acheson
praga dampnys rebee
hag an scrifas y honon
pan eth pylat zy redye
scyle nyn io na gonon
prest y keffy pan vyre
henma yw mygtern ezewon

188 En ethewon a gowsys
henna yw zyn bylyny
bezens ze ves defendis
y vonas mygtern zynny
ha bezens ena gorris
y fense bos dre vestry
han pyth a screfys screfys
yn meth pylat zeze y

186 *The Jews hanged a thief on Christ's left hand and on his right they hanged a great thief also, and Christ in the middle, full of grace, his heart full of sorrow. "He ended with thieves," as it is written about his end.*

187 *Pilate wanted to write a reason for Christ's death, why he had been condemned, and he wrote it himself. When Pilate came to read it, it was not a reason at all. Whenever he looked he always found, "This is the King of the Jews."*

188 *The Jews said, "This is an outrage upon us. Let it be struck out that he is our king and let it be put there that he had wanted to be by domination." "What I have written, I have written," said Pilate to them.*

186 An Edhewon a grogas
Lader dhe Krist a'n barth kledh
Hag a dheghow lader bras
Kregi a wrussons ynwedh,
Ha Krist y'n kres leun a ras,
Leun y golonn a voreth.
"Gans ladron y tiwedhas,"
Dell yw skrifys a'y dhiwedh.

Mt 27 v.38
Mk 15 v.27-28
Lk 23 v.32-33
Jn 19 v.18
P.C. Stage direction following 2784

187 Pilat a vynnas skrifa
A vernans Krist acheson,
Praga dempnys re bia,
Hag a'n skrifas y honan.
Pan eth Pilat dh'y redya
Skila nyns o nagonan.
Prest y kevi pan vira,
"Hemm yw Myghtern Edhewon."

Mt 27 v.37
Mk 15 v.26
Lk 23 v.38
Jn 19 v.19
P.C. 2791-96 & preceding stage direction

188 An Edhewon a gewsis,
"Henna yw dhyn bileni!
Bedhes dhe-ves defendys
Y vones myghtern dhyn ni
Ha bedhes ena gorrys
Y fynnas vos dre vaystri."
"An pyth a skrifis, skrifis."
Yn-medh Pilat dhedha i.

Jn 19 v.21-22
P.C. 2797-2806

187/2 **vewnans** (MS). I have followed (with Hooper and Pennaod) the reading *vernans*. suggested by Stokes and Nance.

187/5-8 Hooper gives this note from Nance: "A miracle story. Pilate might write whatever he chose - it always read the same."

187/8 **hemma** (MS). I have followed Hooper and Pennaod in omitting the final *a* as it represents an excess syllable and is not normal when followed by *yw*.

188/2 **Henna**. In this case, although the final *a* is abnormal, it is necessary to complete the syllable count.

188/3/5 **bedhes**. See Language Notes, page 12; 3rd singular imperative.

189 En lybell a ve tackis
worth en grous fast may zese
hag a vgh pen crist gorrys
may hylly peb y redye
rag bos Ihesus crist crowsys
ogas ze forth an cyte
gans leas yfe redijs
y vonas mygtern zethe

190 Dyllas crist a ve rynnys
pedar ran guris a neze
gans peswar marreg a brys
ze bub marreg ran nayse
y bous ef o mar dek guris
y ny vynsans y ranne
war nethy pren be tewlys
oll an bows pyv an gyffe

191 An barth cleyth neb o cregis
dyveth o ha lader pur
yn ges ef a leuerys
te crist mar sota mar fur
war an bys del omwressys
lemmyn dyswa ha gura cur
ha saw te ha me kyffris
agan bewnans may fen sur

189 *The charge was securely nailed to the cross where he was, and placed above Christ's head so that all could read it. Because Christ was crucified near the road to the city it was read by many that he was their king.*

190 *Christ's garments were divided, four parts being made of them by four soldiers of repute, a share for each soldier. His robe was so beautifully made that they were unwilling to divide it. Lots were cast upon it to see who should get the whole robe.*

191 *The one who was hanged on his left was without shame, an out-and-out thief. In mockery he said, "You, Christ, if you are as clever in the world as you pretended, show it now and perform a remedy, and save yourself and me as well so that we may be sure of our lives."*

189 An libel a veu tekkys P.C. 2807-10
Orth an grows fast mayth esa
Hag a-ugh penn Krist gorrys
May hylli pub y redya.
Rag bos Yesus Krist krowsys
Ogas dhe fordh an sita,
Gans lies y feu redys
Y vones myghtern dhedha.

190 Dillas Krist a veu rennys, Mt 27 v.38
Peder rann gwrys anedha, Mk 15 v.24
Gans peswar marghek a bris Lk 23 v.34
Dhe bub marghek rann ’nedha, Jn 19 v.23
Y bows ev o mar deg gwrys P.C. 2841-60
I ny vynnsons hy ranna. & preceding
Warnedhi prenn ’veu tewlys stage direction
Oll an bows piw a’n jeffa.

191 A’n barth kledh neb o kreghys Mt 27 v.44
Diveth o ha lader pur. Lk 23 v.39
Yn ges ev a leveris, P.C. 2891-96
“Ty, Krist, mars o'ta mar fur
War an bys dell omwrussys,
Lemmyn diskwa ha gwra kur ,
Ha saw ty ha my keffrys,
A’gan bywnans may fyn sur.”

189/2 **fast**. Hooper suggests this might go with *esa* and refer to Jesus rather than *tekkys* and the charge sheet.

190/3/4 **marreg** (MS). See Spelling Notes, page 12.

190/4 **ran nayse** (MS). I have taken this as *rann ’nedha.* Hooper and Pennaod read *ran may fe* but this does not rhyme so well.

191/4 **o'ta**. See Spelling Notes, page 13.

192 In meth an lader arall
drok zen os kepar del ves
ny zowtyth du te yw dall
rag genen cregis neb es
den glan yw a begh heb fall
ynno eff dyfout nyn ges
agan cregy ny yv mall
rag ny rebe laddron dres

193 An lader an barth dyghow
a besys in ketelma
arluth pan dyffy zet pow
predery a hanaff gura
crist pur wek an caradow
an gorzebys yn vrna
te a vyth yn keth golow
yn paradis genama

194 An ezewon a gewsy
a Ihesus rag y scornye
kyns yn ta ef a ylly
tus a bup drok ol sawye
lemmyn gans ol y vestry
ragon ny wor omweze
na gans oll y tretury
ny yll agan dyssaytye

192 *The other thief said, "You are an evil man, just as you were. You do not fear God. You are blind, for he who has been hanged with us is a man who is, without doubt, free of sin. In him there is no blemish. It is fitting that we should be hanged for we have been wicked robbers."*

193 *The thief on the right prayed like this: "Lord, when you come into your land, think of me!" Then Christ, the beloved, answered him very kindly, "You will be with me this very day in Paradise."*

194 *The Jews talked about Jesus to mock him: "Before, he was able to save people from every evil. Now with all his power he cannot protect himself from us, nor with all his treachery can he deceive us."*

192 Yn-medh an lader arall, Lk 23 v.40-43
"Drog dhen os, kepar dell veus. P.C. 2896-2912
Ny dhoutydh Duw. Ty yw dall.
Rag genen kregys neb eus
Den glan yw a begh heb fall.
Ynno ev defowt nyns eus.
Agan kregi ni yw mall
Rag ni re beu ladron dreus."

193 An lader a'n barth deghow
A bysis yn kettellma,
"Arloedh, pan dhyffi dhe'th pow,
Prederi ahanav gwra!"
Krist pur hweg, an karadow
A'n gorthybis y'n eur na,
"Ty a vydh y'n keth golow,
Yn Paradhis genama."

194 An Edhewon a gewsi Mt 27 v.39-43
A Yesus, rag y skornya, Mk 15 v.29-32
"Kyns, yn ta ev a ylli Lk 23 v.35
Tus a bub drog oll sawya. P.C. 2861-90
Lemmyn, gans oll y vaystri,
Ragon ny woer omwitha,
Na, gans oll y drayturi,
Ny yll agan dessaytya."

192/7 **mall**. Clearly used as an adjective though Nance and *G.M.* give only as noun with the basic meaning of 'haste' which does not make much sense here. I have followed Hooper. Cf. Lk 23 v.41 'and we indeed justly' (*A.V.*).

193/8 **genama**. "Probably colloquial: in other texts *gene* is common." (Hooper). I have presumed the K.K. spelling will be the same as the MS and Unified.

195 War aga dewlyn y ze
pe rag Ihesus re erell
aga fen y a sackye
hag a gewsy pur debell
worth Ihesus rag y angre
a wotta omma neb yll
tempell du dowstoll squardye
ha ze voth y zrehevell

196 Hag y ee ze ben dewlyn
ha hager mowys a wre
gweze gozyans aga meyn
orth Ihesus a omgame
hag ef moygha yn y beyn
yn y fas y a drewe
heno zozo calys feyn
agan pegh ny ow prenne

197 Re ze gryst a leuery
a berth yn crows pan ese
mar soge crist mab dauy
des an grows heb pystege
ha ny a grys ze vestry
hag ad syns mester neffre
me yw mab du yredy
crist a leueris thethe

195 *Others went on their knees before Jesus. They shook their heads and spoke very cruelly to Jesus to harass him: "Behold, here is the one who can utterly pulverise God's temple and build it up at will."*

196 *And they went on their knees and made ugly grimaces. As badly as they could they contorted their faces at Jesus. Whilst his pain was at its height they spat in his face. This was a harsh end for him as he redeemed our sin.*

197 *Some said to Christ when he was crucified, "If you are Christ, the son of David, come off the cross unharmed, and we will believe in your authority and acknowledge you always as master." "I am the Son of God indeed," Christ said to them.*

195 War aga dewlin yth e
Dherag Yesus re erell.
Aga fenn i a shakya
Hag a gewsi pur debel
Orth Yesus, rag y angra.
"Awotta omma neb 'yll
Tempel Duw doust oll skwardya,
Ha dh'y vodh y dhrehevel."

196 Hag i e dhe benn dewlin
Ha hager mowys a wre,
Gwettha godhyens a'ga min
Orth Yesus a omgamma.
Hag ev moyha yn y bayn
Yn y fas i a drewa.
Henn o dhodho kales fin
Agan pegh ni ow prena.

197 Re dhe Krist a leveri,
A-berth yn krows pan esa,
"Mars o'ta Krist, Mab Davi,
Deus a'n grows heb pystiga,
Ha ni a grys dha vaystri,
Hag a'th syns mester nevra."
"My yw Mab Duw yredi,"
Krist a leveris dhedha.

195/1-2 **War aga dewlin**. See *G.M.C.* §50; *G.M.C.(2)* §53

195/2 **pe rag** (MS) I have followed Nance, Hooper and Pennaod in reading this as *dherag*.

196/3-4 **a'ga min Orth Yesus a omgamma**. Literally: 'twisted themselves in their faces'. Wella Brown regards this as a use of *a* comparable with *G.M.C.* §126(4); *G.M.C.(2)* §126(4) The nearest example there is *gwenys veuv a'm troes* = 'I was stung in my foot.' Hooper and Pennaod print *y omgamma*. Following the MS, I assume that the subject of *omgamma* is *i* in 196/1 in a compound nominal sentence. *Omgamma* is given in *G.M.* and *G.M.C.* §153(8); *G.M.C.(2)* §152(9) but not in Nance.

196/7-8 The present participle *ow prena* evidently qualifies *dhodho*, probably in imitation of the Latin use of the dative present participle. The literal sense is: 'This was to him redeeming our sin a hard end.' I found the following example of the Latin construction in Nunn. It is a from a hymn by St. Bernard: *Quam pius es petentibus, sed quid invenientibus?*: 'How good thou art to those who seek, but what to those who find?'

197/2 **A-berth yn krows.** See Language Notes, page 10.

197/3 **o'ta**. See Spelling Notes, page 13.

197/3 **Davi**. Retained for the rhyme. *G.M.* gives *Davydh.*

197/6 Cf. the Charter Endorsement line 35: *Y'n eur na y'th syns dhe vos mestres* = 'Then he will acknowledge you to be mistress.'

198 A barth dyghow y zese
ze gryst y vam marya
hay vam ef neb a gare
an barth arall magata
deso benyn yn meza
Iowan ze vab me a wra
na byth moy ken mam neffre
es hyhy te na whela

199 War lyrgh crist enef ze ry
pub onan oll zy gele
Iowan y vam a sensy
marya crist del arse
yn pub maner may hylly
y vam prest asonore
yn delma comfort zyzy
y map a vynnas dygtye

200 Nevngo deuethys an prys
may zo ogas zy zeweth
yn erna y fe dorgis
ha dris ol an bys ef eth
tewolgow bras a ve guris
an houll a gollas y feth
ha moy marzus me a gris
ys an rena ve yn weth

198 *On the right side of Christ there was his mother Mary and on the other side his servant also whom he loved. "For you, lady, he said, I make John your son - and you, do not ever seek any mother other than her."*

199 *After Christ had surrendered his soul, John held Mary as his mother, each to the other, as Christ had ordered. He always honoured his mother in every way he could. In this way her son wanted to provide support for her.*

200 *Now the time had come when he was near to his end. At that time there was an earthquake and it went all over the earth. A great darkness came about. The sun's presence was lost and (there were) more wonders also I believe than these.*

198 A'n barth deghow yth esa — Jn 19 v.26-27
Dhe Krist y vamm Maria, — P.C. 2925-54
Ha'y vaw ev neb a gara
A'n barth arall maga ta.
"Dhiso, benyn," yn-medh e,
"Yowann dha vab my a wra.
Na bydh moy ken mamm nevra
Es hyhi, ty, na hwila."

199 War-lergh Krist enev dhe ri
Pubonan oll dh'y gila,
Yowann y vamm a synsi
Maria, Krist dell arghsa.
Yn pub maner may hylli
Y vamm prest a's enora.
Yndellma konfort dhedhi
Hy mab a vynnas dyghtya.

200 Nans o devedhys an prys — Mt 27 v.51
Mayth o ogas dh'y dhiwedh. — Mk 15 v.33
Y'n eur na y feu dorgrys — Lk 23 v.44
Ha dres oll an bys ev eth. — P.C. 2989-3002
Tewolgow bras a veu gwrys. — & preceding
An howl a gollas y feth — stage directions
Ha moy marthus, my a grys,
Es an re ma 'veu ynwedh.

198/3 **vam** (MS). I have followed Hooper and Pennaod in reading *vaw* which is clearly intended. *M* and *W* are easily confused in MSS.

200/5 **Tewolgow bras a veu gwrys**. 'A great darkness was made' is not natural English and I suspect the Cornish is a word-for-word translation of the Latin *factum est* which literally means 'was made' but can also translate as 'became' or 'took place' and is very common in biblical Latin, e.g. *Verbum caro factum est*: 'The Word was made/became flesh.' (Jn 1 v.14).

200/6 **feth** = 'face'; cf. 115/3 note.

200/7 **marthus**. This appears to be plural through all the dictionaries give it is sing.

201 In della hy a begyas
bys hanter dyth yredy
yn erna crist a vynnas
leuerell ely ely
ze strirya (leg. scrirya) yw a gowsas
arluth prag y hysta vy
mas re war gryst a ynnyas
y zo dewas ar yrghy

202 Gans an ezewon war hast
drok zewas a ve dyzgtys
tebell lycour mur y last
eysyll bestyll kemyskis
yn (un) spong orth gwelen fast
ze gryst hy a ve hezys
gonys oll a wrens yn fast
rag na go crist attendijs

203 Re an ezewon tebell
a leuerys heb pyte
a wottense ow kelwel
hely zozo zy wyze
myrugh mar te drehevell
ay beynys zy delyffre
han scherewys prest a bell
ze worth an gwyr afye

201 *So it went on right up to midday. Then Christ wanted to say "Eli, Eli." What he said is to be interpreted, "Lord, why have you abandoned me?" But some insisted that it was a drink that Christ was demanding.*

202 *An evil drink was hastily prepared by the Jews, a devilish liquor, most loathsome, vinegar mixed with gall. It was held out to Christ in a sponge fixed to a rod. They all worked hastily because Christ was not understood.*

203 *Some of the evil Jews said without pity, "Behold him calling Elias to him to preserve him. See whether he comes and rises up to deliver him from his tortures." Yet all the time the wicked ones had been far from the truth.*

201 Yndella hi a besyas — Mt 27 v.45-46
Bys hanter-dydh yredi, — Mk 15 v.33-34
Y'n eur na Krist a vynnas — Lk 23 v.46
Leverel "Eli, Eli." — P.C. 2955
Dhe styrya yw a gowsas,
"Arloedh, prag y hys'sta vy?" — Ps 22 v.1
Mes re war Krist 'ynnias
Yth o diwes a erghi. — Jn 19 v.28

202 Gans an Edhewon war hast — Mt 27 v.48
Drog dhiwes a veu dyghtys, — Mk 15 v.36
Tebel likour, meur y last. — Jn 19 v.29
Aysel, bystel, kemmyskys, — Stage direction
Yn unn spong orth gwelenn fast. — following P.C. 2964
Dhe Krist hi a veu hedhys.
Gonis oll a wrens yn hast
Rag nag o Krist attendys.

203 Re an Edhewon debel — Mt 27 v.47-49
A leveris, heb pyta, — Mk 15 v.35-36
"Awottensa ow kelwel — P.C. 2959-64
Eli dhodho dh'y witha.
Mirewgh mar teu drehevel
A'y baynys dh'y dhelivra."
Ha'n sherewys prest a-bell
Dhiworth an gwir a via.

201/4 **Eli, Eli**. Mt 27 v.46 has *Eli, Eli.* Mk 15 v.34 has *Eloi, Eloi.* The cry is not mentioned by Luke or John, but John 19 v. 28 quotes Jesus as saying 'I thirst.' (*A.V.*).

201/5 **strirya.** (MS) This was previously read as *scrirya* with the presumed meaning "to describe" but the word is found several times as *styrrya* in the *Tregear Homiles* clearly meaning "to mean". (Nance writing in *Old Cornwall* Summer l951)

201/6 **prag y hys'sta vy?** Hooper points out that this is colloquial for *prag y'm gys'ta vy? P.C.* 2957 has *prag y'm gyssys?* as the cry of Jesus.

201/7 **'ynnias.** I have elided the particle as the long *i* in *ynnias* creates an excess syllable not allowed for in the MS or by Hooper of Pennaod. May be *a ynnyas*?

202/5 **Yn unn spong**. *unn* is necessary to make up the syllable count, though shown only in the *Kernow* MS version and in brackets. It acts as an indefinite article. See Spelling Notes, page 9.

202/7 **yn hast**, accepting the emendment from *fast* made by Hooper and Pennaod.

203/5 Hooper and Pennaod insert *ha* before *drehevel* and create an excess syllable. Grammar requires *ha*, *dhe* or *rag* but I feel poetic licence sanctions the omission.

203/7-8 I have followed Hooper's translation which allows a concessive meaning to the *Ha*. Cf. 86/8 note.

203/8 **Dhiworth**. For *A-dhiworth*. See 12/4 note.

204 I beyn o mar greff ha tyn
caman na ylly bewe
heb dascor y eneff gwyn
bytqueth yn lan revewse
crist a besys del redyn
yn delma yn luas le
ow eneff me a gymyn
arluth yn tre ze zewle

205 Rag gwan spyr(n) hag ef yn ten
caman na ylly gwyze
war nans na bosse y ben
rag an arlont a vsye
mar posse a neyll tenewen
rag y scoth hy a grevye
Ha whath gweth a wre an pren
war zellargh mar an gorre

206 Na war rag ef ny ylly
pose rag own bos megis
yn erna del redyn ny
y(n) lyffrow del yw scrifys
zen nezyn gwyls rag nyezy
tellyryow esa paris
the crist y ben py sensy
teller vyth nyn go kefis

204 *His torture was so intense and cruel that in no way could he live without surrendering his blessed spirit that had ever lived in purity. As we read in many places, Christ prayed like this: "Into your hands, Lord, I commend my spirit."*

205 *Because of the piercing of thorns as he was stretched out, there was no way he could stop his head leaning downward. Because of the wreath he was wearing, if he leaned to one side it hurt him because of his shoulder, and the wood hurt even worse if he laid it backward.*

206 *Nor could he lean forward for fear of being choked. At that time, as we read what is written in the Scriptures, there were places ready for the wild birds to build their nests; for Christ no place was found for him to hold his head.*

204 Y bayn o mar grev ha tynn
Kammenn na ylli bywa
Heb daskorr y enev gwynn
Bythkweyth yn lan re vywsa.
Krist a bysis, dell redyn
Yndellma yn lies le,
"Ow enev my a gemmynn, Lk 23 v.46
Arloedh, yntra dha dhiwla!" P.C. 2985-86

205 Rag gwan spern, hag ev yn tenn,
Kammenn na ylli gwitha
War-nans na boessa y benn .
Rag an arlont a usya,
Mar poessa'n eyl tenewen,
Rag y skoedh hi a'n grevya,
Ha hwath gweth a wre an prenn
War-dhelergh mara'n gorra.

206 Na war-rag ev ny ylli
Poesa rag own bos megys.
Y'n eur na, dell redyn ni
Y'n lyvrow dell yw skrifys,
Dhe'n ydhyn gwyls, rag neythi, Mt 8 v.20
Tylleryow esa parys: Lk 9 v.58
Dhe Krist, y benn py synsi,
Tyller vydh nyns o kevys.

204/3 **enev gwynn**. Hooper has 'spotless soul'

204/4 **yn lan**. See *G.M.C.* §252; *G.M.C.(2)* §267. Normally *yn* causes fifth state mutation which would leave *glan* unchanged. Here second state mutation has occurred

205/2 Note the parallelism with 204/2, which may be the reason for the *na* rather than *ny* as would be normal in a main clause.

205/5-6 **Mar poessa...hi a'n grevya**. A conditional sentence with an imperfect subjunctive in both clauses. Cf. *G.M.C.* §328(3note). This note is omitted in *G.M.C.(2)*

205/7 **a wre an prenn**. Hooper has *a wre a'n pren* and translates 'and still worse it would be from the wood.'

205/7/8 **a wre...mara'n gorra**. Wella Brown suggests that these two imperfect indicative verbs in a conditional sentence imply 'whenever/every time'.

206/4 **dell yw skrifys**. Hooper and Pennaod emend to *yth yw skrifys* and treat the next four lines as direct speech. I take them as the main statement following on from *Y'n eur na,* with *dell redyn ni* and *dell yw skrifys* as parenthetical; cf. 209/2.

206/6/8 **esa parys...o kevys**. See *G.M.C.* §315(3e); *G.M.C.(2)* §332(3e). In both these cases the subjects are indefinite (*tylleryow* and *tyller*) and should therefore require the long form of *bos* as they are followed by past participles. So, does the *o* imply that the place which Jesus lacked was definite, or is it just to fit the metre?

207 Rag porrys rys o zozo
gase y ben zegregy
rag galse glan ze worto
y woys bewe ny ylly
war tu hay vam an pewo
y ben a vynnas synsy
hay eneff eth a nozo
gans garm eyn hag vghel gry

208 Ryp crous Ihesus y zese
vn den henwys sentury
a vernans crist pan welse
kynyuer tra marthusy
han enef del dascorse
erbyn natar gans vn cry
y leuerys heb scornye
hemma (hem) yw mab du yredy
ha leas ganso ene
dozo a zuk dustuny

209 Nango hanter dyth yn wlas
po moy del yma scryfis
dorgis esa ha lughas
han tewolgow kekyffrys
veyll an tempyll a squardyas
yn tre dew zen dor cozys
ena yn weth y torras
en veyn o creff ha calys

207 *For he was compelled to allow his head to hang. Because his blood had completely left him, he could not live. He wanted to hold his head towards his mother to whom he belonged, and his soul went from him with a shrill scream and a loud cry.*

208 *By the cross of Jesus there was a man called a centurion. When he had seen so many marvels concerning the death of Christ, and how he had unnaturally yielded up his soul with a cry, he said, without mockery, "This is God's son indeed." And many there were with him bore witness to it.*

209 *Now it was midday or past in the land. As it is written, there was an earthquake and lightning and darkness as well. The veil of the temple was rent in two and fell to the ground. Then also the stones that were strong and hard broke up.*

207 Rag porres res o dhodho
Gasa y benn dhe gregi
Rag galsa glan dhiworto
Y woes, bywa ny ylli.
War-tu ha'y vamm a'n piwo
Y benn a vynnas synsi,
Ha'y enev eth anodho Mt 27 v.50
Gans garm yeyn hag ughel gri. Mk 15 v.37
Lk 24 v.46

208 Ryb krows Yesus yth esa Jn 19 v.30
Unn den henwys senturi. Mt 27 v.54
A vernans Krist pan welsa Mk 15 v.39
Keniver tra marthusi Lk 23 v.47
Ha'n enev dell daskorrsa, P.C. 3079-80
Erbynn natur, gans unn kri,
Y leveris, heb skornya,
"Hemm yw Mab Duw, yredi."
Ha lies ganso ena
Dhodho a dhug dustuni.

209 Nans o hanter-dydh y'n wlas Mt 27 v.51
Po moy. Dell yma skrifys, Mk 15 v.38
Dorgrys esa, ha lughes, Lk 23 v.45
Ha'n tewolgow kekeffrys. P.C. 2990;2995
Vayl an tempel a skwardyas
Yntra dew, dhe'n dor koedhys.
Ena ynwedh y torras
An veyn o krev ha kales.

207/4 **ny ylli**. Hooper and Pennaod have emended this to *na ylli* and treated it as a subordinate clause dependent on the previous one. It seems better to treat it as a main clause.

207/5 **War-tu ha**. The somewhat surprising alteration of *wor'tu ha* to *war-tu ha* in G.M. is supported by the MS in this case.

207/8 It is difficult to convey the pathos of this line. I have borrowed Hooper's translation on which I cannot improve.

208/2 **Unn den**. See Language Notes, page 9.

208/4 **Keniver**. Followed by a singular noun; see *G.M.C.* §70(4); *G.M.C.(2)* §72(4).

208/4 **marthusi** is used as an adjective qualifying *tra*. Nance gives it in its K.U. spelling, *marthusy*, as a plural noun, though *G.M.* gives the form *marthusyon* as plural of marthus.

209/2 **dell yma skrifys**. See *G.M.C.* §316 (*del*) *G.M.C.(2)* §332(6 *dell*). *Yma* is used with a past participle when the subject is indefinite, but here 'what is written' seems pretty definite. Cf. 206/4 which has *dell yw skrifys*. Maybe the *yma*, here, is just a line filler.

209/3 **Dorgrys esa**. See Language Notes, page 11 (Long forms of *bos* in nominal sentences).

210 En bezow yn lower le
a pert a ve egerys
han corfow esa ynne
a ve yn ban drehevys
hag eth poran zen cyte
gans luas y fons gwelys
en gwyr ze zustynee
bos mab du neb o lezys

211 Dowr ha ler ha tan ha gwyns
houl ha lour ha steyr kyffris
a gryst ow cozaff mernans
anken y a wozevys
natur scyle me a syns
arluth da mar pyth peynys
ol y sogete kyn fons syns
rag y beyn ze vos grevijs

212 Enaff crist ze yffarn eth
hag a dorras an porzow
dre y nerth bras hay sleyueth
ena golmas dewolow
lucyfer kelmys yv whath
pur fast yn y golmennow
hag ef a dryk heb fynweth
yn yffarn yn tewolgow

210 *The graves in many places were opened wide, and the bodies that were there were raised up and went directly to the city. They were seen by many to bear witness to the truth that he who was slain was the Son of God.*

211 *Water and earth and fire and wind, sun and moon and stars likewise suffered distress from Christ suffering death. Nature causes, I maintain, if a good lord is put to torture, all his subjects, even if they are saints, to be afflicted because of his suffering.*

212 *The soul of Christ went to hell and broke down the doors. By his great strength and skill he bound devils there. Lucifer is still bound very tightly in bonds and he dwells interminably in hell, in darkness.*

210 An bedhow yn lower le — Mt 27 v.52-53
Apert a veu igerys, — P.C. 2999
Ha'n korfow esa ena
A veu yn-bann drehevys,
Hag eth poran dhe'n sita.
Gans lies y fons gwelys
An gwir dhe dhustunia
Bos Mab Duw neb o ledhys.

211 Dowr ha leur ha tan ha gwyns,
Howl ha loer ha ster keffrys,
A Krist ow kodhav mernans,
Anken i a wodhevis.
Natur skila, my a syns,
Arloedh da mar pydh paynys,
Oll y sojets kyn fons sens,
Rag y bayn dhe vos grevys.

212 Enev Krist dhe ifarn eth — 1 Pr 3 v.18-20
Hag a dorras an porthow, — 1 Pr 4 v. 6
Dre y nerth bras ha'y sleynedh, — R.D. 97-124, preceding &
Ev a golmas dewolow. — following stage directions
Lusyfer kelmys yw hwath — Rev. 20 v.2-3
Pur fast yn y golmennow,
Hag ev a dryg heb finwedh
Yn ifarn, yn tewolgow.

210/7 **dhustunia**. The *i* needs to be long to make up the syllable count and to assonance with *ena* and *sita*. It is marked long in Nance but *G.M.C.* §188(6); *G.M.C.(2)* §23(4) and *G.M.* give it as short, with the spelling *dustunya*. G.M. points out the permanent lenition from the Latin *testimonium.* The MS spelling here *zustynee* shows that a secondary lenition has now taken place. The final double *ee* suggests the long *i* of *dhustunia,* as *-ya* is commonly used in the MS spelling for the ending with the short i sound, as in K.K..

211/7 **sogete** (MS). Hooper and Pennaod have *sojta* which they take as plural as required by the context, though Nance gives it as sing. *G.M.* emends this to *sojets*. I have followed this though in previous prints I have suggested *soj'ta* and I still prefer this. One syllable has to be removed to fit the syllable count. The only other occurrence of the word is in *C.W.* where it is used as an adjective and spelt as in English.

211/8 **grevys**. Both Hooper and Pennaod print *grewys*, presumably a misprint.

213 Ena crist a thelyffras
a breson adam hag evef
suel a wressa both y das
man geffo tregva yn nef
pan eth yn mes yn sewyas
en dus vas del vynne ef
an scherewes a dregas
yn yffarn yn tormont creff

214 Vn burges Iosep hynwys
a baramat an cyte
yn mernans crist a gewsys
bytqueth dremas re bee
ol y doul ef o tewlys
ganso yn nef rag trege
Ihesus ganso o keris
ha nyn io hard zy notye

215 Iosep eth bys an Iustis
ze bylat mester treus o
ha pur hardh a wovynnys
corf Ihesus worto yn ro
rag bos Iosep den keris
grontis ef a ve zozo
pylat a woromynnys
meras crist marow mar so

213 *Then Christ freed Adam and Eve from prison, so that all who had done his Father's will would have a dwelling in heaven. When he went out the good people followed him as he wished. The wicked stayed in hell in relentless torment.*

214 *A citizen called Joseph of the City of Arimathaea said, on Christ's death, that he had always been a holy man. He intended by all his planning to dwell with him in heaven. Jesus was loved by him but he was not bold enough to make it known.*

215 *Joseph went to the magistrate, to Pilate, who was a perverse authoritarian, and very boldly asked him for the body of Jesus as a gift. Because Joseph was a favourite it was granted to him. Pilate gave orders to see whether Christ was dead.*

213 Ena Krist a dhelivras R.D. 155-306
A bryson Adam hag Ev,
Seul a wrussa bodh y Das
Ma'n jeffa trigva yn nev.
Pan eth yn-mes y'n sywyas
An dus 'vas, dell vynna ev.
An sherewys a drygas
Yn ifarn yn torment krev.

214 Unn burjes, Yosep henwys Mt 27 v.57-60
A Baramat, an sita, Mk 15 v.43-46
Yn mernans Krist a gewsis Lk 23 v.50-53
Bythkweyth dremas re bia. Jn 19 v.38
Oll y dowl ev o tewlys P.C. 3099-3138
Ganso yn nev rag triga.
Yesus ganso o kerys
Ha nyns o hardh dh'y notya.

215 Yosep eth bys y'n justis,
Dhe Pilat, mester treus o,
Ha pur hardh a wovynnis
Korf Yesus orto yn ro.
Rag bos Yosep den kerys
Grontys ev a veu dhodho.
Pilat a worhemmynnis
Mires Krist marow mars o.

213/2 **evef** (MS). Normally *Eva* in *O.M.* and *C.W.* The strange spelling here appears to be intended to rhyme with *nef*, *ef*, and *creff* but it creates an excess syllable. Maybe it suggests that the final *f* in such words was becoming inaudible. Hooper and Pennaod have *Ef* which I have followed, changing it to the K.K. form.

213/4 **geffo** (MS). The present subjunctive ending used for the imperfect. See Language Notes, page 9.

214/1 **Unn burjes**. *Unn* used as indefinite article. See Language Notes, page 9.

214/2 **A Baramat** follows the *Kernow* reading. Pennaod, following Stokes, reads *a haramat* and gives *A Aramat* in his Unified version. Hooper prints *Ab Aramat*. *P.C.* 3099 has *Josep Baramathya,* and *Josep Baramathia* in the preceding Latin stage directions. As Hooper's version suggests, the *b* probably arose from *ab Arimathaea* ('from Arimathaea') in the Latin gospel.

214/8 **hardh dh'y notya** = 'bold enough to...'. See Language Notes, page 10.

215/7 **worhemmynnis**. Hooper and Pennaod have *worhemmys,* which is a syllable short. The MS *woromynnys*, though a little strange, does have the correct number of syllables, as do the normal K.U. and K.K. spellings.

215/8 **Mires ... mars o**. See *G.M.C.* §328(5); *G.M.C.(2)* §344(6).

216 En ezewon skyntyll keth
resteffo mur vylyny
ze veras worth crist y eth
hag ef yn crous ow cregy
y a welas war y feth
y vos marow yredy
yttaseffsons oll yn weth
dre an golon y delly

217 In aga herwyth y zese
vn marreg longis hynwys
dal o ny wely banna
ef rebea den a brys
gew a ve yn y zewle
gans an ezewon gorris
ha pen lym rag y wane
ze golon Ihesus hynwys

218 Longis sur an barth dyghow
ze grous Ihesus y zese
zen marreg worth y hanow
y a yrhys may whane
yn corf Ihesus caradow
en gew lym ef a bechye
pur ewn yn dan an asow
dre an golon may zese

216 *The crafty caitiff Jews - great shame be upon them - they went to look at Jesus as he was hanging crucified. They saw by his face that he was indeed dead. They even had the presumption, all of them, to pierce him through the heart.*

217 *In their company was a soldier called Longis. He was blind. He could not see at all. He had been a man of rank. A spear with a sharp point was put into his hands by the Jews to pierce the heart of Jesus, the Holy One.*

218 *Longis, indeed was on the right hand of the cross of Jesus. They ordered the soldier by name to pierce the body of beloved Jesus. He thrust the sharp spear exactly beneath the ribs so that it went through the heart.*

216 An Edhewon skentyl keth -
Re's teffo meur vileni! -
Dhe vires orth Krist i eth
Hag ev yn krows ow kregi.
I a welas war y feth
Y vos marow yredi,
Y tesevsons oll ynwedh
Dre an golonn y delli.

217 Y'ga herwydh yth esa Jn 19 v.34-37
Unn marghek, Longys henwys. P.C. 3006-30
Dall o, ny weli banna.
Ev re bia den a bris.
Guw a veu yn y dhiwla
Gans an Edhewon gorrys,
Ha penn lymm rag y wana
Dhe golonn Yesus henwys.

218 Longys, sur, a'n barth deghow
Dhe grows Yesus yth esa.
Dhe'n marghek orth y hanow
I a erghis may hwana
Yn korf Yesus karadow.
An guw lymm ev a bechya
Pur ewn yn-dann an asow
Dre an golonn mayth eth e.

216/1 I am indebted to Hooper for his brilliant translation of this line.

216/4 **yn krows**. See Language Notes, page 10.

216/4 **ow kregi**. Hooper and Pennaod omit the *ow*. It is difficult to see why.

216/5 **war y feth**. Hooper and Pennaod emend to *worth y feth*. Maybe the original writer used *war* to avoid repeating the *worth* in line 3. See 115/3 note on *feth*.

216/7 **Y tesevsons**. None of the meanings for *desevos* in Nance or *G.M.* seems adequate here. Hooper has 'presumed'. Perhaps 'dared' might be better as also in *C.W.* 630 quoted in Gendall's *A Students' Dictionary of Modern Cornish.*

216/8 Notice the parallel mention of the heart of Jesus here and in 217/8 and 218/8.

217/2 **Unn marghek**. *Unn* used as indefinite article. See Language Notes, page 9.

217/2; 218/3 **marghek**. See Spelling Notes, page 12.

217/8 **golonn Yesus henwys**. Hooper translates 'the sacred heart of Jesus' and Pennaod's Breton is similar. Presumably *henwys* is taken as a transferred epithet, anticipating the modern devotion to the Sacred Heart which dates from the eighteenth century. (*Chambers*)

218/8 **mayth eth e**. I have followed Hooper's and Pennaod's emendation.

219 An golon y zeth stret bras
dour ha goys yn kemeskis
ha ryp an gyw a resas
ze zewle neb an gwyskis
y wholhas y zewlagas
gans y eyll leyff o gosys
dre ras an goys y whelas
Ihesus crist del o dyzgtis

220 Eddrek mur an kemeras
rag an ober re wresse
zy ben dowlyn y cozas
arluth gevyans yn meze
dall en ny welyn yn fas
ow bos mar veyll ow pewe
Ihesus zozo a avas
pan welas y edrege

221 Mam Ihesus marya wyn
herd(h)ya an gyw pan welas
yn y mab yn tenewyn
dre an golon may resas
ha zen dor an goys han lyn
an nozo dell deveras
angus bras ha peynys tyn
ha gloys creff askemeres (leg. askemeras)

219 *From the heart there went a great stream of water and blood mixed together which ran along the spear to the hands of him who struck him. He washed his eyes with his one hand that had been made bloody. By virtue of the blood he saw how Jesus Christ had been treated.*

220 *Great remorse overcame him for the deed that he had done. He fell on his knees. "Lord, forgiveness!" he said. "I was blind. I could not see properly that I was living so vilely." Jesus forgave him when he saw his repentance.*

221 *When the mother of Jesus, Blessed Mary, saw the thrusting of the spear into her son, into his side, so that it ran through the heart, and how the blood and the water ran from him to the ground, great anguish, cruel pain and a powerful spasm seized her.*

219 A'n golonn yth eth stredh vras
Dowr ha goes yn kemmyskys
Ha ryb an guw a resas
Dhe dhiwla neb a'n gweskis.
Y hwolghas y dhewlagas
Gans y eyl leuv o goesys.
Dre ras an goes y hwelas
Yesus Krist dell o dyghtys.

220 Edrek meur a'n kemmeras
Rag an ober re wrussa.
Dh'y benn-dewlin y koedhas.
"Arloedh, gevyans!" yn-medh e,
"Dall en, ny welen yn fas
Ow bos mar vil ow pywa."
Yesus dhodho a avas
Pan welas y edrega.

221 Mamm Yesus, Maria Wynn,
Herdhya an guw pan welas
Yn hy mab y'n tenewen,
Dre an golonn may resas
Ha dhe'n dor an goes ha'n lin
Anodho dell dheveras,
Angus bras ha paynys tynn
Ha gloes krev a's kemmeras.

219/6/8 **o goesys**; **o dyghtys**. See Language Notes, page 11.

220/5 **ny welen yn fas**. See Language Notes, pages 9.

221/2/6 **pan welas...dell dheveras** = 'when she saw how it poured'. See Language Notes, page 10.

221/6 **dell dheveras**. The MS, Hooper and Pennaod all miss this mutation.

222 Ffest yn tyn hy a wole
ze wherzyn nysteva whans
hay dagrow a zevera
hay dew lagas pur zewhans
hay holon whek a ranne
me a leuer rag trystans
rag an grayth yn hy ese
nas gweze an spyrys sans

223 Dre y holon y zeth seth
y mab syndis pan welse
moreth an seth ha pytet
natureth a ha denseth
ha pen arall o pytet
tackis fast gans kerense
ny wozevys den bythqueth
kymmys peynys ow pewe

224 An seth yw rag leueris
as gwyskis tyn gans mur angus
war hy holon may crunys
dre nerth an bum fynten woys
ha hy a wolas kymmys
gans mar ver nerth ha galloys
an fynten may trehevys
ran yn ban du droka loys

222 *She wept very bitterly. She had no desire to laugh and the tears flowed from her eyes very freely. Her sweet heart would have broken for sadness, I say, if the Holy Spirit had not protected her because of the grace that was in her.*

223 *An arrow went though her heart when she had seen her son destroyed. Grief, compassion, natural and human feeling was the arrow, and the other end, compassion secured fast with love. No man has ever suffered so much pain in his lifetime.*

224 *The arrow which had been foretold struck her cruelly with great anguish, so that by the force of the blow a well of blood gathered upon her heart, and she wept so much with such great strength and force that a part of the well rose up - God! What a wicked pang!*

222 Fest yn tynn hi a oela;
Dhe hwerthin ny's teva hwans.
Ha'y dagrow a dhevera
A'y dewlagas pur dhehwans,
Ha'y holonn hweg a ranna,
My a lever, rag tristans
Rag an gras ynni esa
Na's gwittha an Spyrys Sans.

223 Dre hy holonn yth eth seth Lk 2 v.35
Hy mab shyndys pan welsa.
Moreth an seth ha pyteth,
Natureth o ha densa,
Ha'n penn arall o pyteth
Tekkys fast gans kerensa.
Ny wodhevis den bythkweyth
Kemmys paynys ow pywa!

224 An seth yw ragleverys Lk 2 v.35
A's gwiskas tynn gans meur angus
War hy holonn may kreunis
Dre nerth an boemm, fenten woes.
Ha hi a oelas kemmys
Gans mar veur nerth ha galloes
An fenten may trehevis
Rann yn-bann - Duw, drog a loes!

222/5 **a ranna**. Imperfect subjunctive used for conditional. See *G.M.C.* §328(3) note. This note is omitted from *G.M.C.(2)*.

222/6 **tristans**. "Used for the rhyme: elsewhere always *trystyns.*" (Hooper). *G.M.* says *tristyns* is apparently a variant of *tristans.*

223/2/6 The metaphor seems to take the arrow-head as being 'grief, compassion, natural and human feeling,' and the tail 'compassion secured fast with love,' bearing in mind that it is the tail that keeps the arrow straight. Maybe it is inspired by the 'clothing' metaphors in the Epistles, e.g. Colossians 3 v.12 & 14: *Ytho, yn tus dewisys gans Duw, sans ha meurgerys, gwiskewgh tregeredh, kuvder, uvelder, klorder, godhevyans ... ha dres oll an dillas ma, gwiskewgh kerensa, yw kolmenn a gowlwra pub tra.* (*R.E.*) The *A.V.* does not bring out the metaphor clearly.

223/4 **densa**. I have followed Hooper and Pennaod in emending fom *denseth* for the sake of the rhyme though the dictionaries do not recognise this spelling in this sense.

224/1 **yw ragleverys**. Cf. Lk 2 v.35, 'Yea, a sword shall pierce through thy soul also.' (*A.V.*) It must mean more than just 'already mentioned' as in Stokes and Hooper.

224/2 **tynn**. Omitted by Hooper and Pennaod, presumably because it is an excess syllable.

224/8 **droka loys** (MS). The MS spelling suggests the *g* of *drog* is unvoiced. Perhaps it should be spelt *drok a loes* in the K.K. version. In Cornish Studies 7 and 9, 1978/ 9 Oliver Padel quotes five cases including this one of *drog* and *teg* followed by *a* in similar constructions, ending in g in only one case in the MS spelling, but he says g is the correct sound. He says the MSS show the *drog/teg* and *a* as separate words, though three of them are shown as one word in the printed editions I have.

225 An goysna dagrennow try
dre y ij lagas y zeth
ny go comfort na yly
a wrello y holon hueth
hay veynys mar drewesy
askemar ha kymmys cueth
yn oll an bys ny ylly
den cafos kymmys anfueth

226 I feynys o bras ha creff
yn ioy zezy trylys yw
rag mygternes yw yn nef
ze vos gorzijs hy yv gyw
Eleth ze rygthy a seff
leas myll y both a syw
hay mab as gorth del vyn ef
tecke ys houl yv y lyw

227 In corff Ihesus y zese
hag ef yn crows ow cregy
pymp myll strekis del iove
ha pedergwyth cans goly
ha tryvgons moy ganse
ha pymzek pur wyr ens y
hag ol rag pur gerense
worth mab den ys gozevy

225 *Of that blood three tears went through her eyes. It was not a comfort or a salve to make her heart glad and her ills beset her woefully with so much sorrow that in all the world so much wretchedness could not be found.*

226 *Her pains which were great and intense are turned to joy for her for she is Queen in Heaven. She is worthy to be adored. Angels stand before her. Many thousands follow her will and her Son honours her as he wishes. Fairer than the sun is her brightness.*

227 *In the body of Jesus, as he was hanging crucified, I hear there were five thousand weals and four times a hundred wounds and with them seventy-five more. They were absolutely authentic and he suffered them all for pure love towards mankind.*

225 A'n goes na dagrennow tri
Dre hy dewlagas yth eth.
Nyns o konfort nag eli
A wrella hy holonn heudh,
Ha'y faynys mar druesi
A's kemmer ha kemmys keudh,
Yn oll an bys na ylli
Den kavoes kemmys anfeudh.

226 Hy faynys o bras ha krev
Yn joy dhedhi treylys yw,
Rag Myghternes yw yn Nev.
Dhe vos gordhys hi yw gwiw.
Eledh dherygdhi a sev,
Lies mil hy bodh a syw,
Ha'y mab a's gordh dell vynn ev.
Tekka es howl yw hy liw.

227 Yn korf Yesus yth esa
Hag ev yn krows ow kregi
Pymp mil strekys dell j'oue
Ha pedergweyth kans goli,
Ha triugens moy gansa
Ha pymthek. Pur wir ens i
Hag oll rag pur gerensa
Orth mab-den y's godhevi.

225/1 **dagrennow tri**. See *G.M.C.* §105(4), *G.M.C.(2)* §105(4).

225/3 **Nyns o konfort**. Hooper has 'there was no comfort', but this assumes the long form of *bos*.

225/4 **a wrello** (MS). Present subjunctive used for the imperfect. See Language Notes, page 9.

225/8 **anfeudh**. "alternative form of *anfus* like *feth* and *fas* in *Ordinalia* and 115/3." (Hooper). It is retained for the rhymes though *G.M.* recognises only *anfeus*.

226/5 **dherygdhi**. For *a-dherygdhi*.

227/2 **yn krows**. See Language Notes, page 10.

227/3 **j'oue**. Hooper says "French *j'ai ouï* " (= 'I have heard') but it seems more likely to be the present tense. The Old French verb *ouïr:* 'to hear' became *oyer* in legal Anglo-Norman of the fourteenth century (Pope), which could give *jou-e*, pronounced as two syllables, as 1st sing. present tense = 'I hear'. This gives the correct syllable count and the final unstressed and neutral *e* fits the rhyme scheme.

227/6 I have introduced a full stop after *pymthek*. Hooper takes the following *pur wir* as adverbial and the whole verse as one long sentence.

228 Pub tezoll neb a vynne
leuerel pymzek pater
a leun golon rag gorzye
pascon agan arluth ker
yn blyzen y a vye
ha bederow keneuer
hag a owleow ese
yn gorf Ihesus worth neuer

229 En ezewon ny vynne
bos an laddron ow cregy
ternos rag pasch o zeze
dyth vghel y a sensy
an ezewon yn treze
a rug may wrellons terry
aga morzosow whare
hag a lena aga dry

230 Erbyn bonas henna guris
nanso prys gwespar yn wlas
yn erna yn weth kemeas
ze Iosep y a rontyas
hag an grous del o prys
corf Ihesus a gemeras
tyr marya me a gris
pur ylwys an gweresas

228 *Anyone who would say fifteen Our Fathers every day with a full heart to glorify our dear Lord's Passion - in a year these would be as many Our Fathers in number as there were wounds in the body of Jesus.*

229 *The Jews did not want the thieves to be hanging overnight because it was their Passover. They celebrated it as a high day. The Jews among them arranged that they should break their thighs at once and carry them away from there.*

230 *By the time this was done it was already evening in the land. At that time also they gave permission to Joseph and, as it was time, he took the body of Jesus from the cross. Three Marys, I believe, helped him when he called.*

228 Pub dydh oll neb a vynne
Leverel pymthek Pader
A leun golonn rag gordhya
Passhyon agan Arloedh ker,
Yn blydhen i a via
A bederow keniver
Hag a woliow esa
Yn korf Yesus orth niver.

229 An Edhewon ny vynna Mk 15 v.42-47
Bos an ladron ow kregi Lk 23 v.50-56
Ternos, rag Pask o dhedha. Jn 19 v.38-42
Dydh ughel i a'n synsi. P.C. 3099-3210
An Edhewon yntredha
A wrug may hwrellens terri
Aga mordhosow hware
Hag alena aga dri.

230 Erbynn bones henna gwrys
Nans o prys gwesper y'n wlas,
Y'n eur na ynwedh kummyas
Dhe Yosep i a wrontyas
Hag a'n krowsprenn, dell o prys,
Korf Yesus a gemmeras.
Teyr Maria, my a grys
P'eur helwis, a'n gweresas.

228/6 **A bederow**. I have followed Hooper and Pennaod in reading the *Ha* of the MS as *A* followed by soft mutation.

228/7 **a woliow**. The metathesis *owleow* in the MS looks like a scribal error. Hooper and Pennaod print *olyow* but I cannot find any justification for this form.

229/6 **A wrug** followed by *may* and the subjunctive; see *G.M.C.* §141(6); *G.M.C.(2)* §141(7). The subjunctive has the form of the present in the MS though the imperfect is needed here. See Language Notes, page 9.

229/7 **hware**. *G.M.* points out that *hware* frequently rhymes with words like *tressa*.

230/5 **krowsprenn** follows Hooper's and Pennaod's emendation to make up the syllable count.

230/8 **P'eur**. One would expect *pan* as this is not a question, direct or indirect.

230 has the rhyme scheme; a b b b a b a b instead of the usual repetition of the a b pattern.

231 Mam Ihesus Cryst amme
corf y mab pur drewesy
hay daggrow a zevere
a nozo pan predery
han anken mur asgrevye
pan vyre worth y woly
yn tenewen y zese
dre an golon astylly

232 Iosep ze gryst a vynnas
y arrow hay zeffregh whek
yn vaner del yn whas
hag as ystynnas pur dek
a dro zy gorff y trylyas
sendall rych yn luas pleg
ha marya leun a ras
ganso trest ha morezek

233 Ena vn lowarth ese
ha ynno nyn io parys
den marow rag receve
newyth parrys nyn io vsijs
corff Ihesus crist yn treze
zen logell a ve degys
hag a heys ze wroweze
ynno ef a ve gesys

231 *The mother of Jesus Christ kissed her Son's body very sadly and her tears ran when she thought of him, and the great grief that oppressed her when she looked at his wound (it was in the side) pierced her through her heart.*

232 *Joseph straightened Christ's legs and his sweet arms as was customary and extended them very becomingly. Round his body he wound rich linen in many folds, while Mary, full of grace, was with him, sad and sorrowful.*

233 *There was a garden there and in it a grave had been prepared to receive a dead man. Newly prepared, it had not been used. The body of Jesus Christ was carried between them to the sepulchre and was left in it to lie outstretched.*

231 Mamm Yesus Krist a amma
Korf hy mab pur druesi
Ha'y dagrow a dhevera
Anodho pan brederi
Ha'n anken meur a's grevya
Pan vira orth y woli
(Y'n tenewen yth esa)
Dre an golonn a's telli.

232 Yosep dhe Krist a ewnas Mt 27 v.59
Y arrow ha'y dhiwvregh hweg
Y'n vaner dell o yn hwas
Hag a's ystynnas pur deg.
A-dro dh'y gorf y treylyas
Sendal rych yn lies pleg,
Ha Maria leun a ras,
Ganso trist ha morethek.

233 Ena unn lowarth esa Mt 27 v.60
Hag ynno bedh o parys
Den marow rag resseva.
Nowydh parys, nyns o usys.
Korf Yesus Krist yntredha
Dhe'n logel a veu degys
Hag a-hys dhe wrowedha
Ynno ev a veu gesys.

231/1 **amma** is usually followed by *dhe;* cf. 65/6.
(Verses 232 and 233 are discussed at some length by J.C. Zeuss in his *Grammatica Celtica* as an example of *poetica britannica.* His version differs from the MS I am using and, according to Stokes. comes from the Davies Gilbert edition of 1826.)

232/1 **a vynnas** (MS). Zeuss, Hooper and Pennaod all take this as *a ewnas* but Stokes translates as "whitened".

232/2 **Y arrow.** *G.M.C. (1)* §41 and *G.M.C. (2)* §45 point out that the dual is more usual than the plural for parts of the body.

232/3 **del yn whas** (MS). Hooper and Pennaod read *ef del vewas.* Zeuss says that *whas* means 'custom' according to an old English translation (Keigwin's?) but is otherwise unknown, and compares the word with Breton *boas* with this meaning. He also inserts *ve* after *del* to make up the syllable count. I have replaced this with *o* which seems more appropriate, and followed Zeuss.

232/4 **ystynnas pur deg**. Curiously Zeuss' Latin translation is *detersit pure* ('washed cleanly'). It is hard to see how he gets this but it makes more sense of the *pur deg.*

233/1 **unn lowarth**. *Unn* used as an indefinite article. See Language Notes, page 9.

233/2 **nyn io parys** (MS). I have followed Zeuss, Hooper and Pennaod in emending this to *bedh o parys*, although Zeuss points out that two English versions have 'now' and 'not'.

233/4 **Nowydh parys**. Hooper and Pennaod read this as *Noweth o,* presumably to avoid the excess syllable. Zeuss follows the MS.

233/4 **nyns o usys**. See Language Notes, page 11.

233/5 **yntredha**. Cf. 176/3.

233/7 Curiously again, Zeuss corrects this line to *Hag a heys the c̲rowethe*, wrongly comparing it with 25/5, *ow crowethe,* and saying the metre is faulty. He seems to be under the impression that the initial *w* resulting from mutation counts as a syllable.

234 Vn den da c(ri)st a gara
Nycodemus y hanow
eff nyn io hardh zy notya
rag own cafos y ankow
dworennos yn pur brena
ef eth zen corff o marow
gans vnnient zozo esa
ha spycis a vur rasow

235 Nycodemus a vras
corff Ihesus hay esely
oynment o a gymmys ras
may weze corf heb pedry
nagonon ef ny asas
heb vre ay esely
yn delma ef an dyzgtyas
mey eyn sur o y wely

236 Ha spycis leas ehen
ef a worras yn y veth
ze gryst a bub tenewen
hag a zyghow hag a gleth
worth y dreys ha worth y ben
ha war ol y gorf yn weth
dysquezyens war lyrgh anken
beze mygtern yn deweth

234 *A certain good man, Nicodemus by name, loved Christ. He was not bold enough to make it known for fear of being slain. At night, simply in expiation, he went to the dead body with ointment which he had, and spices of great virtue.*

235 *Nicodemus anointed the body of Jesus and his limbs. The ointment was of such great virtue that it preserved a body from putrefaction. He did not leave any one of his limbs without anointing it. In this way he prepared him. Cold stones indeed were his bed.*

236 *And he put spices of many kinds in his grave on each side of Christ, both right and left, on his feet and on his head and all over his body also, a demonstration after pain that he would be King at last.*

234 Unn den da Krist a gara Jn 19 v.39
Nykodemus y hanow.
Ev nyns o hardh dh'y notya
Rag own kavoes y ankow
D'wor'an nos, yn pur brena
Ev eth dhe'n korf o marow
Gans unyent dhodho esa
Ha spisys a veur rasow.

235 Nykodemus a uras
Korf Yesus ha'y eseli.
Oynment o a gemmys ras
May hwitha korf heb pedri.
Nagonan ev ny asas
Heb ura a'y eseli.
Yndellma ev a'n dyghtyas.
Meyn yeyn sur o y weli.

236 Ha spisys lies eghenn
Ev a worras yn y vedh
Dhe Krist a bub tenewen
Hag a dheghow hag a gledh,
Orth y dreys hag orth y benn
Ha war oll y gorf ynwedh.
Diskwedhyans, war-lergh anken,
Bedha myghtern yn diwedh.

234/3 **Ev nyns o hardh**. = 'He was not bold enough.' See Language Notes, page 10.

234/4 **own kavoes y ankow** = 'fear of being killed.' See 174/8 note.

236/8 **Bedha myghtern**. The habitual imperfect of *bos* showing the future in the past, i.e. what was going to happen. *Y fedha* would be normal but this would create an excess syllable.

237 Han ezewon a worras
a vgh Ihesus crist vn men
leden o ha poys ha bras
moy agis gauel tredden
ganso drys nos y zolyas
yn y seruys neb o len
an nosna a dremenas
hag oll y drok hay anken

238 Ternoys y sordyas bresel
gans an ezewon goky
lauarow tyn hag vghel
fest yn foll y a gewsy
may zens y parys zen well
ny wozyens y zystrowy
rag Ihesus ze leuerell
yn tressa dyth y sevy

239 In vn stevya oll y eth
bys yn pylat o Iustis
vn ezow zozo yn freth
yn delma a leuerys
ny a yll yn nos haneth
fest dystough bonas kellys
ha may fo dynny ze weth
rag bonas Ihesus lezys

237 *And the Jews placed a stone over Jesus. It was broad and heavy and big - bigger than could be held by three men. One who was faithful in his service kept watch with him through the night. That night passed by with all its evil and wretchedness.*

238 *The next day strife arose among the foolish Jews. They spoke sharply and loudly and very foolishly so that they were prepared for what they would see. They could not destroy him because Jesus had said he would rise on the third day.*

239 *They all rushed to Pilate who was a magistrate. One Jew spoke to him eagerly like this: "Tonight we may be lost, here and now, and the death of Jesus may be the worse for us.*

237 Ha'n Edhewon a worras Mt 27 v.60
A-ugh Yesus Krist unn men. Mk 15 v.46
Ledan o ha poes ha bras, Mt 27 v.62
Moy ages gavel tredden.
Ganso dres nos y hwoelyas
Yn y servis neb o len.
An nos na a dremenas
Hag oll hy drog ha'y anken.

238 Ternos y sordyas bresel
Gans an Edhewon wokki.
Lavarow tynn hag ughel
Fest yn fol i a gewsi
Mayth ens i parys dhe'n wel.
Ny wodhyens y dhistrui
Rag Yesus dhe leverel
Y'n tressa dydh y sevi.

239 Yn unn stevya oll i eth
Bys yn Pilat o justis.
Unn Edhow dhodho yn freth
Yndellma a leveris:
"Ni a yll y'n nos haneth,
Fest distowgh bones kellys
Ha may fo dhyn ni dhe weth
Rag bones Yesus ledhys.

237/4 **gavel**. Does this mean more than they could hold (pick up, carry) or more than they could encircle with arms outstretched and hands joined?

237/4 **tredden**. "Perhaps the words used for singers of 'three men's songs.' (*Old Cornwall*, April 1929, R.M.N.)" (Hooper) It is in Nance but not *G.M.*

237/8 "**hy** refers to Mary Magdalene: John XX. 1 (R.M.N.)" (Hooper) I see no reason for assuming this and have taken the *hy* as referring to *nos* which is a feminine noun.

238/5 Hooper and Pennaod read: *Ma's yth ens parys dhe well*, and Hooper translates: 'that unless they were better prepared.' He also gives a note: "or, *Mar nyns ens*: 'if they were not'". My reading depends on *gwel* being feminine. Nance gives it as m. or f. but *G.M.* as m. I take it to mean that, after discussion, the Jews realise more fully what the disappearance of the body of Jesus might entail. Wella Brown suggests: *Mayth ens i parys dhe well,* = 'so that they would be better prepared.'

238/8 **y sevi**. A good example of the imperfect showing the future in the past.

239/1 **Yn unn stevya**. See *G.M.C.* §228(2). *G.M.C.(2)* §243(5)

240 Rag an traytor a gewsys
ha ze rag leas huny
war lyrgh y vonas lezys
zen tressa dyth y seuy
mars mara peza degis
gans y dus nan caffan ny
yn vrna byth leuerys
ef ze sevell dre vestry

241 Pylat a yrghys zeze
war beyn kylly an bewnans
monas zen corf zy weze
nan kemerre y yskerans
hag yn nos oll aspye
ha gwyze tam na guskens
y eth yn vn fystene
peswar marrek yrvys ens

242 Pan dezens y bys yn beth
y zeth vn marrek zy ben
hag arall zy dreys yn weth
yrvys fast bys yn zewen
hag a zyghow hag a gleth
onon a bub tenewen
bost a wrens tyn ha deveth
yn gwezens worth y ehen

240 *"For the traitor said before many that he would rise the third day after being slain. But if he is carried off by his people so that we do not find him then it will be said that he has risen through supernatural power."*

241 *Pilate commanded them, on pain of losing their lives, to go to the body and guard it so that enemies would not take it, and to keep watch all night and take care they did not sleep a moment. They went in haste. They were four armed soldiers.*

242 *When they reached the grave, one soldier went to his head and another to his feet as well, armed right up to the teeth, and on the right and left, one on each side. They made a direct and shameless boast that they would guard him in spite of anything he could do.*

240 “Rag an traytour a gewsis Mt 27 v.63
A-dherag lies huni,
War-lergh y vones ledhys
Dhe’n tressa dydh y sevi.
Mes mara pydh ev degys
Gans y dus, na’n kyffyn ni,
Y’n eur na bydh leverys
Ev dhe sevel dre vaystri.”

241 Pilat a erghis dhedha Mt 27 v.64-65
War bayn kelli an bywnans R.D. 334-422
Mones dhe’n korf dh’y witha
Na’n kemmerra eskerens
Hag y’n nos oll aspia
Ha gwitha tamm na goskens.
I eth yn unn fistena.
Peswar marghek ervys ens.

242 Pan dheudhons i bys y’n bedh Mt 27 v.66
Yth eth unn marghek dh’y benn
Hag arall dh’y dreys ynwedh,
Ervys fest bys y’n dhiwen.
Hag a dheghow hag a gledh,
Onan a bub tenewen.
Bost a wrens, tynn ha diveth,
Y’n gwithens orth y eghenn!

240/2 **A-dherag**. Hooper and Pennaod print *Ha dherag*.

240/4 **y sevi**. Future in the past; cf. 238/8.

242/8 **Yn gwithens**. ditto.

240/6 **caffan ny** (MS). Imperfect subjunctive for present. See Language Notes, page 9.

241/4 **eskerens**. The *y* which precedes this word in the MS creates an excess syllable and is confusing. What would ‘his enemies’ mean? Whose enemies? I am therefore assuming it is a scribal error and omitting it. Hooper and Pennaod keep it but elide the first vowel of *eskerens* to avoid the excess syllable. This does not explain to whom ‘his’ refers.

241/7 **yn unn fistena**. See *G.M.C.* §228(2). *G.M.C.(2)* §243(5).

241/8; 242/2 **marghek**. See Spelling Notes, page 12.

242/4 **y’n dhiwen**. I feel my translation is an appropriate idiom. Hooper has, more literally, ‘armed right up to the jaws.’

242/8 **orth y eghenn**. See *G.M.C.* §153(5); *G.M.C.(2)* §152/6 A useful phrase!

243 En varogyon a guskas
myttyn han gyth ow tarze
ha Ihesus a zezoras
hag eth yn le may fynne
den a pert ha mur y ras
golow cleyr ow tewynnye
ef e wre oll y vynnas
y ny yllens y weze

244 Pan o pur holergh an gyth
y tefenas vn marrek
del deth an nef war y fyth
ef a welas golow tek
han meyn vmhelys yn weth
ese a vgh Ihesus whek
ha warnozo a yseth
ell benegas lowenek

245 En marrek na a sevys
oll yn ban y goweze
ha zeze a leuerys
a Ihesus fatell vye
an denma re drehevys
gallas ny wozan pele
lemman na veny lezys
nyn ges forth ze omweze

243 *The soldiers slept in the morning as day was breaking and Jesus rose again and moved wherever he wanted, manifestly a man with great grace and with a bright light shining. He did everything he wanted and they could not prevent him.*

244 *When it was very late, one soldier awoke as the daylight came from heaven upon his face. He saw a beautiful light and the stone that was over sweet Jesus overturned also, and sitting upon it a blessed, joyful angel.*

245 *That soldier got his comrades up completely and told them what had happened about Jesus: "This man has risen. He has gone we know not where. Now there is no way to protect ourselves from being killed."*

243 An varghogyon a goskas
Myttin, ha'n jydh ow tardha,
Ha Yesus a dhassorghas
Hag eth y'n le may fynna. R.D. Stage direction
Den apert ha meur y ras following 423
Golow kler ow tewynnya.
Ev a wre oll y vynnas.
I ny yllens y witha.

244 Pan o pur helergh an jydh R.D. 511-678
Y tifunas unn marghek
Dell dheuth a'n nev war y feth.
Ev a welas golow teg
Ha'n men omhwelys ynwedh
Esa a-ugh Yesus hweg,
Ha warnodho, a'y esedh,
El bennigys lowenek. Mt 28 v.2-3

245 An marghek na a sevis
Oll yn-bann y gowetha
Ha dhedha a leveris
A Yesus fatell via:
"An den ma re dhrehevis.
Gallas ny wodhon pyla.
Lemmyn na ven ledhys
Nyns eus fordh dhe omwitha."

243/1 **varghogyon**. See Spelling Notes, page 12.

244/2; 245/1 **marghek**. ditto.

243/5 **Den apert**. Hooper and Pennaod read *Dew apert*, but it is the humanity, not the divinity, of Jesus that is emphasised here. *R.D.* follows with a long speech from Mary emphasising her human love and grief for her son.

244/1 **helergh**. In their translations, Hooper and Pennaod avoid saying it was late, although Mt 28 v.1-4 indicates the soldiers were still there when the women arrived and this also occurs in the *York Resurrection* (Cawley).

244/3 **feth**. Cf. 115/3 note.

245/6 **Gallas**. Perfect of *mos*. See *G.M.C.* §203; *G.M.C.(2)* §205.

246 Marrak arall a gowsas
gony vyth pan veyn genys
tru a thu elhas elhas
gans vn huyn re ben tullys
an bewnans ny re gollas
hag yn weth agan fleghys
om zyghtyn trussen anwlas
fyan na veny kefys

247 An peswore a gewsys
na whelyn gwevye an pow
kepar del ve zen Iustis
dun leueryn war anow
ay veth del yw drehevys
na leueryn vn ger gow
y a ruge a zesympys
oll war lyrgh y arhadow

248 I eth yn vn fystene
ze pylat aga Iustis
en deskyens del vye
ha zozo a leuerys
re safse crist heb strevye
ol zy voth gans golowys
ha na yllens y gwyze
y voth na vo colenwys

246 *Another soldier spoke: "Woe to us that we were ever born. Alas, O God, alas, alas! A sleep has caught us out. We have lost our lives and our children also. Let us get ready. Let us cross over away from the land. Let us escape so we are not caught."*

247 *The fourth spoke: "Let us not try to escape from the country. Let us go to the magistrate. Let us tell plainly as it was how he rose from his grave. Let us not tell one word of a lie." They did at once entirely according to his bidding.*

248 *They hastened to Pilate their magistrate. They would advise him what had happened. And they told him Christ had risen without great effort entirely at his pleasure with radiance, and they could not prevent him doing exactly as he wished.*

246 Marghek arall a gowsas,
"Go-ni vydh pan ven genys!
Tru, a Dhuw, ellas, ellas.
Gans unn hun re ben toellys.
An bywnans ni re gollas
Hag ynwedh agan fleghes.
Omdhyghtyen, treussyn a'n wlas.
Fien na vyn ni kevys."

247 An peswara a gewsis,
"Na hwilen gwevya an pow.
Kepar dell veu, dhe'n justis
Deun, leveryn war anow
A'y vedh dell yw drehevys.
Na leveryn unn ger gow."
I a wrug a-dhesempis
Oll war-lergh y arghadow.

248 I eth yn unn fistena
Dhe Pilat aga justis.
Y'n dyskens dell via.
Ha dhodho a leveris
Re savsa Krist heb strivya
Oll dh'y vodh, gans golowys,
Ha na yllens i gwitha
Y vodh na ve kollenwys.

246/1 **Marghek**. See Spelling Notes, page 12.

246/1 **gowsas**. Cf. 247/1 ending in *gewsis*. These two verbs have the same meaning and give the two verses parallel first lines, but fit in with *-as* and *-is* rhymes respectively in their verses.

246/2 **Go-ni**. I have followed Hooper and the *Kernow* MS. Pennaod follows his own reading *govy*.

246/4 **unn hun**. *unn* used as an indefinite article. See Language Notes, page 9.

246/7 **treussyn**. Hooper takes this as from *troessa* = "to pack" (truss). However Stokes takes it as treusi = to cross and I have followed this as it makes better sense. I am indebted to Keith Syed for drawing this to my attention.

247/4 **war anow**. Cf. 170/5.

248/1 **yn unn fistena**. See *G.M.C.* §228(2); *G.M.C.(2)* §243(5).

248/3 **Y'n dyskens**. Hooper and Pennaod read *Y'n dustunsons* = 'They testified to it.' It seems more likely to be the imperfect of *dyski*, probably showing the future in the past, although *dyski* is normally followed by *dhe* rather than a direct object.

248/8 **na vo colenwys** (MS). The present subjunctive used for the imperfect. See Language Notes, page 9.

249 Ena pylat pan glewas
yn delma y ze gewsell
prederow an kemeras
rak own y ze leuerell
ha zy notye drys an wlas
sur a ogas hag a bell
may teffe tus gans nerth bras
erbyn rag gustle bell

250 Rag henna pylat a ros
zen vorogyon aga ro
may lavarsans hadolos
yn pub tyller dris an vro
ze vos tus yrvys yn nos
warneze kymmys a dro
na gens y hardh ze wortos
lemmen oll monas zen fo

251 En varogyon pan glewas
pylat ov cows yn della
mur a ioy askemeras
y ze zeank yn della
an peynys o creff ha bras
ha cafos rohow ma za
both pylat y a notyas
yn le may zens rak henna

249 *Then when Pilate heard that they were talking like this, he became worried for fear that they would tell it and make it known throughout the land for certain, close at hand and far away, so that men would come in great force to wage a war of rebellion against him.*

250 *Because of that Pilate gave the soldiers their gift so that they said and falsely publicised everywhere throughout the land, that in the night so many armed men came upon them and surrounded them that they were not bold enough to stay, but all took flight.*

251 *When the soldiers heard Pilate talking like this they were delighted that they would escape in such a way from the pains that were great and intense and get such good gifts. So they made Pilate's wish known wherever they went.*

249 Ena Pilat pan glywas R.D. 669-78
Yndellma i dhe gewsel,
Prederow a'n kemmeras
Rag own i dhe leverel
Ha dh'y notya dres an wlas,
Sur, a-ogas hag a-bell
May teffa tus gans nerth bras
Er y bynn rag gustla bell.

250 Rakhenna Pilat a ros
Dhe'n varghogyon aga ro
May lavarsons, ha dolos
Yn pub tyller dres an vro,
Dhe vos tus ervys y'n nos
Warnedha, kemmys a-dro,
Nag ens i hardh dhe wortos
Lemmyn oll mones dhe'n fo.

251 An varghogyon pan glywas
Pilat ow kows yndella,
Meur a joy a's kemmeras
I dhe dhiank yndella
A'n paynys o krev ha bras,
Ha kavoes rohow mar dha.
Bodh Pilat i a notyas
Yn le mayth ens rakhenna.

250/2; 251/1 **varghogyon**. See Spelling Notes, page 12.

250/3 **lavarsans** (MS) Read as *lavarrens* (imperf. subj.) by Stokes, Hooper and Pennaod to form a purpose clause rather than a result cluse.

250/3 **dolos**. Hooper says "Mordon suggested 'to give out falsely' as Latin *dolose*". On this basis, presumably, it is included as such in GM and Nance's dictionary. I wonder, however, whether it is not just a form of *dyllo* = "to publish" which is how Stokes translates it.

250/7 **hardh dhe**. See Language Notes, page 10.

250/8 **Lemmyn**. See Spelling Notes, page 13.

251/5 **krev ha bras**. Cf. 226/1. In each case the *paynys krev ha bras* are contrasted with sharp relief from them in the following line, though in the case of Mary the suffering actually occurred but was only feared in the case of the soldiers.

252 In keth gythna pur avar
han houll nowyth drehevys
tyr marea cleyr ha whar
a zeth zen beth leuerys
ha ganse oynment heb par
rag corf Ihesus o prennys
whath yn erna nyn gens war
bonas mab du drehevys

253 Pan o an tyr marya
ogas zen beth deuethys
an meyn esa a warza
y an guelas drehevys
en benenas yn delma
yn treze a leuerys
ze worth an beth an meynma
zynny pu an ommelys

254 En benenas leun a ras
gans an beth fast powessens
worth an pen y a welas
zen beth yw leueris kens
vn flough yonk gwyn y zyllas
eyll o ha y ny wozyens
scruth own mur askemeras
rag an marthus re welsens

252 *On that same day, very early, when the sun was newly risen, three Marys, pure and humble, came to the said grave, bringing ointment without equal which had been bought for the body of Jesus. At that time they were still not aware that the Son of God had risen.*

253 *When the three Marys had come close to the grave, they saw the stone that was on top raised up. So the women said to each other, "Who has overturned the stone for us from the grave?"*

254 *The women, full of grace, had paused close by the grave. At the head of the grave, which has been mentioned before, they saw a young person in white clothing. It was an angel and they did not know. A shudder of great fear seized them because of the wonder they had seen.*

252 Y'n keth jydh na, pur a-varr Mt 28 v. 1-5
Ha'n howl nowydh drehevys, Mk 16 v. 1-5
Teyr Maria, kler ha hwar, Lk 24 v.1-4
A dheuth dhe'n bedh leverys, Jn 20 v.1
Ha gansa oynment heb par R.D. 679-780
Rag korf Yesus o prenys.
Hwath y'n eur na nyns ens war
Bones Mab Duw drehevys.

253 Pan o an teyr Maria
Ogas dhe'n bedh devedhys,
An men esa a-wartha
I a'n gwelas drehevys.
An benynes yndellma
Yntredha a leveris,
"Dhiworth an bedh an men ma
Dhyn ni piw a'n omhwelis?"

254 An benynes leun a ras
Gans an bedh fast powessens.
Orth an penn i a welas
Dhe'n bedh yw leverys kyns
Unn flogh yo'nk gwynn y dhillas.
El o hag i ny wodhyens.
Skruth own meur a's kemmeras
Rag an marthus re welsens.

252/3 **cleyr** (MS). Hooper reads as *clor* and translates the phrase 'meek and mild'. I have followed Pennaod who reads *cler* though his Breton translation *sklaer* ('bright') does not seem appropriate.

252/4; 254/4 **leverys**. How could the writer so belittle a noble theme with such trite line fillers!

254/2 **powessens**. Presumably a pluperfect. Hooper reads as a simple past tense.

254/5 **Unn flogh**. See Language Notes, page 9.

254/6 **i ny wodhyens**. Cf. 152/6.

255 En eyll a gewsys zeze
na vezough dyscomfortis
Ihesus crist a nazary
del welsough a ve lethys
sevys gallas ze gen le
den a pert ha mur y breys
a wotta an le may zese
vmma nyn gew ef tregis

256 Eugh yn fen zy zyschyblon
ha leuerough wy zeze
ha ze pedyr dos yn scon
erbyn ze alyle
ena crist an kuf colon
wy an kyff yn lowene
del leuerys y honon
yn kyg yn goys ow pewe

257 Gans henna y a drylyas
confortis ha lowenek
hag eth tus crist rag whelas
hag as cafos morezek
y lauarsons ol an cas
y zezons yn vn tonek
bys yn galyle zy whelas
ha ze gows worth Ihesus wek

255 *The angel spoke to them: "Do not be discouraged. Jesus Christ of Nazareth who was slain as you saw has risen and gone to another place, clearly a man of great worth. Behold the place where he was. He does not remain here.*

256 *"Go immediately to his disciples and tell them and Peter to come quickly to meet him in Galilee. There, Christ the Beloved you will find in joy as he himself said, alive in flesh and blood."*

257 *With that they turned away, reassured and joyful, and went to look for Christ's people and found them grieving. They told them the whole story. They went in one gathering to look for him and to speak to sweet Jesus.*

255 An el a gewsis dhedha, Mt 28 v.5-8
"Na vedhewgh diskonfortys. Mk 16 v.6-8
Yesus Krist a Nasara, Lk 24 v.4-9
Dell welsowgh, a veu ledhys, R.D. 781-99
Sevys, gallas dhe gen le,
Den apert ha meur y bris.
Awotta'n le mayth esa.
Omma nyns yw ev trigys.

256 "Ewgh yn fen dh'y dhyskyblon
Ha leverewgh hwi dhedha
Ha dhe Beder dos yn skon
Er y bynn dhe Galila.
Ena Krist an kuv kolonn
Hwi a'n kyv yn lowena,
Dell leveris y honan,
Yn kig, yn goes, ow pywa."

257 Gans henna i a drelyas,
Konfortys ha lowenek,
Hag eth tus Krist rag hwilas
Hag a's kavas morethek.
Y lavarsons oll an kas.
Yth ethons yn unn tonnek
Bys Galila dh'y hwilas
Ha dhe gows orth Yesus hweg.

255/1 **a gewsis dhedha**. *kewsel orth* or *gans* is more usual. Perhaps *dhe* is used here because the angel is thought of as addressing the women formally. Cf. *gows orth* in 257/8 where the disciples would converse with Jesus informally.

255/3 **Nasara**. I have followed the spelling of Hooper and Pennaod, just altering the *z* to *s* for the K.K. spelling. The rhyming suggests the last syllable is a neutral vowel.

255/5 **gen le**. Similarly it appears that the *le* has a neutral vowel. Maybe it should be spelt *la* as in *dornla*. It is a pity K.K. does not have a unique symbol for the neutral vowel.

255/6 **Den apert**. Cf. 243/5. Again Hooper and Pennaod emend this to *Dew apert*. The *Kernow* MS. shows the *den* as contracted in the original MS. but not in 243/5. This may introduce some doubt but 'God' is almost always *du* in the MS, not easily confused with *den* unless it is contracted. The angel's words are quite similar in all four gospels but they offer no help here.

256/4 **Galila**. Cf. 85/4. The MS now has the mutation for the first time. It seems more acceptable following *dhe* than *a* which is often the case.

256/5 **kuv kolonn**. Cf. 101/1 and note.

256/8 **Yn kig yn goes**. Cf. *yn kig yn kneus,* e.g. *R.D.* 199, which seems to mean the same.

257/7 **Bys Galila**. I have followed Hooper and Pennaod in omitting the *yn* to fit the metre, though its omission is not normal after *bys.*

258 Pan dezons ze alyle
Ihesus crist y a welas
yn y zensys ow pewe
den apert ha mur y ras
ol y beyn yntremense
ha trylys ens yn ioy bras
hag a vyth zynny neffre
mar a cresyn ha bos vas

259 Del sevys mab du ay veth
yn erna zen tressa dyth
yn della ol ny a seff
deth brues drok ha da yn weth
obereth dremas a dyff
yn erna rych ef a vyth
drok zen yn gythna goef
ze gryst y fyth anbarth cleth

258 *When they came to Galilee they saw Jesus Christ alive in his humanity, manifestly a man and full of grace. All his pain had passed him by. And they were transported into great joy, a joy which shall be ours for ever if we believe and are good.*

259 *As the Son of God then rose from his grave on the third day, likewise we all shall rise on Judgment Day, bad and good alike. The good man's work shall grow. Then he will be rich. Woe to a wicked man on that day. He will be at Christ's left hand.*

258 Pan dheudhons dhe Galila — Mt 28 v.16-18
Yesus Krist i a welas — Jn 21 v.1
Yn y dhenses ow pywa, — R.D. 1139-44
Den apert ha meur y ras
Oll y bayn y'n tremensa.
Ha treylys ens yn joy bras
Hag a vydh dhyn ni nevra
Mara krysyn ha bos 'vas.

259 Dell sevis Mab Duw a'y vedh
Y'n eur na dhe'n tressa dydh
Yndella oll ni a sev
Dydh breus, drog ha da ynwedh.
Obereth dremas a dyv.
Y'n eur na rych ev a vydh
Drog dhen y'n jydh na, go-ev.
Dhe Krist y fydh a'n barth kleth.

258/1 **Galila**. Cf. 256/4 note.

258/4 **Den apert**. Cf. 255/6 note. Here the *Kernow* MS does not show contraction. The mention of *denses* in the previous line also suggests that *den* rather than *Duw* is the correct reading.

258/5 **bayn**. Hooper reads *bayns* and translates 'pains'. Pennaod reads *bayn* but translates plural *boaniou.*

258/6 **Ha treylys ens**. Hooper and Pennaod emend to *treylys o*, and refer the verb to *bayn* in the previous line. I have taken the *ens* as referring to the disciples who have come to Galilee. Cf. Lk 24 v. 52; '...and returned to Jerusalem with great joy.' (*A.V.*). Admittedly, this was not in Galilee but the idea could easily have been transferred. This makes a literal translation awkward so I have repeated 'joy' which I hope will make it clearer.

However, Wella Brown is of the opinion that *bayn(s)* should be taken as plural and *ens* referred to it to mean: 'All his pains had passed him by and were turned into great joy.'

259/1 Hooper emends this line to *Del sevys Cryst a'y veth-ef* with a note saying that Nance suggested this as probably restoring the original, or alternatively, *Cryst del sevys a'y veth-ef.* Pennaod prints the second suggestion. I have kept to the MS. Although *ev* rhymes better with the *b* rhymes in the rest of the verse, the final syllables of all the lines assonance together more or less, within the normal toleration limits of the poem and add a certain *gravitas* to the final verse.

ENVOI

"Dewedhys lemmyn yu an ober-ma.

"Oll an Kernewek re-be gwythys nyns yu mes boghes, hag yma'n *Pascon* un ran vras anodho: betegens, namna ve gyllys an Gan-ma a wel tus, hag yn-whyr kellys dhe'n re-na a-s-teva moyha ethom anedhy. Pur gales yu cafos dascryf an *Philological Society's Transactions, 1860-1*, le may fe dyllys an mamscryf gans Stokes. Mes mar pe war an varghas lyes dascryf a'n mamscryf, py gemmys ahanan a-alsa y redya? Dornscryf a'n drocca y'n bys yn-teffry yu henna an *Pascon*, ha ny-alsa mes dyscajor skentyl y redya. Yn gwella prys, yma genen y'gan renkyow dyscajor a'n par-na. Mordon a-allas y redya, ha'n pyth yu moy a vern dhen-ny, ef a-allas ynweth ry dhen oll an Gan yn tavas es genen convedhys.

"Lowena a-m-be ow-pryntya kettep gwers yn *Kernow*: my a-leverys yn ow holon, 'Otomma un wers moy - otomma un lyven moy - re-be sawyes,' ha dhe voy y-whodhyen gras dhe'n den, nep a fethas caletter uthek an mamscryf. Py lyes ur y-fe res dhodho omdewlel y'n vaner ma, ny-won leverel. Mes alemma rak, ny a-yl omlowenhe yn frut y lafur bras, ha gwyw ny-vya dewedha an dyllans-ma a *Gernow* hep ger a rassyes colon dhe Vordon, a'm govys-vy kepar ha'gan redyoryon erel oll."

With these words, A.S.D. Smith ended Nance's edition of the Manuscript in *Kernow* in May, 1936. May this new edition be found worthy of those two great *dyskadoryon skentyl*, Mordon and Caradar.

Bibliography

Reference is made to the following books either by the title in full, or by the name of the author/translator/editor, or by the abbreviation shown in brackets.

Anderson M.D.	1971	Drama and Imagery in British Churches. Murray.
Brown Wella	1984	A Grammar of Modern Cornish. The Cornish Language Board. (G.M.C.)
Brown Wella	1993	A Grammar of Modern Cornish (Second Edition) The Cornish Language Board. (G.M.C.(2))
Cawley A.C. (ed.)	1959	Everyman and Medieval Miracle Plays. E.P. Dutton and Co. Inc.
Davidson C. (ed.)	1982	The York Cycle of Mystery Plays. Ams Press, New York.
Edwards Ray	1989	Biblical Names beginning with J in English. (Circulated paper)
Edwards Ray (ed.)	1992	The Charter Fragment. Kernewek dre Lyther.
Edwards Ray (tr.)	1986	Dysquedhyans Jowan hag Unnek Epystol. Kernewek dre Lyther. (R.E.)
Ellis Peter Berresford	1974	The Cornish Language and its Literature. Routledge and Kegan Paul.
Evans H. & Thomas B.	1976	Y Geiradur Mawr. Christopher Davies.
Fudge Crysten	1982	The Life of Cornish. Truran Publications.
Geddie William	1964	Chambers Twentieth Century Dictionary. W. & R. Chambers, Ltd. (Chambers)
Gendall Richard	1972	Kernewek Bew. Cornish Language Board.
Gendall Richard	1990	A Students' Dictionary of Modern Cornish. Cornish Language Council.
George Ken	1986	The Pronunciation & Spelling of Revived Cornish. Cornish Language Board. (P.S.R.C.)

George Ken 1983 Devedhyans Sen Pawl yn Bro Leon.
Cowethas an Yeth Kernewek.

George Ken 1991 Gerlyver Kernewek Kemmyn, Dyllans Servadow
Cornish Language Board. (G.S.)

George Ken 1993 Gerlyver Kernewek Kemmyn, An Gerlyver Meur
Cornish Language Board (G.M.)

Grandsaignes D'Hauterive R. 1947 Dictionnaire d'Ancien Français.
Librairie Larousse. Paris. (Larousse)

Halliday F. E. 1954 The Legend of the Rood.
Gerald Duckworth & Co. Ltd.

Hardie D.W.F. 1948 A Handbook of Modern Breton.
University of Wales Press, Cardiff.

Hooper E. G. R. (ed.) 1972 Passyon agan Arluth.
Cornish Language Board.

Hooper E. G. R. (ed.) 1972 Cornish Simplified.
Truran Publications. (C.S.)

Hooper E. G. R. (ed.) 1984 Cornish Simplified Part Two.
Truran Publications. (C.S.II)

Hooper E. G. R. (ed.) 1985 Gwryans an Bys.
Truran Publications. (C.W.)

James M. R. (ed.) 1924 The Apocryphal New Testament.
Oxford Clarendon Press.
(The Gospel of Peter; The Book of the Resurrection of Christ by Bartholomew the Apostle)

Kim H. C. (ed.) 1973 The Gospel of Nicodemus.
Pontifical Inst. of Medieval Studies, Toronto.

Lhuyd Edward 1707 Archaeologia Britannica.
F. Trull, Lerryn. (Photocopy Edition)

Lyon R. & Pengilly J. 1987 Notes on Spoken Cornish.
Truran Publications.

Mâle E. 1949 L'Art Religieux de la Fin du Moyen Age en France.
Armand Colin. Paris.

Mardon E. G. 1970 The Narrative Unity of the Cursor Mundi.
Wm. Maclellan, Glasgow.

Murdoch Brian 1979 The Medieval Cornish Poem of the Passion.
Institute of Cornish Studies, Redruth.

Murdoch Brian	1993	Cornish Literature D. S. Brewer. Cambridge	
Nance R. M.	1978	An English-Cornish and vv.Dictionary. Cornish Language Board.	
Nance R. M. (ed.)	1934/36	Pascon agan Arluth. Kernow.	(Kernow)
Nance R. M.	1951	Old Cornwall, Summer 1951 (writing in)	
Nunn H. P. V.	1952	An Introduction to Ecclesiastical Latin. Alden & Blackwell (Eton) Ltd.	
Pennaod Goulven	1981	Passyon agan Arluth/Pasion hon Aotrou. Preder. Quimper.	
Pope M. K.	1934	From Latin to Modern French. Manchester University Press.	
Sandercock G. (ed.)	1982	Christ's Passion. Cornish Language Board.	(P.C.)
Sandercock G. (ed.)	1984	Resurrection. Cornish Language Board.	(R.D.)
Stokes Whitley	1860-61	Pascon agan Arluth Transactions of the Philological Society.	
Sandercock G. (ed.)	1989	Origo Mundi. Cornish Language Board.	(O.M.)
Smith A. S. D.	1936	Kernow.	
Toorians Lauran	1990	De Middelcornische *Passie van Onze Heer* Kruispunt 129	
Williams N.J.A.	1995	Cornish Today Kernewek dre Lyther	
Woolf Rosemary	1972	The English Mystery Plays. Routledge and Kegan Paul.	
Zeuss J. C.	1853	Grammatica Celtica. Weidmann, Leipzig.	